ANATOMY
OF A
JURY

By the same author

Nothing Personal, a novel
Confessions of a Criminal Lawyer

ANATOMY OF A JURY

THE SYSTEM ON TRIAL

SEYMOUR WISHMAN

Times BOOKS

Library of Congress Cataloging-in-Publication Data

Wishman, Seymour.
   Anatomy of a jury.

   Includes index.
   1. Jury—United States.   I. Title.
KF8972.W57   1986   347.73'752   85-40845
ISBN 0-8129-1260-8   347.307752

Designed by Marjorie Anderson
Manufactured in the United States of America
9 8 7 6 5 4 3 2

To Pauline and Isadore Wishman

Truth and Progress

PREFACE

I HAVE BEEN A CRIMINAL LAWYER for twenty years. I have tried hundreds of cases before juries, both as a prosecutor and as a defense lawyer. Juries have fascinated me not only for what they reveal about our idea of justice, but for what they tell us about ourselves. I decided to write a book that would show something about how we administer justice, and, perhaps just as important, how we judge others and how others perceive and judge us.

Every year more than 1,200,000 people in America place their hands on Bibles and swear they will decide with fairness whether or not thousands of their fellow citizens are guilty of murder, rape, robbery, or other crimes. Twelve strangers without special skill or training are called upon to exercise their sense of justice and draw on their most astute perceptions of people. Each jury in its own way represents the best and worst of us as a society.

The jury system—our substitute for trial by ordeal—has been venerated over the centuries by respected authorities. To William Blackstone, the great English legal commentator of the eighteenth century, the jury was a "palladium of liberty"; Jefferson called it a "touchstone" ensuring our peace and safety; more recently, the British jurist Patrick Devlin has described the jury system as "the lamp that shows that freedom lives." To thousands of lawyers, judges, and average citizens, however, the jury is seen as twelve prejudiced, gullible dolts incapable of understanding the evidence or law involved in a case.

While the merits of the jury are hotly debated in legal and nonlegal circles, these "ordinary" people are deliberating in

secret and announcing, without explanation, verdicts affecting the lives and sometimes the deaths of perfect strangers. If
any of us are ever accused of a crime, these "ordinary" people
will determine our guilt or innocence. Their power is enormous, far greater than any power most of us exercise either
before or after jury service. And when it is over, after this
most intense, often humbling, experience, they resume their
normal routines.

When I was considering how to write a book about the
jury system, I soon realized that it could not be a dissertation
full of legal abstractions. If I restricted myself to my own past
dealings with juries and exhaustive research, the book would
lose the immediacy and vividness of the actual experience of
jurors.

I decided to describe a real trial through all its stages, using
that case as a vehicle to discuss along the way the various
issues involving juries. A criminal trial is inherently dramatic.
The plot unfolds in regular scenes of neat acts, all leading to a
climax of great consequences. The actors in the trial—the
lawyers, the judge, the witnesses, the jurors—have clearly defined roles, and whether or not they perform well, all are
interesting.

In many respects it didn't matter which case I chose. The
basic legal principles and procedure are the same for all criminal trials, and the jurors' involvement is the same regardless
of the charge. I decided on a murder case because of the high
stakes, and I felt it was important to have a trial that was
"typical" so as to be representative, yet complex enough to
involve a range of questions affecting the jury.

So I chose a case that seemed to suit my purpose, and followed the trial. When it was all over, I realized that several
important issues had simply not come up. It had been unrealistic of me to think that any one trial could furnish the opportunities to cover all the topics I wanted to discuss. At that
point I decided to observe several more trials and then bring

in some of my personal experiences, and in this way tailor a more "perfect" case.

The result is a composite case, most of which is derived from a single trial. All the characters are real, but a few have been drawn from different cases. I cannot claim that this is a documentary case, but I can assert that I have seen all of the events described in it at one time or another. The trial is intended only as a vehicle to illustrate aspects of the jury system as a whole. The names of all the characters in the trial have been changed.

ACKNOWLEDGMENTS

I WANT TO THANK a number of people who helped me write this book. I could not have written it without the cooperation and assistance of Judge Julius Feinberg, an honest, decent, and terrific judge; Norman Menz and Leslie Mann of the Essex County Prosecutor's Office; Allen Marra, Norman Fishbein, and a number of other defense lawyers; and, mostly, the jurors in this case and the large number of jurors in dozens of other cases who trusted me with their experiences.

I also want to thank the following people for their valuable and wise suggestions during the seemingly endless writing process: Alan Axelrod, John Galagher, George Hobson, Leonard Klein, Peter Passell, Peter McCabe, Helen Whitney, Harvey Wishman, Hans Zeisel. And most of all, yet again, Nancy Evans.

I owe a great debt of appreciation to Leonard Klein, David Slater, and the Palisades Institute for Research Services for so graciously allowing me to use their facilities; I simply could not have written this book without their support.

I also want to thank Wendy Lipkind, my literary agent, for her professionalism, encouragement, and good counsel, without which I would have never finished; Jonathan Segal, my editor, who convinced me to write the book and to write it in the structure of its present form; Ruth Fecych, for her significant editorial contributions; and Victoria Hobson, who served as so much more than a line editor and whose sensitivity to language and generosity toward my intentions enormously improved the writing. I am also deeply grateful to my friends George and Victoria Hobson for their warm hospitality and friendship and for allowing me to spend some time with them in Puy del Claux, France.

CONTENTS

PART

ONE

WHO SHALL
JUDGE
ME?

CHAPTER

I.

JOHN MINTON, alone in his police car, drove slowly through the quiet streets of Glen Ridge, New Jersey, in the middle of a hot, humid afternoon. It was September 5, 1982, the day the case against Leander Rafshoon began.

Minton had been on the police force of this wealthy residential community for eighteen years, and an air-conditioned vehicle—the prize for years of faithful service—had still, somehow, eluded him. His blue short-sleeved shirt, now soaked with sweat, stuck to the vinyl of the back of the seat.

Minton glanced admiringly, protectively, at the stately fifty-year-old mansions of red brick with stone turrets and gray slate roofs, Tudor or Colonial in design—or the best of both—each house, he knew, with its own carpeted recreation/family room in the basement, many of the houses with brick patios and colorful umbrellas over round white tables, some of the homes with pools in the backyard, and all surrounded by high, carefully trimmed hedges. Glen Ridge is a town of bankers and brokers and business executives whose wives fill their days preparing for charitable events and interesting cultural projects and programs of physical fitness. When the children are at school, the streets are silent except for an occasional delivery, or the mailman, or the coming or going of a maintenance man.

John Minton knew the town, virtually every family and every street within the two square miles. They were good people and it was a good community, a peaceful world totally foreign to the danger of violence so common in a place like Newark, only a few miles to the east.

In another four years Minton was to retire from the force and settle into a sedentary job as a guard in a cool, quiet bank. But in a few minutes he would become involved in the most brutal crime of his career, an act of bloody violence that would horrify the good people of Glen Ridge and leave them unable ever again to feel fully secure in their homes.

As Minton's car edged along the tree-lined street, Adam Collins, two blocks away on a parallel street, walked up the slate path to the main entrance of a large brick house. Adam had decided to skip swimming practice and go directly home from school. He was a shy, strikingly handsome, well-behaved boy of fourteen just starting his sophomore year in high school.

Adam closed the front door behind him. From the center hall he saw on the bottom step of the staircase the end of a black and white rope. He called for his mother. No one answered. He followed the rope around the doorframe to the corridor leading to the kitchen. He started to reach down to pick up the rope, but something kept him moving forward in the direction of the kitchen toward which the rope snaked a path.

What Adam then saw was a scene of horror worse than any nightmare. The kitchen table and one of the chairs were knocked over. Pools of blood covered parts of the black tile floor. In the center of the room was his mother . . . naked, on her stomach, with blood all over her back. Her head, just above her right temple, was smashed in, and her blond hair was soaked in coagulating blood. The long rope he had followed from the staircase in the center hall ended around her neck.

Adam began to scream.

Ten minutes later loud static forced its way through John Minton's car radio. In rasping patches, as if the radio were clearing its throat, the dispatcher's voice reported that someone was yelling for help at a residence on Ridgewood Avenue, 1326.

Minton pushed the accelerator to the floor—no need for a noisy siren—and within seconds he was at the house. Adam Collins was standing in the middle of the front lawn, pulling on his shirt, screaming, "Mother!"

Minton jumped out of his car and ran to the boy. He put his arm around him and tried to comfort him.

Adam pointed to the house. He was shaking, crying, gasping for breath, trying to speak. "My mother! My mother!"

"It'll be okay," Minton said, unaware of what awaited him in the house. He ran up the path to the front door.

In the next hour dozens of men arrived from various law enforcement agencies, some in uniform, others in plain clothes, almost every one with a gun. Forensic specialists from the state police combed the house, while someone from the Medical Examiner's Office tended to the body. An electric storm seemed to be exploding inside the house as flashbulbs went off while photographs were taken of the body and the objects in the rooms. Dr. William Collins, the husband of the victim, arrived and ran to the body of his wife. John Minton stayed with Adam, his arm around the boy in a pathetic gesture of comfort. A small crowd of news reporters and neighbors had gathered outside the house.

At this point a short, portly man with a smooth, round face and gray hair, wearing a light gray suit with wide lapels and jutting shoulder pads, pushed his way through the knot of people. It was Leslie Ryan, the head of the homicide squad of the Essex County Prosecutor's Office. He entered the house and took charge of the proceedings. At thirty-eight he already had eighteen years in law enforcement, four years as an investigator while he attended law school at night before he became an assistant prosecutor. Ryan had seen hundreds of victims of violence, but most were black and in Newark or the poorer towns next to it. The Collins woman looked like his wife's best friend, and Glen Ridge, with its powerful and wealthy residents, was a community he had always envied.

An hour after the body was carried out, two detectives of the Essex County Prosecutor's Office brought the suspect, Leander Rafshoon, a thirty-three-year-old black male, to the scene. The detectives led him into the living room.

"We got him at the store where the doctor told us he'd be," one of the detectives said.

Leslie Ryan looked up and down at the tall, powerful figure standing between the two detectives. Ryan thought that Rafshoon looked like a frightened Mr. T. "You have the right to remain silent and have a lawyer. Do you understand?" Ryan said.

Rafshoon nodded.

"Did you know Mrs. Collins?"

"I knew her," Rafshoon said. "I worked for her, or for her husband. I was like her bodyguard."

"We have witnesses who saw you here today."

"I was here. I was here this morning, but when I left she was okay."

"These witnesses, Leander, they say you were the only one here when she was killed."

"There had to be somebody else."

"I called into the record room," one of the detectives said.

"He's got an armed robbery. He did three, and he's been out about two."

"Is that right?" Ryan asked Rafshoon.

Rafshoon nodded. He couldn't deny it, but he was sure that with his criminal record the police would be convinced they had their man. He was tempted to tell them he was also a decorated Vietnam veteran, but he didn't think that would make a difference.

Ryan took Rafshoon into the kitchen where the body of Carolyn Collins had been found. "Is this where you last saw her when she was okay, Leander?"

"I don't want to answer no more questions," Rafshoon said.

"Dr. Collins was here a little while ago. He told me you did it. He said you were having an affair with his wife, and she was going to break it off with you today. What do you say to that, Leander?"

"No more questions. I want to see a lawyer. I have a right to see a lawyer."

"Hold him here tonight," Ryan said to the detective. "Bring him down to Newark tomorrow." And with that Rafshoon was led away to the Glen Ridge Police Station.

Six hours later John Minton sat at a scarred oak desk at police headquarters typing a report on an old machine. He spun the report out of the typewriter. Too bad the search of the guy's apartment didn't turn up the weapon, but at least we got the guy who did it, Minton said to himself. And a gullible jury better not let him get away with it.

At the time Adam Collins's mother was murdered, the names of 650,000 neighbors, friends, and strangers, law-abiding citizens living in the same county, were already encoded on magnetic tape and stored in a large, well-lighted room on the first floor in the rear of a large office building six miles from the scene of the crime. The tapes were wound on ten-inch reels and enclosed in tin containers that were stacked upright on shelves lining the walls from floor to ceiling. The names were waiting to be retrieved.

Two squat printers clicked names and addresses onto a wide roll of paper, while spokes extending through holes along the paper's edges moved the roll, hesitated while a new name was being printed, and advanced the roll. A four-inch pile of key-punch cards filled the jaws of another machine.

In the center of the room, seven tape drives hummed as white, green, and red buttons flashed. Glass doors enclosed the upper third of the tall beige machines. Behind the glass, the names of 400,000 voters and 400,000 licensed drivers had been translated into millions of electronic bits of information that were now silently moving onto 1,600 feet of dark tape. The information was being transferred from one reel to another as the machine merged, updated, and eliminated duplicates to produce a single list of 650,000 potential jurors, called the master wheel.

The day after the murder, the medical examiner performed the autopsy and prepared a report:

> I hereby certify that I, Graciela H. Linares, M.D., have performed an autopsy on the body of Carolyn Collins at the Essex County Morgue, Belleville, N.J., on 6th day of September 1982 at 11:00 A.M. and said autopsy revealed Homicide by stabbing, stab wounds of chest, neck and back involving heart, lungs and aorta; internal hemorrhage. . . .

> Samples of hair from scalp; smears from vagina, rectum and mouth. Blood for typing; blood, urine, stomach and contents, liver, gall bladder, lungs, kidneys and brain for toxicological investigation of alcohol and drugs. Tissue for histology. . . .

> The clothing included a short-sleeved nylon T-shirt, green front and blue-violet back, a pair of BonJour blue jeans, mustard-colored lace panties. . . .

The body is that of a well-nourished, well-developed, middle-aged white female. Skin is pale and cold, with average turgor and average elasticity. Rigidity is present in muscles of mastication, upper and lower extremities. . . . Abdomen is flat, there is an old appendectomy scar. . . .

Two weeks later the autopsy report was on the desk of Vince Altieri, the detective in charge of the homicide investigation. Altieri studied the autopsy report, and then turned to the lab reports. Sperm found on the vagina smears made rape seem clearly established. No evidence of drugs or alcohol was found. That was good news. Altieri knew that juries are often more lenient with a defendant when the victim was drunk or on drugs or was otherwise unlikable.

Altieri looked at the color morgue shots of the naked body of Carolyn Collins. The number and location of wounds eliminated self-defense as a justification for the killing. In fact, the victim had been stabbed so many times that the defendant might claim he had gone berserk. In Altieri's fifteen years in homicide, he had been involved in only one case where insanity was even claimed, and the jury had brought back a conviction of murder anyway. As it happens, the insanity defense is raised in less than 2 percent of all criminal cases, and the more serious the charge, the tougher it is to convince the jury that the defendant did not know what he was doing.

Too bad they couldn't get a confession out of Rafshoon, Altieri thought. That would have made the case easy. Jurors like confessions. But usually only scared and stupid defendants give confessions, and Rafshoon didn't seem either scared or stupid. Juries, in fact, hear confessions at trial in about a fifth of all cases; almost half the homicide cases but virtually none of the narcotics cases involve confessions.

The Collins woman was certainly beautiful, Altieri thought. Rafshoon looked like a black stud. Maybe there was a love triangle in the case. Altieri had seen a number of cases where the infidelity of the victim was the trigger for the murder. Juries may be more lenient with defendants who had been emotionally wronged by the victim. Altieri shoved the morgue shots back into the folder.

He looked again at the police report submitted by the first officer on the scene, John Minton. A search of the defendant's apartment had turned up no evidence. There was no mention of a search warrant, so Altieri was sure that the search had been done without one. He knew that his boss, Leslie Ryan, was going to hit the roof. As soon as Ryan had decided on the arrest, these local cops had run off to Rafshoon's apartment in Newark. They were so eager to find the murder weapon, they hadn't waited to get a warrant or tell Ryan they were going on a search. They hadn't even told the Newark police. If they had found the weapon, it would most likely have been excluded as evidence at the trial because the search had been illegal.

Small-town cops, Altieri knew, are usually less competent than city cops. The illegal search in this case would never become known. Since no evidence had been recovered, the jury would never even hear that there had been a search. Fortunately, an illegal search keeps evidence from a jury much less often than the public realizes; it happens in less than 2 percent of all cases.

While Altieri was reviewing the status of his case against Leander Rafshoon, Leonard Klein, a widowed father of two, was in his Hoboken office flipping through the mail he had thrown into his briefcase at his house the night before. With the training in time efficiency he had received as an industrial engineer, Leonard felt compelled to deal with his personal and business mail at the same time. He often made fun of this compulsive behavior to his staff, but he also knew that his "habits of orderliness" had probably had something to do with the fact that he had been able to build a multimillion-dollar business out of a one-desk, one-telephone office.

Leonard Klein was unaware that the bloody body of Carolyn Collins had been found a week earlier in the adjacent town, just two miles away from his home. He read *The Wall Street Journal* and *The New York Times,* but neither had made any mention of what must have been considered just another routine crime story. A local television station had carried a ninety-second broadcast from the Collins house, but he had not been home from work in time to see it. This sort of thing could never happen in small towns of rural America where people know from personal contacts what is going on in their community. It would be another ten months before Leonard Klein learned about what had happened to his neighbor.

In the upper-left corner of a computer-printed envelope, his eye caught the words The Jury Commission. Across the bottom of the envelope was printed JURY SERVICE . . . A PRIVILEGE AND YOUR DUTY!

He tore off the stub along the perforated line near the edge of the envelope and peeled back the thin front skin of the envelope. "Prospective Juror Questionnaire" said the line printed across the top of the page inside. The computer's printer had typed Leonard Klein's name and address on the envelope, at the same time making the impression through the carbon on the inside of the envelope onto the form.

Leonard decided not to postpone answering the questions. In the first space he wrote "40 years old—3/17/42." Next to occupation he entered "Industrial Engineer" rather than "Chief Executive Officer" because that was really how he saw himself. The remaining questions, he felt, were less likely to provoke an identity crisis. "Yes," he'd lived in New Jersey for more than two years. "Yes," he could read, write, and understand the English language. "No," he was not connected, directly or indirectly, through office, position, or employment with the administration of justice. "No," he had no mental or physical disability. "No," he'd never been convicted of or pleaded guilty or no contest to a crime. And "No," he had never previously served as a juror.

These same questions are asked in virtually every state of every person on the master wheel to determine his or her qualifications as a potential juror. Some 15 to 30 percent of the people asked have died or moved or otherwise do not respond. The answered questionnaires are used to prepare another list, the "qualified wheel," from which a certain number of people will be randomly selected and summoned to court.

Leonard Klein was surprised at how meaningless the information to determine the qualifications of jurors seemed. What he regarded as the central facts of his life—that he was a devoted father of two teen-age boys, that three nights a week he went to a nursing home to visit his mother who was suffering from Alzheimer's disease, and that even after two years he was still reeling from the devastating loss of his wife—were not asked for anywhere in the questionnaire.

He shoved the answered questionnaire into the envelope and placed it in his out box. His secretary would make sure it would be in the afternoon mail. He had no idea that if he had not sent back his answers, he would have simply avoided jury duty. The failure to fill out a jury questionnaire is a crime almost everywhere, but prosecutions are practically unheard of. It is easier to mail questionnaires to a new set of names than to go after those who do not answer.

Leonard Klein dreaded the thought of losing two weeks of work, but he, like most Americans, would have sent the questionnaire back even if he had known that by holding on to it he would have removed himself from the selection process.

The Newark jail was a modern building, twelve stories of gray cinder block with black, screened gun slits for windows all the way up. The thick bulletproof glass door gave a slight blue tint to the objects inside. Fluorescent lights glared into every corner of the lobby. All prisons were the same, Michael Bernstein thought to himself, except some were more modern than others. Bernstein had been to a lot of them. They were all warehouses, warehouses of shelved criminals regularly serviced with all their basic needs except hetero sex; they were foolish and vicious places, and too depressing, too overwhelmingly depressing to contemplate.

The guard unlocked the door, holding it partly ajar as Bernstein identified himself. The guard explained that some "disturbance" had occurred the previous night but that the ban on visitors did not apply to lawyers.

Bernstein followed the guard to the large glass control booth and watched him disappear behind a steel door. Inside the booth three guards were engaged in an animated conversation, but Bernstein could not hear any of it, as no sounds penetrated the thick glass.

Bernstein wrote his name and address and "Leander Rafshoon" and "homicide" on a three-by-five card. He dropped the card into a metal drawer and pushed the drawer into the booth. A guard in the booth retrieved the card; he flipped through a black loose-leaf book of inmates, each on a separate, removable sheet. He walked over to the fancy intercom and called to have the inmate brought down. The guard dropped the card back into the metal drawer and pushed it to Bernstein.

The guard cupped his hand around his ear and pointed to the six-inch perforated silver disk cut into the glass separating himself from Bernstein. Bernstein pressed his ear against the metal disk. It was cold.

"It may take a couple of minutes. The inmates are feeding," the guard said.

Bernstein nodded and reached for the card in the drawer. He moved several feet to his left and waited behind a solid metal door. The guard inside standing next to the switches was talking to another guard. Bernstein waited.

Looking back over his shoulder at the main door through which he had entered, Bernstein noticed several benches to the side of the door where visitors could wait. A wooden desk was on the other side of the doorway. On top of the desk was a rectangular box, the size of a walkie-talkie, with an eight-inch metal coil protruding from it; it was a weapons detector of the sort that is passed up and down a few inches from the body. Next to the desk, leading to the elevator, was a short runway with tall posts on each side—another weapons detector. All the walls were cinder block painted gray. All the floors were concrete with a heavy layer of shiny gray paint. And the bright fluorescent lights beamed everywhere, illuminating everything with the same cold white glare.

Finally the guard in the booth, nearly convulsed with laughter at his own story, turned the switch, and a red bulb flashed on his large control panel. A lock clanked, and the metal door slid rasping to the left with a loud motorized hum. All sounds were harsh and echoed off the gray walls and floors. When the space was large enough, Bernstein turned sideways and slipped through. The door stopped, then jerked, then rasped its way back to the closed position.

Bernstein stepped forward ten feet to a barred door. He could see through the glass of the control booth to the guard standing by the switch waiting for the first door to clank shut. *Clank.* The guard pushed another button. Again the motorized hum, and the barred door began to open. Bernstein slipped through. Then the barred door reversed directions and shut. *Clang.*

Bernstein walked another ten feet to another barred door and passed the three-by-five card through the bars to a guard. The guard opened the door. Bernstein deposited his briefcase and signed the register. The guard unlocked the door to the lawyers' conference room. Bernstein entered and the guard slammed the solid door shut. The sound echoed off the walls. The room was about three times the size of a jury box. Five-foot dividers formed a narrow corridor separating a series of small cubicles. The cinder-block floors and walls were all painted the same glossy gray; there was a low ceiling of pockmarked white masonite, no window; the usual bright white fluorescent bulbs—Bernstein hated these places.

He entered the first cubicle. All the cubicles were the same. Each had two or three unmatched chairs and an old wooden desk, scratched and gouged. He took off his jacket, sat down, and waited.

About ten minutes later, the door opened and a black man in bedroom slippers appeared. "Rafshoon?" Bernstein asked.

"Yes, sir."

"My name is Michael Bernstein. I have been assigned your case from the Public Defender's Office."

"Yes, sir."

"I'm a private attorney. I specialize in criminal work. I get about a third of my cases from the Public Defender's Office."

"Yes, sir. Thank you for coming. I been here three weeks. Since they arrested me, three weeks and I only seen an investigator from your office. He came the first day."

"I'm sorry, but you were just assigned to me. I wanted to meet with you and tell you that I'm on the case now, and we'll be seeing a lot of each other from now on."

"I didn't do it. I didn't kill that woman, Mr. Bernstein."

"They have a kid who was working across the street where the woman was killed. He says that he saw you running out of the back of the house. And no one else came or left during the time she was killed."

"I was there. But I didn't kill her. I didn't."

Bernstein spent the next hour going over the details of what his client said he did on the day of the murder. Bernstein listened and took notes and wondered if this was yet another desperate, lying defendant. In the fifteen years he had practiced criminal law, he had found that most of his clients lied to him. He realized that many felt they could not trust him, or maybe they thought he would not work as hard for them if they told him they were guilty. Sooner or later most of them admitted the truth.

During his first few years as a defense lawyer, Bernstein had found that, guilty or not, his clients, in their helplessness and dependence on him, would evoke protective feelings in him, and he would often find himself wanting to shield them from the prosecutor and the cops and anyone else trying to harm them. That was in the beginning, but at this point in his career he no longer had any emotional reaction to a person claiming to be innocent. Bernstein would do his job for Rafshoon, and do it better than just about anyone he knew, but he was not about to be taken in again. He would postpone any conclusion as to whether or not his new client was guilty, postpone it to the time he got all the evidence, postpone it, perhaps, until a jury announced its verdict.

Two months after the murder of Carolyn Collins, nearly two months after Leonard Klein and approximately thirty-five thousand other neighbors had responded to the juror questionnaire, an Essex County grand jury, the body with the power to indict an individual for a crime, took up the case against Leander Rafshoon. Rafshoon had been in custody since the day of the murder. Detective Altieri had prepared the case for the grand jury. John Minton testified about what he had found as the first police officer on the scene. A forensic specialist from the state police told the grand jurors that the blood and hair found on a sledgehammer traced back to Rafshoon. A young man testified that he had seen the defendant running out of the house at the time of the murder. After hearing the testimony of the witnesses, the twenty-three citizens sitting around the large table in the grand jury room watched the young prosecutor place a check mark on a yellow legal pad next to the name of the defendant, Leander Rafshoon.

"All those in favor of returning an indictment against . . . what's his name?"—the prosecutor looked down at his pad—"Leander Rafshoon, please raise your hand."

Twenty-three hands went up. As most people looked to see what the others were doing, one of those voting said to the person next to him, "This is the worst one we've had so far, don't you think?"

"Not as bad as the beheading last week," the person answered.

At the same time the grand jury was coming to its decision to indict Leander Rafshoon, five middle-aged women sat at their desks in a large office off the jury control waiting room, directly across the hall from the grand jury room on the same fourth floor of the courthouse. The women were sifting through answered juror questionnaires.

A seemingly endless stream of people every week sent these women the basic information about their lives. Each questionnaire was read. Questionnaires claiming some basis for exemption had to be separated from the others. About 25 percent were thrown into the basket of "ineligibles." Similar civil servants all over America were throwing similar questionnaires onto similar piles. One of the women scanned Leonard Klein's response and placed it onto the pile for "eligibles."

Two weeks after the grand jury indicted Leander Rafshoon, Michael Bernstein was in court with his client for the arraignment, the time when a defendant formally responds to the indictment by pleading either guilty or not guilty to the charges. Bernstein had read the indictment to Rafshoon at a meeting at the jail earlier in the week, and they had decided to plead not guilty.

Leander Rafshoon was led into the courtroom in handcuffs and placed in a seat in the jury box. When his name was called, he stood up. Bernstein, who had been waiting in the first row of the spectators' seats, stepped up to counsel table and stood next to Leslie Ryan.

"Your Honor," Bernstein began, "I have read and reviewed the indictment with my client. We waive the reading of it now."

"Very well. Mr. Rafshoon is charged with first-degree murder and rape. How does the defendant plead?"

"Not guilty," Bernstein said.

"Very well. The trial will be set for February first."

"Your Honor, may I make an application for bail?" Bernstein asked.

The judge turned to Ryan. "Mr. Prosecutor?"

Ryan opened a folder on the table in front of him. "The defendant has a prior record, and this was a particularly brutal murder. I also have the statement of a witness who claimed the defendant had said he intended to leave the country."

"My client has roots in the community. He's lived here all his life. His mother lives here. His wife and two kids are here. He's still presumed innocent. Bail is only to assure his presence at the trial. He's not going to run away."

"No bail," the judge said. "Next case."

Bernstein looked over at Rafshoon with a shrug that said, We tried. He had told him not to expect bail. Rafshoon nodded back: Thanks for trying. A guard led Rafshoon out of the courtroom. The defendant would have to wait in jail.

Six months after Bernstein pleaded not guilty on behalf of his client, three months after the trial was supposed to begin, a judge was about to play the next part in the process of bringing together the twelve strangers who would decide the fate of Leander Rafshoon. It was a late spring day, almost summer, a beautiful day for the judge and his sergeant at arms to walk down the hill from the courthouse to the twelve-story office building in downtown Newark where the jury lists were held on tapes.

The judge in his finely tailored blue pin-striped suit walked quickly alongside his beefy, square-shouldered companion into the lobby. Turning right at a bank of elevators facing them, the two men approached a guard from a private detective agency seated at a bridge table. Loud soul music from the guard's radio heralded their arrival.

The gray-haired judge nodded at the guard, who straightened himself in his chair. The two men turned left at the end of the lobby and headed down the long, dimly lit corridor. The metal taps on the judge's companion's shoes clicked on the stone floor and echoed off the black marble walls. Pieces of plaster that had fallen from the ceiling lay here and there on the floor; doors to empty offices were unhinged. Once luxurious, the building was now in a state of disintegration, almost vacant.

The two men turned left at the end of the corridor, through a glass door, into a brightly lighted room with a wall of tin containers. There they were greeted by several men in polyester suits with some smiles, some small talk, and the judge was escorted to a waist-high computer, one of several in a line that looked like high-tech washing machines, each with six buttons across the top; two buttons white, two green, two flashing red.

These machines held the lists of potential jurors that had resulted from the screening of the questionnaires. The "ineligibles" had been eliminated from the master wheel, and a new, reduced list, the qualified wheel, had been composed. Now, by means of a modern technological ritual—by simply pushing a key on a computer keyboard—the judge would instruct the machinery to narrow the pool of people available for the Rafshoon trial to a twentieth of its size. In each group of twenty among the thousands of groups of twenty, the person who was given the number the judge selected would be summoned to court. Although in some states judges or clerks still blindly pull slips of paper or capsules from a drum, many states, like New Jersey, use judges and computers to make the selection of jurors who are to be summoned for jury duty.

The judge stepped up to the machine. He'd been through this before, twice the previous year. One to twenty. He pushed the keys. An orange "11" appeared in the small screen on the face of the machine.

"Maybe eleven will be some defendant's lucky number," the judge said, and pushed the key marked "Execute." The people around him laughed politely.

Behind the glass door, two 10-inch reels began to spin, one pulling the tape from the other. Soon there would be twelve people of those hundreds of thousands on the tape, twelve who were unaware, at this point, that the microchips and gears of justice were bringing them toward a duty they would never forget.

Three weeks after the computer selected every eleventh name on the qualified wheel, Carl Copco was too hung over to go to work. He was sick of his pet shop, and for all he cared, the parakeets could starve, and the gerbils and the business could die with them. It had been more than a year now, so it wasn't just a matter of waiting for the neighborhood to learn of his presence. It was clear the neighborhood did not care about his presence.

Carl prepared a glass of tomato juice with wheat germ. Maybe that would settle his stomach. The house was a mess—filthy, with clothes thrown all around. It had been that way for more than a month, ever since Patty had decided she couldn't stand any more of his beatings and had run out on him.

He heard someone on the front porch. Through the window he could see the postman dripping wet in a raincoat and ridiculous cap.

"More bills," Carl said to himself, but he couldn't resist seeing if there was a note from Patty. As soon as the postman left, Carl went outside into the rain.

He ran back into the house with several letters. Nothing from Patty. A few bills. A small computerized letter with OF-FICIAL BUSINESS printed in red across the top. His eye flicked to the upper left-hand corner: Petit Jury Control.

With his hands shaking from the aftereffects of too much drink, he tore off the stub along the perforated line near the edge of the envelope and peeled back the front of the envelope:

SUMMONS FOR JURY SERVICE— ESSEX COUNTY

You are hereby summoned to appear on September 9, 1983, at the Superior Court of New Jersey, at the Essex County Courts Building, Room 410, Newark, New Jersey, to serve as a Petit Juror.

The form gave him a six-digit number, the date to appear, and four "Instructions for Jurors":

(1) Only the Assignment Judge is empowered to excuse a juror from jury service.
(2) Requests to be excused from jury service must be in writing to the Assignment Judge, not later than 10 days before reporting date. Telephone requests are not acceptable.
(3) Parking facilities are available on Howard Street. Enter by South Orange Avenue.
(4) The anticipated period of service is two weeks.

In a box at the bottom of the summons was a warning:

> Every person summoned as a grand or petit juror who shall either fail to appear or refuse, without reasonable excuse, to serve or be sworn, shall be fined by the court in an amount not to exceed $50, to the use of the county where such offense was committed; and may be punished as for contempt of court.

"Terrific," Carl mumbled. "Contempt of court, that's just what I need. I should have told them the truth about that army conviction."

Not always, but often, people are reluctant to tell the truth about their backgrounds. The complicated rules and lists and machinery for jury selection cannot deal very well with the simple fact that people sometimes lie. The penalty for falsely swearing about such information is serious—it's a crime punishable by fine or imprisonment—but the judge or the lawyers trying a case do not routinely verify the statements of prospective jurors at any stage of the process. No one would check to see if Carl Copco had a criminal record, and even if they did check, the records—often inaccurate or incomplete—probably would not reveal it.

Most states would exclude felons like Carl Copco from serving on a jury in the belief that such people, as a California court put it in 1979, "might well harbor a continuing resentment against 'the system' that punished them or hold an equally unthinking bias in favor of the defendant on trial."

On September 9, 1983, Maureen Whalen drove to the courthouse early, pulling in at about seven-thirty. The summons didn't require her to appear until eight-twenty, but she wanted to be sure not to be late. She pulled into the nearly empty parking lot with the large sign in front marked JURORS.

Maureen went to the room indicated on her summons. Eagerly she opened the door marked Jury Control and stepped inside. Passing a bank of pay telephones, she walked down a hallway that led into a large room. Four rows of black folding chairs, six chairs in each row, were arranged on either side of a center aisle. A thirty-foot counter ran across the front of the room.

Alone in the jury control room, she sat down in the third row on the aisle. The large clock on the wall behind the counter said 7:45. To the left of the counter, an American flag was planted next to a coat rack; a brown bulletin board hung on the wall to the right. A door to the left of her row was marked LADIES; to the right of her row was a door marked MEN. Everything seemed very symmetrical and orderly. Maureen liked that.

She wondered what kind of people would be on the jury with her. Except for church activities and, of course, her gardening club, she wasn't getting out very much to social functions, not since her younger sister Dorothy had gotten married eight years ago and left her. She had thought of selling their house. It was a much bigger house than she needed, but her father had built it, and she had been born there sixty-eight years ago. The neighborhood had changed so much over the years, with all the blacks moving in and everything. She could move to a nice apartment in a clean, safe neighborhood.

Maureen wondered if her flower-print dress was serious enough. The lawyers would certainly want a serious person. Maybe the lawyers would think she was too serious, too proper. She was startled to notice a young woman, maybe in her late twenties, with short black hair and a bright, smiling face, walking down the center aisle.

"Good morning," Maureen said as she glanced again at the clock: 8:03.

"If you'll step up to the counter, there's a juror button and an instruction sheet for you," the young woman said as she passed Maureen on her way to the front of the room.

Maureen carefully smoothed her white linen jacket neatly folded on her lap and watched the young woman walk behind the brown Formica counter.

The woman noticed that Maureen hadn't responded. "There's an instruction sheet for you," she said again, pointing to a pile of papers on the counter. "And a juror button."

Maureen realized the woman must be a clerk. She rose quickly and moved to the counter.

"Your name, please, and number?"

"I'm sorry . . ." Maureen felt alarmed. She hadn't seen the woman's lips.

"On your summons," the clerk said, removing the envelope from Maureen's hand.

After placing a check mark next to Maureen's name on a long list, the clerk gave Maureen an instruction sheet and a white oval button marked JUROR. "You have to wear the button so that it's visible at all times."

Soon after Maureen returned to her seat, another woman clerk arrived and went behind the counter, and within minutes dozens of people were lining up to receive their buttons and instruction sheets.

"Form one line," the woman who'd given Maureen her button said loudly. "Have your summons out, and form one line."

By eight-fifteen most of the chairs were taken and people were filling up the lounges behind both sides of the counter. About three hundred people had arrived. Maureen had had no real problem hearing the clerk's instructions. She felt reassured about her decision not to wear her hearing aid. She was sure it would have lessened her chances of being picked as a juror, and she was confident that she'd be able to hear most of the trial without it. Besides, Maureen knew that she compensated for her disability with her keener remaining senses.

She could notice something in body language or a gesture that would betray a lie, something that a person without a hearing problem would miss altogether. And she was not about to be denied the opportunity to be a juror and be cast as a second-class American.

Maureen had not thought she had answered her questionnaire untruthfully when she said she had no physical disability. In fact some states now allow the deaf or the blind to sit on a jury, and several blind persons, and a deaf person assisted by a signer, have served on civil juries in Seattle, Washington.

Most lawyers, however much they may support the idea of not discriminating against the handicapped, would not want to run the risk that a deaf juror would fail to detect some subtle but highly significant nuance in a defendant's tone of voice, or that a blind juror would fail to infer something important from the posture or dress of a witness. As a result, even if the handicapped were not disqualified by law, it is unlikely that a blind or deaf person would be chosen by the lawyers at the time of the trial to serve on a particular jury if the lawyers knew of the disability.

Alex Butler's first two books had been novels. "Character studies of young Americans," the critics had called them; his agent had called them barely commercial. Having two books published by the age of twenty-three should be enough to satisfy most people, Alex thought, but no, not his agent—and not himself.

As his next project, Alex was determined to write something sensational that would earn him enough to return to serious writing. The call to jury duty had seemed like a good way to spend a last couple of weeks of his free time before figuring out the source of his future economic independence.

Alex read from the instruction sheet about the locations of the parking area, vending machines, cafeteria, lavatories, and lockers. He smiled when he saw that a juror was paid five dollars per day for each day he appeared for service. The same day Alex had read in a newspaper that the average full-time writer earned less than five thousand dollars a year, his agent had called to remind him that she got 10 percent of his earnings. At least he'd get to keep 100 percent of his daily fiver.

Alex did not know that the national average is ten dollars per day, twice what he would be receiving. On the other hand, he might have received a mere two dollars per day in some South Carolina counties—or the princely twenty dollars per day paid out by the federal courts. And, of course, if he were earning the forty dollars per day paid by Middlesex County, Massachusetts, Alex would be among the better-paid writers in America.

It would have been little solace to Alex that the cost to the country of compensating jurors comes to $200 million annually, not including the estimated $1 billion lost to the nation's economy by the absence of jurors from their regular jobs. Unfortunately for Alex, he was not among the 80 percent of jurors who were salaried workers compensated by their employers for jury service.

The instruction sheet informed Alex that the jurors summoned to the courthouse were divided into twelve panels, A through L, and that his panel was designated on his jury summons. He took out the folded summons from his back pocket. He was in panel E.

He had debated with himself whether he would prefer to pass the two weeks on a jury or spend it reading and relaxing. While an undergraduate at Yale, he had sat as a member of a mock jury at the law school, and that had been fun. It might be interesting to see how justice was really done, and to participate in it, watching the human drama unfold. On second thought, he would just as soon relax. Besides, he had heard that during the selection process lawyers usually knocked young people off the juries.

Alex Butler was correct in believing that young people are discriminated against in jury selection. In the 1970s people between twenty-one and twenty-five constituted 13 percent of the population but made up only 3 percent of juries.

When Julius Solars stepped off the elevator, someone directed him into the waiting room for the grand jury. He sat there for more than ten minutes. The number of policemen, and the horrible stories he overheard in snatches of conversation among the other people waiting, made him increasingly anxious about whether or not he was in the right place.

Finally he built up enough nerve to approach the guard at the desk, and in the Yiddish accent of which he had always been so self-conscious, he asked if he might not have made a mistake and come to the wrong room. As a young man just before the war, Julius had escaped from Poland at great risk to come to America. Now, in spite of all the years in his adopted country, it seemed to him he still spoke as a foreigner. While very proud of his citizenship, in many ways he still felt like a recent immigrant.

"Across the hall, mister," the guard said gruffly.

He hurried out the door and rushed to the jury control room. The big room was crowded with people seated in rows facing the front counter. They were all wearing white buttons and listening to a man talking about an orientation film that was about to start.

Julius felt flustered. They must have taken some sort of attendance. He hoped no one would think badly of him. It was an honest mistake. He would be very careful to follow the rules from now on.

Julius was seventy-two, close to the maximum allowable age in New Jersey for jurors, seventy-five. There is a powerful prejudice in the United States against the elderly—an assumption of senility or other disability—and this prejudice is reflected in our laws about jury duty: twenty-one states prohibit for jury duty people beyond a certain age, generally sixty-five or seventy.

And where do the people come from who are considered qualified to judge their neighbor, Leander Rafshoon? Under our Constitution a defendant's fate is supposed to be decided by people randomly drawn from a "fair cross section of the community." The compilation of jury rolls, as for example the gathering of bits of encoded information on computer tapes in Essex County, is the beginning of an elaborate process that ends with a group of twelve who constitute a "jury of peers."

As Leonard Klein realized from the material in the questionnaire, the rules make *almost* every adult American citizen eligible. But is a system of drawing by chance from an all-inclusive pool the best way to come up with the most reliable jurors to judge Leander Rafshoon?

Sixteen states in New England and the South use the once more popular "key-man" system to assemble "better-than-average" jurors: jury commissioners ask prominent members of the community—the head of the Kiwanis, the chamber of commerce, or other community organizations, for example—to supply the names of people they think would make good jurors. Seems simple enough.

The "key-man" method has often produced white, comparatively affluent, better-educated jurors who very much resembled the profiles of the key men making the selections. In the South the key-man method managed for years to virtually eliminate blacks from serving as jurors.

In 1968 federal legislation replaced key men with voter lists. Today the federal courts and thirty-four states put their faith in the common sense of the randomly selected "average" citizen over the community leaders' subjective judgments of who might be the "best" jurors. Under the key-man method, perhaps Leonard Klein and Maureen Whalen would have been included; Alex Butler and Julius Solars might not have been; and if it worked properly, Carl Copco would have been excluded.

Unfortunately, reliance on voter lists creates its own biases. Less than three quarters of the people eligible to vote in 1984 were registered; in some states the level was below 60 percent. And those who do register are not a random group: whites, the middle-aged, and the better educated are overrepresented, while nonwhites, the poor, the young, the old, and the less educated are underrepresented.

Ironically, some people (a *Los Angeles Times* survey in 1977 found 6 percent, and a Rutgers University poll in 1980 found 5 percent) do not vote in order to avoid jury duty, but in some twenty states, like New Jersey, these people still wind up being called as jurors because other lists such as those of licensed drivers or taxpayers are added to voter registrants to constitute the jury rolls.

When Maureen Whalen headed to the courthouse to begin her service as a juror, she was one of over three million people summoned every year in America, one of 137,000 people called in New Jersey for the court year of 1983–84, to determine a neighbor's guilt or innocence.

If the process of selecting the people to be summoned to jury duty is not truly random, the profile of the jury picked for a particular case can be distorted. If more people, for example, are called from a Jewish neighborhood than other neighborhoods, or Hispanic or Italian names are overlooked, the jury panel will favor one group of people over another. In a more heavy-handed example of stacking the deck at this stage of the process, until 1955 the names of white potential jurors in Georgia were put on white cards and the names of blacks were put on yellow cards; when the names were "randomly" drawn to determine who would be summoned, few blacks were called. A Georgia trial court and the Georgia Supreme Court found nothing wrong with the procedure; it took the United States Supreme Court to stop the charade. The use of a computer such as the one in Essex County can avoid this kind of obstacle in arriving at a fair jury.

It is interesting to speculate what differences result when a particular group in our society is absent from juries. The Supreme Court has referred to the underrepresentation of women on juries as the loss of "a flavor, a distinct quality," and the absence of the young or the old has a similar impact on jury deliberations.

Different age groups differ in a variety of ways. Older people differ sharply from younger in many of their attitudes about such basic aspects of life as health, personal problems, and death. The old also tend to be more intolerant of political and social nonconformists than the young and more inclined toward favoring tougher law enforcement.

Prosecutors and defense lawyers should be wary of using stereotypes and statistics in picking juries because there is no way to be sure whether the individual juror is typical of the class to which he might belong. Though young, Alex Butler, for example, wrote sympathetically in his first novel about a teen-ager driven to revenge because legal technicalities had prevented the prosecution of the man who had killed his father. A lawyer would be mistaken simply to pigeonhole Alex as a juror who fell into the category of "young people."

On the other hand, while it is impossible to be sure that an individual is representative of his group, a lawyer must make decisions on probabilities. And a lawyer defending someone accused of murder should be interested to know that 44 percent of those between eighteen and twenty-four opposed the death penalty, while only 27 percent of those over fifty opposed it.

Should our concept of a jury of peers require that Leander

Rafshoon be tried by young, urban blacks? Most people would agree that a brilliant professor is not entitled to a jury composed entirely of brilliant professors, but should he be allowed to be judged only by college graduates, or at least high school graduates? Most people would also agree that a dangerous felon is not entitled to a jury of dangerous felons. Does a young Korean have a right to expect a jury of young Koreans, or a percentage of young people, or of Koreans corresponding to the percentage in the community? If not Koreans, is it fair to confront him with a jury composed predominantly of white, middle-class, average-educated, native-born Americans?

Foreigners have not always been denied the right to jurors from their own countries. The issue of where jurors come from is at the heart of the very concept of a jury of peers. On April 10, 1201, in England, King John signed a charter giving Jews on trial the right to have juries composed of equal numbers of Jews and Christians. King John adopted this charter to protect Jews from the loss of their property, which was being jeopardized in trials because of prejudice against them. This special treatment was afforded less as a favor to Jews than out of self-interest, since the king regarded the property of Jews as belonging to him. Later statutes granted foreign merchants this same right to "mixed juries" in order to encourage merchants to continue doing business in England.

These mixed juries, also called juries *de medietate linguae,* composed half of native jurors and half of jurors speaking the defendant's native language, were allowed, as it was put in the 1880 Supreme Court ruling in *Virginia* v. *Rives,* "probably as much because of the difference of language and customs between the foreigner and Englishmen, and the greater probability of his defense being more fully understood, as because it would be heard in a more friendly spirit by jurors of his own country and language."

Mixed juries were used on several occasions in previous

centuries in America. Four Italians charged with murder in Pennsylvania requested and received a mixed jury in 1783. In 1807 an alien in New York received a mixed jury in his trial for murder. An alien charged with piracy was tried in 1823 by a mixed jury (he was convicted and sentenced to death). In 1841 an Englishman requested a mixed jury from the Virginia court that was about to try him for perjury. His request was granted, but only three Englishmen responded to the summons to court. One of the Englishmen was excused for legal reasons, and the judge went on with the trial, with the two remaining jurors representing only one sixth of the jury of twelve. The defendant's conviction was upheld after he appealed on the grounds that he had not had his proper "half-English" jury.

The basic issue raised by mixed juries was considered by the Supreme Court as recently as 1961. The Court rejected the arguments of a woman convicted of murdering her husband when she claimed that she had been denied a fair trial because her jury had been all male. The defendant had argued that women jurors would have been more understanding than men in assessing her behavior. The right to an impartially selected jury, said the Court, "does not entitle one accused of crime to a jury tailored to the circumstances of the particular case, whether relating to the sex or other condition of the defendant, or to the nature of the charges to be tried."

Legal scholars continue to debate endlessly the merits of the various methods of constituting our juries. Civil rights lawyers have succeeded in changing the way some of the state systems compile lists or select panels from them. But the average criminal lawyer has never challenged the jury lists, and while he may have tried hundreds of cases, it is likely that he barely knows how all those people have turned up in the courtroom waiting to be selected as the final twelve to decide a specific case.

While there may be biases built into the system, their significance is minimal when compared with the kind of distortions accomplished later at the voir dire, that part of the selection process in which the lawyers choose the particular twelve they want for their trial. The last thing the prosecutor and the defense lawyer in a case like that of Leander Rafshoon would want would be a truly random jury. Both would want jurors they thought favored their side.

CHAPTER

II.

WHILE STRANGERS WERE COMING TOGETHER from all directions to take on their new roles as jurors, about a dozen lawyers were assembling five floors above them in Judge Harlan Whitaker's court to go through the weekly ritual of the calendar call.

Assistant Prosecutor Leslie Ryan and his detective, Vince Altieri, headed down the center aisle of the courtroom. Ryan walked over to the prosecutor's side of counsel table and put down his files. He went over to Mike Bernstein, Rafshoon's defense lawyer, who was seated against the wooden rail.

"Mike, we can't go today," Ryan said.

"What's with you guys?" Bernstein was instantly steaming. "This is the third damned time you've had me get everything ready. I screw up my whole schedule. You give me no goddamned notice."

"It's the medical examiner. He's in the hospital having

a hernia fixed." Ryan was unaware that his detective had mistakenly attached the last page of another victim's autopsy report done by the absent medical examiner to Carolyn Collins's report and that the woman pathologist who had actually performed the autopsy on Carolyn Collins, Dr. Linares, was available.

"You mean you just found out about that?"

"He'll be ready by next week. We can start the case Wednesday. I'll need him about the following Monday. I'm talking about two days."

"You want to explain it to my client? He's been sitting in the can for a year already."

"Tell him it'll all be credited to his life sentence," Ryan said, smiling.

"There isn't going to be any sentence. I'm going to win this one," Bernstein said without a smile.

"All rise," the court officer said loudly.

There was no one in the courtroom except lawyers and the personnel assigned to the court. As everyone rose to his feet, Judge Whitaker emerged from a door behind and to the right of his desk. His black robes fluttered as he quickly climbed the three steps to his seat.

"Be seated," he said.

All the lawyers except Ryan sat down.

The man seated next to Bernstein leaned over to him. "I was in court here one day a few years ago," he whispered, "when Ryan and another lawyer were waiting to argue a motion. Judge Whitaker came out of his chambers and took his seat on the bench. Before opening the proceedings, he announced to a courtroom full of lawyers, 'I just heard on the radio that they've elected a Polish pope.'"

Bernstein arched his eyebrows to ask what happened.

"There was a dead silence in the courtroom for a few seconds and then Ryan stood up. 'I'm sorry, Judge,' he said. 'So

they elected a Polish pope. I don't get it.' He thought the
judge had been telling a new Polish joke."

Bernstein began to shake in silent laughter.

Ryan was now tentatively addressing the judge. "Your
Honor, I know we were counting on starting today in the
Rafshoon murder case, and—"

"That's right," the judge said with a snap in his voice, "and
that's what we're moving. We've already adjourned that case
twice. Today was set down weeks ago. I cleared my calendar
of all my other cases. Now, what did you want to tell me, Mr.
Prosecutor?"

"We will be ready Wednesday."

Judge Whitaker placed a pencil in his mouth and bit down.
"How dare you?" the judge finally said after removing the
pencil. "This man has been locked up almost a year. Do you
know what kind of directives I get from the supreme court
about moving jail cases?"

"Yes, sir," Ryan said.

"What am I supposed to tell the chief justice?" The judge's
face flushed with anger. "Our jails are bursting, and this is
the third time now you can't get your act together. If this
weren't a murder case, I'd dismiss it. What's your excuse this
time?"

"Our medical examiner is in the hospital."

"Splendid. Can't you get someone else?"

"He's the guy who did the autopsy, and his assistant has
just left for a job in California."

"Are you telling me that the Medical Examiner's Office has
only one person who can testify from a simple autopsy report
that the victim is dead? Is that what you're telling me?"

"No, sir. The forensic evidence is critical in this case. The
nature and extent of the wounds played a large part in identifying the perpetrator. And we don't have anyone with the
courtroom experience of Dr. Carbona or his former assistant."

"What does that mean?" the judge asked. "Are you telling me that you have a weak case?"

"No, sir. It means one of the witnesses will be the murder victim who will announce in open court who her killer was—but the victim will have to speak through the mouth of the medical examiner. We need the medical examiner to be her voice, if you get my drift, Judge." Ryan wasn't going to be intimidated by anyone, not even an infuriated judge.

"Save it for the jury, Mr. Prosecutor."

"I'm only asking for two days."

The judge shook his head in disgust. He turned to his court clerk. "Fred, do we have a short gambling case or something?"

"I think we can find something," a bald man in a charcoal black suit answered.

"You know, Mr. Ryan, I have to report my bench time, and if I can't find a case to occupy these two days, I'm going to send my sergeant at arms downstairs to your office to physically bring you back to start this case."

"Yes, Judge."

"And another thing. If you're not ready on Wednesday, I am going to dismiss this case, murder or no murder. Do you get *my* drift?"

"Yes, Judge."

"Why are you smiling, Mr. Bernstein?" Judge Whitaker asked. "Perhaps you would like to consider waiving the jury and having a bench trial." Waiving the jury and having a trial by a judge alone is called a bench trial. About 10 percent of all defendants go to trial before judges without juries. "It would certainly speed things up once we got started," the judge added.

Defendants waive juries when they think they would be better off with a judge. They more often opt for a bench trial when they have bad criminal records, where there has been prejudicial pretrial publicity, or where the charges involve

outrageous behavior such as the rape of a young girl. Blacks
in the South frequently waived juries when they feared the
racial prejudice of jurors, particularly if the charge involved a
crime against a white woman.

Bernstein stood. "No, Judge. I don't think I'll waive the
jury."

"I'm not surprised," the judge said.

There is an old and cynical piece of lawyer's advice: if not
guilty, be tried by a judge; if guilty, be tried by a jury. The
theory behind the advice is that judges are more rational and
predictable than juries. Bernstein never seriously considered
waiving the jury. He had genuine respect for the common
sense of the "average" people of the jury. Although he felt
they were at times susceptible to being swayed by emotion, he
preferred to entrust the fate of his client to nonprofessionals
trying to be fair rather than to a hardened judge like Whitaker who had seen it all.

As Judge Whitaker was juggling his calendar of cases, the
orientation program was beginning in the jury control room
on the fourth floor.

"The origin of the jury is unclear," a tape-recorded bari-
tone voice announced as the American flag disappeared from
the wall, leaving the room in darkness. "It may have roots in
Greece as far back as 450 B.C., when the guilt or innocence of
an accused was decided by a jurylike assembly of two thousand members." The projector flashed a painting of Socrates
on trial. Many states now have similar orientation programs
for jurors, providing handbooks describing the juror's role,
and even showing movies, or, as here in New Jersey, a slide
show.

Laura Sayres sat near the two slide projectors; the one that
had flashed a color photograph of the American flag on the
green wall and the other that had shown the picture of Socrates. Laura, at thirty-three, had just been promoted to Ex-

ecutive Vice-President of Cross-Cultural Communications. The promotion meant to her that she had been right in her decision to commit herself to her career. Had she married David straight out of college, she would always have felt she had missed an opportunity. The string of unhappy relationships with men had been one of the consequences of her decision, but at least she had been right about the work. She loved it, and she was good at it, and her success was not simply because of her good looks.

Laura tried to concentrate on the slide show. "In the early days of the jury system in England, jurors made judgments as representatives of the king." Darkness for a moment, then the machine projected the picture of a king. "If the king was unhappy with those judgments, he punished the jurors. But gradually this perilous aspect of jury duty faded away, in no small part because of the difficulty of finding people willing to serve as jurors." Several people in the audience laughed.

Now a series of inspirational images was projected on the green wall. Laura leaned back and tried to relax.

A Colonial building was flashed on the wall. "To encourage settlements in the American colonies," the voice announced, "the English kings found it necessary to promise the colonists that they and their descendants would forever enjoy all the privileges of Englishmen—which included the right to trial by jury. But as the colonies prospered, King George the Third became convinced that American juries would not enforce such unpopular laws as the Stamp Act of 1765 imposing heavy taxes. And so power was transferred to admiralty courts, whose judges served without juries at the king's pleasure."

Here a scene of boats in the Boston harbor was projected on the wall, and the narrator talked about the Continental Congress, while Laura thought about her looks. In the past she had felt that most of the attention she'd received in her life had had nothing to do with her real worth, but had re-

sulted from the fact that she was uncommonly beautiful. All
the fawning she'd been exposed to had served only to undermine her self-confidence. Being elected to Phi Beta Kappa and
all the awards in college and graduate school hadn't been
enough to rid her of that gnawing feeling that if she lost her
looks, she'd be worthless. Now, with her new position in the
company, she knew she had arrived where she was because of
ability, not because of superficial appearances.

"The Declaration of Independence called the right to a trial
by jury inalienable," the rich voice announced. Darkness for
a moment, then the machine flashed the face of George
Washington.

"The subject of trial by jury was brought up in the last few
days of the Constitutional Convention. Few records docu-
ment what went on when the provision for juries was drafted.
The following wording was eventually adopted under Article
Three of the Constitution: 'The Trial of all Crimes, except in
Cases of Impeachment, shall be by Jury.'

"The failure to include more detailed guarantees of impartial procedures for juries in criminal cases or to provide at all
for juries in civil cases became a heated issue in the acceptance of the Constitution. Thomas Jefferson, Patrick Henry,
and others opposed the adoption of the Constitution on the
grounds that the jury provisions did not go far enough."

From Laura's standpoint, her jury duty came at just the
wrong moment. She felt that she needed to spend most of her
time at the office from now on, dealing with clients rather
than handling paperwork. And there were so many things to
do at the office before she would feel truly organized.

"In response to the critics' demands for more guarantees,
Madison, who drafted the Bill of Rights, included the Sixth
Amendment: 'In all criminal prosecutions, the accused shall
enjoy the right to a speedy and public trial, by an impartial
jury of the State and district wherein the crime shall have
been committed.' The Seventh Amendment extended jury

trials to all civil cases, 'suits in common law where the value in controversy shall exceed twenty dollars.' And so trial by jury became the only right to be triply guaranteed in our Constitution.

"In spite of its long history and place in our fundamental documents, the jury doesn't function in the same way throughout our country, nor has it finished evolving as an institution. Some states have juries made up of less than twelve members, and not every state requires verdicts to be unanimous. In fact it was only as recently as 1968 that the United States Supreme Court ruled that a jury trial was constitutionally required in all criminal cases in which the penalty could exceed six months.

"Your responsibility as a juror is nothing less than the safeguarding of our liberty."

The slide show abruptly ended with the image of the American flag and a recording of "The Star-Spangled Banner" playing loudly in the background.

Patricia Stewart thought the documentary slide show was impressive. At twenty-eight, she felt she had been too absorbed in herself and her career as an actress to learn much about such things as the history of the jury system. She had once played a juror in an experimental off-off-Broadway play, but all she had done was sit silently in the jury box dressed as a cauliflower. She was sure it would be interesting to study the performances of the real characters in an actual trial. Some of the witnesses would probably lie, and she wondered—being an actress herself—if she would be able to tell who was telling the truth. Lying, after all, was a performance. But as Patricia thought about it, it occurred to her that everyone involved in a trial was performing—the lawyers, the judge, even the honest witnesses had probably rehearsed.

The supervisor of jury control was about to speak. Patricia tried to take careful note of his public-speaking ability.

"Some of you may have legitimate reasons to be excused as jurors," the supervisor said, "but I can tell you that less than one percent of the people who reach the point of sitting in this room get excused. People are excused in New Jersey, as in courts throughout the country, if their jury service would cause a genuine personal hardship either to them or to the public. We don't have specific criteria which govern the granting of excuses. We deal with problems on a case by case basis. If you still feel entitled to an excuse, please see me after the orientation program is over."

The jury supervisor may never have heard the story of the prospective juror who had reported to a San Francisco court toting two birdcages containing twenty canaries, asking to be excused on the grounds that her birds would become depressed if she was absent from them. The judge was happy to let the woman go, commenting that the possession of twenty canaries probably indicated more serious problems anyway.

"In a few moments," the supervisor went on, "you will be sworn in as jurors. Unfortunately, there doesn't seem to be a way to run this enormous undertaking without involving juries in some waiting. The Essex County Bar Association has donated books, puzzles, and games that you are welcome to use while you are waiting to be called.

"Please don't use the freight elevators.

"If your employer needs a certification of your service here, we can furnish that for you.

"In a few minutes I will have the privilege of introducing the Honorable Charles G. Samuelson, who will make a few introductory remarks, and then you will be sworn in as jurors. Unfortunately, Judge Samuelson has been delayed, and I must ask you to be patient."

Twenty minutes later Judge Samuelson was standing in his black robes in front of the long counter in the jury control room. "On behalf of our County of Essex, it is my privilege to welcome you to your present tour of jury service," he said.

"Your jury service represents your contribution to the perpetuation of our democratic way of life. Your willingness to support our legal system protects all of our liberties. Your service is an assurance that if chance or design brings you to a court of law in a civil or criminal entanglement, your rights will be protected by the same mantle of consideration that you will administer here in the faithful discharge of your duties. These statements are not platitudes, but are real and meaningful in terms of your role as jurors.

"Not only must juries exonerate the innocent and convict the guilty, they must *appear* to be doing that. If the public loses confidence that juries are rationally settling violent disputes between society and those accused of offending it, personal acts of vigilantism, revenge, lynchings, and riots are not farfetched consequences.

"From grammar school on we have learned about our rights as Americans, but aside from voting, most of us have had few opportunities to participate in the democratic process. Most of our governmental institutions derive their power as representatives of the electorate, but in a criminal trial the citizens themselves make fateful decisions in a direct expression of power.

"Your service as a juror should command your pride and pleasure. The sacrifice it compels enlarges the value and worth of its rendition. Jury service will bind you in morality and justice to render verdicts that are above reproach and beyond suspicion.

"Your duty requires that you be prompt in your attendance, attentive to your duties, faithful to your oaths, considerate and tolerant of your fellow jurors, sound in your evaluations, and firm but not obdurate in your convictions.

"In taking the juror's oath you will be agreeing to fulfill the important functions of your high duties with dignity, propriety, and integrity.

"If you do your duty as you are instructed and expected to do, you will reap the rich reward reserved for those who rise to the call of public service and will obtain a sense of deep satisfaction for having borne, with honor and distinction, the obligations and duties of your great responsibility in the cause of common good. We hope that this service will be an interesting and meaningful experience for all of you.

"Will the clerk please swear the panel."

"All please rise," the clerk announced.

Everyone stood.

"Do you solemnly swear," the clerk said, "that you will support the Constitution of the United States and the constitution of this state, so help you God? Please respond 'I do.'"

Some people placed their right hands over their hearts in the way they had done when they saluted the flag as children. Everyone said, "I do."

"Oh," the clerk said, "I forgot to mention that you are asked to wear your juror buttons at all times. And if you see your panel leaving for a courtroom, please join them."

In New Jersey as in most states, judges take turns delivering similar speeches to new jurors. Patricia Stewart was moved by the importance of her new role as a real-life juror. Leonard Klein was sure there must have been a less pompous way of conveying the same information, but in spite of his reluctance to submit to this two-week intrusion into his life, he had to admit to himself that performing this "civic duty" did seem like the right thing to do.

Two days passed and, for panels E and F, nothing happened. On Wednesday, the morning of the third day of jury duty, while those who would soon be caught up in the decision of who was responsible for the brutal killing of Carolyn

Collins waited in the fourth-floor jury control room, Leander Rafshoon, the man who was accused of that killing, was told to step out of his cell. He wore the dark suit his mother had brought to the jail the last time the trial had been scheduled to begin. The guard clicked the handcuffs around his wrists.

"They're too tight," Rafshoon said.

The guard stared coldly at him.

"Please. They're too tight."

The guard shrugged and loosened them a bit. "We'd better get going," he said, pointing down the corridor. "The judge goes bullshit when we're late with prisoners."

They walked down the corridor and stood together waiting for the elevator.

"You think it'll really go this time?" Rafshoon asked.

"This ain't your first trial date?" the guard asked.

Rafshoon shook his head.

The guard shrugged.

When the elevator arrived, Rafshoon entered first and, without being told, moved to the far corner. The guard unfolded the six-foot-high metal screen, locking it to cut the elevator's small space in half on the diagonal.

The guard stood on the side of the screen closest to the doors as they rose to the ninth floor.

When they arrived, Rafshoon was led out of the elevator and a few feet to the left to the dimly lit holding pen. He entered the cell without being instructed, and the guard locked the heavy, barred door.

Rafshoon watched the guard step back into the elevator and vanish. He was alone in a cell again. He sat on the metal bench and looked through the bars at the solid door on the far side of the elevator. He knew the courtroom was on the other side of that door. He waited for the door to open. A few minutes passed. Rafshoon's gaze swept across the cell and the space between the barred door and the door to the courtroom. The wall opposite the elevator was cinder block painted a shiny gray. The cement floor was painted the same color. A metal bench, similar to the one he sat on, was against the wall across from the elevator. The outside bench was intended for lawyers talking to their clients, but it was rarely used. A single exposed bulb protected by a wire mesh cage lighted the area. Rafshoon wondered why the wire mesh did not cast a shadow on the gray wall. He had not yet realized that the jury room was on the other side of the wall he was leaning against. The jury room had an entrance into the courtroom. The jurors would never see his cell. They would see him enter and leave the courtroom, but they would have no idea of how stark and frightening his cage was. And Rafshoon would never see the inside of the jury room, where twelve strangers would argue over his fate.

The handle turned slightly. Rafshoon saw it immediately. Prisoners can sense a finger flick from across a room, even if their backs are turned.

The heavy door slowly opened. He could see the bright courtroom on the other side. Mike Bernstein entered and the door closed behind him.

"They're bringing a panel up in a few minutes," Bernstein said, his words bouncing off the shiny walls. "Once we start picking a jury, the D.A.'s offer is over. Do you understand that?"

"I'm not pleading to anything. I'll take my chances with the jury," Rafshoon said.

"You understand they can find you guilty of first degree. That's life in prison plus the time for the rape if they find you guilty for that. You wouldn't be out for twenty-five years, at the earliest. You'd be close to sixty."

Rafshoon had been offered a chance to plead to second-degree murder, which, as Bernstein had told him months earlier, meant that if the judge imposed the maximum sentence, he would be released from prison in about eight years. The terms of plea bargaining are usually based on the way the prosecutor and the defense lawyer believe a jury will decide the case. In trying to predict a jury's verdict, each side weighs the evidence for and against a conviction, imagining the impact of each piece of evidence on the jury, given the skills of the adversaries. The more likely it seems that the jury will convict, the closer the terms of a plea bargain usually are to the sentence a judge would impose after a jury's verdict of guilty.

"I understand," Rafshoon said. "But how could they come back with first? When the jury hears that the state's offered me second degree . . ."

"No. They never hear anything about plea bargaining."

"I wouldn't even take manslaughter."

"It doesn't matter. They don't hear about it. I'll see you in a couple of minutes. It looks like we're really going to go today."

Rafshoon watched the door close behind Bernstein, then waited. Bernstein had told him the trial could take two weeks. It was hard to judge time when nothing was happening except waiting.

He lit a cigarette. He took several long drags.

The decision that confronted Rafshoon—whether or not to accept a plea bargain—comes up in almost every case throughout the country, not only in urban areas, but in small cities and rural areas as well. Plea bargaining has been the principal means of settling criminal cases in the United States since the mid-1800s, and today defendants in about three quarters of all cases plead guilty to something rather than face a jury. Less than 10 percent of all felony charges and an even smaller percentage of misdemeanor charges are tried before a jury.

Leander Rafshoon was very much aware that an acquittal at trial would be a total victory, but he also knew that the price of defeat would be enormous. Not only could he be convicted of more than what he would have been allowed to plead guilty to, he knew that Judge Whitaker had a reputation of imposing a stiffer sentence on a convicted defendant who had been offered a plea bargain but insisted on a trial anyway. Many judges offer incentives to defendants in order to save money from taxpayers' pockets that guilty defendants often waste by lengthy jury trials; this may seem commendable, but people accused of a crime should not be punished for exercising their constitutional right of making the government prove its case to a jury.

While Rafshoon waited in his cell, Alex Butler sat in one of the small cubicles in the rear of the jury control room. He was reading *The Song of Smoky Sea*, a book he had taken from the bookcase in the lounge. Stamped on the first page of this story about a small fishing village in Alaska were the words *Please do not remove from petit jury control. A gift of the Essex County Bar Association.* Alex could have taken a novel called *A Flag Full of Stars,* a biography called *Cavanaugh, The Forest Ranger, Hoboken: A Tale of Two Cities,* or any of the other fifty dog-eared books. Alex had decided that when his term of jury duty was over he would donate a copy of his latest novel.

Without having met, Maureen Whalen and Carl Copco sat next to each other in the half-empty lounge, watching the twenty-four-inch color television, on which an effeminate chef was demonstrating how to make a chocolate soufflé. The lounge was thick with cigarette smoke. A few people were reading newspapers, magazines, and books. An older woman was knitting.

Patricia Stewart was in the corner of the lounge, trying to memorize the lines of the scene she was going to do for her acting class that night. After listening to the judge's speech at the orientation, she had decided to perform for her class a portion of the Marlene Dietrich role in *Witness for the Prosecution,* but it was proving hard to get the nuances down.

Patricia was growing anxious about the possibility that she would never be called to a jury. At the coffee stand in the basement the day before, she had heard two jurors from a different panel talking about their trial. A local mayor was on the sixth floor defending himself against the charge of political corruption. That must be fascinating, she thought. The days were slipping by and she hadn't even been called to a courtroom.

Almost a quarter of the people called for jury duty every year never wind up serving on an actual jury but spend their entire jury service sitting around waiting: watching the clock, knitting, playing cards, reading, staring at a television set, bored and waiting.

"If you tell them too much," Patricia had heard the woman say, "they'll find something they don't like. You just have to tell them enough of what they want to hear."

"I can't imagine what they're looking for," the other woman had said. "I saw the same lawyer excuse a guy in a business suit and a fellow in jeans. A young man and an old man. A janitor and a professor. I don't know what he was looking for."

Carl Copco, the pet shop owner, was never very good at waiting. Being cooped up for two days with nothing to do was a kind of torture for him. He couldn't stop thinking about his girl friend. Patty hadn't called yet, and he'd spent every minute after court for the last two days looking for her. He'd gone to all the bars they'd frequented. There was no place else he could think of. Maybe she really had gone back to Minneapolis to live with her sister as she'd threatened, but when she'd left before, she'd always called.

"Well, somebody has to do it."

Carl looked to his right. "You talking to me, lady?"

"Yes," Maureen answered. "I was saying that a certain number of people have to be waiting to be called. Somebody has to do it."

"That's right, lady," Carl said.

"You know what they always say, 'They also serve who only stand and wait.'"

Carl thought about walking out. He did not know how much more of this hanging around he could stand. He stood up. The old lady who had just spoken to him smiled. She had introduced herself the day before, trying to be friendly, but he was never any good at small talk. With her lower jaw extended forward, she looked like one of his ugly Pekingese that no one wanted to buy.

He headed for the back of the lounge. He had to get out of there. He walked down a corridor of small cubicles. In the first one he saw the beautiful woman he had noticed every day. She had a terrific body. She was working on some papers. Every time he saw her, she was working on papers. Good for her. On the first day, Carl had watched some creep try to pick this one up. She put him down with a look. She was a tough one.

In the next cubicle there was a well-dressed dude concentrating on a picture puzzle. He was holding a piece of the puzzle in his fat fingers as if it were the most important thing in the world for him to find the right place for it.

In the last cubicle a man was reading a book. Carl looked over the guy's shoulder to read the title, *The Song of Smoky Sea*. He must be some kind of intellectual or fag or something, Carl thought.

Beyond the line of cubicles was the other lounge, the one where smoking was not permitted. Another large television was showing the same cooking program. On leaving that lounge, Carl reentered the large front room where he'd heard the boring judge give his boring speech. No one was behind the long counter. He walked over to the bank of telephones and called his answering service. Patty hadn't called yet.

Carl headed back to his lounge but paused in front of a bulletin board. A notice posted on it about which radio station to listen to for snow reports was yellowing with age. Next to the notice was a *Peanuts* cartoon with Charlie Brown carrying a suitcase and a stepladder; the caption said he'd decided to take his case to a higher court. Someone had tacked up next to the cartoon a drawing of a stick figure being hanged from a scaffold.

The loudspeaker requested, as it periodically did, that a particular juror report to the counter to receive a message. This time Laura Sayres was being called. Half an hour earlier the loudspeaker had announced that various jury panels should assemble in the hallway to be brought up to a courtroom, but Carl's panel was yet to be called. He felt as if he were on a subway, locked in with strangers. He didn't know how much longer he could take it. He headed back to his seat in front of the television.

Proposals and experiments aimed at dealing with the boredom and frustration of jury duty have included reduced service time, improvement in predicting the number of jurors needed, and daily call-in systems to alert jurors who need not come to the courthouse. None of these alternatives had been instituted to save Carl from the imprisonment he felt.

Julius Solars sat in the last row of the lounge. He was relieved that he hadn't yet been called to a courtroom, and he would just as soon spend the duration of his jury service in front of the "telly." Not that he had any interest in the programs, but it was a safe place to be. It seemed a little funny to be watching cooking lessons when he still had heartburn from the meal he had eaten in the cafeteria the day before. He'd always liked eggplant, but he had never had it before with cheese and tomato sauce. It must have been the tomato sauce. He would be more careful from now on. He had noticed they sold yogurt, and that's what he should have had in the first place. He shook his head. He always had second thoughts about everything. How could he ever be a juror deciding an important case?

Leonard Klein, in his little cubicle, always enjoyed puzzles, but he hadn't had the time to assemble one in years. He'd been working for the two days of his jury service on five thousand interlocking pieces of a geometric design. Before starting the puzzle, Leonard had noticed that a note had been written in parentheses on the front of the box, "24 missing," but that hadn't deterred him. It had become important for him to finish the puzzle and find out if there really were twenty-four pieces missing, and if so, where in the puzzle they belonged.

The most common complaint about jury duty is the frustration of wasting time in sheer waiting, but the complaint is not entirely justified. The pressure of a waiting jury forces a large number of settlements in civil cases and plea bargains in criminal cases, which dispose of those cases just as completely as a jury trial. In order to have a number of courts in continuous operation, a pool of jurors has to be available to start the next case.

The door opened. A court officer entered. "Okay," he said, and unlocked the barred door.

Rafshoon threw the cigarette into the seatless toilet. It made a brief hiss. He stepped on the handle. A thunderous *whoosh* echoed in the room.

Stepping into the glare of the courtroom was like stepping out of a gritty black and white photograph into a Technicolor movie. Rafshoon blinked several times and squinted until his eyes adjusted to the brightness.

Two guards were standing by the jury room, laughing. The court reporter was speaking into a tape recorder. The court clerk was reading a thick paperback book. Bernstein was talking to the prosecutor. Rafshoon's mother was sitting in the first row beyond the well of the courtroom. She looked so frightened. He tried to smile at her.

The guard led him to his seat at counsel table. He unlocked the handcuffs and slipped them off Rafshoon's wrists. "We can't let the jury see you in these, can we?" The guard smiled sympathetically.

The guard pointed to a chair, and Leander Rafshoon sat down. The jury panel would enter in a few moments. He looked for them through the little window of the door in the back of the courtroom. They hadn't arrived yet. They were his only hope. He was betting his life on them. He felt he was right not to enter into a plea bargain. Of course he was right. He was almost sure he was right.

Not so many years ago, orientation programs would indoctrinate jurors about the "epidemic" of crime and the need to convict "perpetrators." They would say such things as "Don't be taken in by bogus ploys like claims of insanity or self-defense."

Today, with the encouragement of the upper courts, we are more evenhanded. The pressure to avoid statements about the jurors' being the "best instrument for law enforcement" or, on the other hand, being the "last defense against the oppression of the state" has resulted in inoffensive and boring productions like "To Be a Juror." The jurors who would try Leander Rafshoon could not possibly have been prejudiced by the neutral language to which they had been subjected.

But as a general rule the orientation functions as a ritual that communicates portentously the idea that jury service is important and should be taken seriously. On that modest level it is usually effective, as it was with Patricia Stewart and even Leonard Klein.

What the orientation programs leave out are facts revealing that the history of the jury in the United States has not been uniformly filled with profiles in integrity. New jury panels are not told about the racism, sexism, and discrimination against anyone different that has marked the selection and performance of juries from the beginning of the Republic.

This untold history of the jury is about the struggle to de-

termine who shall have the power to decide guilt or innocence within the meaning of that extraordinary notion of "an
impartial jury of peers." For our first hundred years, blacks
were explicitly denied the right to be jurors, which meant that
if a black defendant was not lynched on the spot, an all-white
jury would later decide what to do with him. In 1880 the
Supreme Court decided that under the then recently adopted
Fourteenth Amendment, state statutes explicitly barring
blacks as jurors were unconstitutional. In that 1880 opinion,
however, the Court specifically recognized that women could
be excluded from juries.

After the Supreme Court disallowed in noble-sounding language any explicit statutes authorizing lily-white juries, public officials accomplished the same kind of discrimination for
the next fifty-five years simply by the way they went about
their duties in selecting jurors. And many all-white juries in
the South continued to hang black defendants. In 1935 the
Supreme Court finally declared that public officials could not
use their authority to exclude blacks.

For more than the first 175 years of the Republic, women
were also officially excluded from most juries. At last, in
1940, the Supreme Court decided that juries must reflect a
fair cross section of the community, and that a selection was
unconstitutional if it resulted in a significant underrepresentation of a recognized group in our society, such as women.

Since that decision, the Court has struggled to determine
just which other groups in our society are entitled to be pro-
portionately represented in that "fair cross section." Blacks,
women, various ethnic groups, the poor, wage earners, atheists, and those with moral scruples against capital punishment have, over the years, been considered "cognizable" and
entitled to be included on juries. Groups based on education
and age have not been regarded as entitled to proportional
representation on jury rolls.

From the time of the Constitution's adoption until 1968,

its jury provisions were interpreted as applying minimum standards only to the federal government; the states were permitted to make their own decisions about who had a right to a jury trial.

Over the years, state courts around the country adopted widely different policies as to who was entitled to a jury. Most states provided juries in cases exposing a defendant to more than six months in jail, but some states such as New York had trials without juries where punishments of one year in jail could be imposed, and Louisiana had nonjury trials in which life sentences were possible.

The right of a state to limit jury trials ended in 1968 in a Louisiana case in which a black teen-ager was accused of slapping a white boy. Gary Duncan, a nineteen-year-old black, had stopped his car by the side of a road where his two cousins were being confronted by four white boys. Gary got out of his car, spoke to the white boys, and encouraged his cousins to leave with him. The whites testified at the trial that just before getting into the car Gary slapped one of the white boys on the elbow. The slap was prosecuted as a battery punishable by up to two years' imprisonment and a $300 fine. The defendant had requested a jury trial, but the trial judge denied that request because the Louisiana Constitution required juries only in cases in which the punishment could include death or imprisonment at hard labor. The defendant was convicted and sentenced to serve sixty days in the parish prison and to pay a fine of $150.

Duncan appealed to the Louisiana Supreme Court, which found nothing wrong with the conviction. His last chance was to take his case to the United States Supreme Court. "The jury trial provisions in the Federal and State Constitutions," the Supreme Court said, "reflect a fundamental decision about the exercise of power—a reluctance to entrust plenary powers over the life and liberty of the citizen to one judge or to a group of judges. Fear of unchecked power, so

typical of our State and Federal Governments in other respects, found expression in the criminal law in this insistence
upon community participation in the determination of guilt
or innocence." The Supreme Court reversed the conviction.

After *Duncan* v. *Louisiana,* the Sixth Amendment's guarantee of the right of trial by jury would apply to all criminal
cases, including those in state courts. But to say that there is a
right to a jury in all criminal trials overstates the scope of the
provisions of the Constitution. Crimes considered "petty"—
and there is quite a squabble among legal scholars over what
constitutes "petty"—are disposed of by a judge without a
jury. Nor have juries been generally used in military trials,
and the Supreme Court, over vehement dissenting opinions,
has permitted the states to try juveniles without juries.

In a sense, the greatest value to society of the right to a jury
trial is its effect as a deterrent to sloppiness or wrongdoing on
the part of the police, prosecutors, and judges, who know
that their work may be scrutinized in a public trial. In this
way the jury, in effect, acts as a randomly selected civilian
review board. But this deterrent is undermined if improper
conduct can be concealed by a plea bargain. As the system
now works, the terms of a bargain, or the reasons for those
terms, are often concealed from the public when the prosecutor and the defense lawyer avoid a jury trial by sitting
down alone together in a room and "negotiating," a process
that too often seems more appropriate for rug merchants.

Prosecutors are sometimes eager to avoid a jury trial. Concerned about their reputations for winning cases, they may
not want to risk a loss. By avoiding a public trial with a plea
bargain, a prosecutor can also avoid the public disclosure of
an illegal search conducted by the police, or some bungling
by the police chemist in the analysis of evidence, or a mishap
of the police photographer or the medical examiner.

There was a time when defendants had reason to refuse to
plead either guilty or not guilty to a charge. In the thirteenth

century, if a defendant stood mute when asked to plead to a crime or submit to a trial jury, he was subjected to punishment. The defendant was sent to prison and put in a low, dark chamber; he was laid on his back, on the bare floor, naked, and a great weight of iron was placed on his body. He was fed only on alternate days, "three morsels of the worst bread and . . . three draughts of standing water . . . and in this situation the person should remain til he died or til he answered."

A defendant would consider standing mute and facing those consequences because if a jury found him guilty, his lands and goods were forfeited to the crown and his family would have nothing to survive on, but if the defendant died before trial, he could, at least, avoid the forfeiture. In 1827 this practice was abolished. Today, if a defendant stands mute, the judge enters a plea of not guilty on his behalf and the trial proceeds.

PART

TWO

THOSE
CHOSEN TO
JUDGE

CHAPTER

III.

WITH HER WHITE OVAL JUROR BUTTON pinned to her lapel, Maureen Whalen waited outside the courtroom. She stood next to Laura Sayres, who had just said hello to her in the jury assembly room downstairs. The court officer had led the panel to the end of the corridor, but before the group could enter the courtroom, they had to wait for the elevators to bring up a second panel, another forty people.

A woman on the other side of the corridor said she'd been a juror before. "The lawyers were so rude when they picked us. Rude and obtuse, I must say," the woman said, her high-pitched laugh echoing down the corridor.

The court officers finally ushered the group into the courtroom. Twenty rows of benches on each side of the center aisle filled the large room. In the front section, on the other side of a wooden rail running the width of the courtroom, a long table faced the judge's bench. To the left, the jury box contained two rows of eight chairs.

Just like the movies, it seemed to Patricia Stewart as she took her seat with the other members of the panel. It was this courtroom and all the other courtrooms like it in America that separated us from barbarians, she mused with pride. Without plain folks like us willing to serve on juries, our whole system of justice would collapse and we'd be no better than the communists.

While the physical characteristics vary, courtrooms, in general, are cold, formal rooms staged with props clearly marking the roles assigned to the cast of characters who perform there. The formality and "hardness" of the courtrooms must affect the responses of jurors in unmeasured ways.

Two men sat together at the right end of the long table in front of the judge's bench. One man sat alone at the other end of the table, next to the jury box. Carl Copco knew right away that the black guy was the defendant, and the guy next to him was his lawyer. Carl had lived and worked around blacks all his life. He knew how often they wound up in court—and, as he thought about it—usually with some smart Jew lawyer, who must be the guy with the big nose sitting next to him up there.

Carl was right to believe that there was a higher likelihood of finding a black male defendant in a Newark courtroom, but nationally 73 percent of those who face juries are white. An even more surprising statistic is that 93 percent are male.

Alex Butler took a seat at the far end of a row, next to a tall, narrow gun slit of a window. He noticed that the only way to open the window was with a key inserted into its metal frame. He imagined a long rifle being slipped into the gun slit to hold off invaders. Alex was surprised at how much he hated being herded around by these court officers. He tried to analyze what was so upsetting for him, and decided it was the authority the guards had over him—it was the pressure of being under their constant supervision.

The courthouse had been built ten years earlier, about the same time the new jailhouse next door had been finished. Both buildings were long rectangles, about twenty yards away from each other, twelve stories high. Viewed from above, the two buildings formed a T, the jailhouse being the head of the T and the courthouse constituting the support. The courtrooms ran along the length of the courthouse, which meant that not a single window of any of the twenty courtrooms viewed the jail.

Leonard Klein looked out the ninth-floor window at Newark's devastated ghetto. Remnants of burnt houses rose up like black spikes from the open lots, lots that he knew were filled with garbage, broken liquor bottles, and rats. He had grown up in Newark. The city had never had much charm, but it was a place of important memories for him. Now it was in ruins, with nothing for today's kids to recall later with nostalgia.

"It looks like a full house," Carl said from his seat in the last row. "Must be a good show."

Several people around Carl laughed nervously. Although he did not find any humor in the remark, Julius Solars started to smile politely but stopped when he realized that the court officer in the aisle might have heard the man.

"It's a murder case, a rape and murder," Patricia Stewart, in the row in front of Julius, turned around to say. "I heard the guard say so when we were in the hall."

Julius felt his heart race. This would be too upsetting. He couldn't do it, he said to himself. Maybe I won't be called, he thought. It would be too complicated. I couldn't make that kind of decision. I'm just a simple worker. I even have trouble deciding if I should wear galoshes, he thought. I would never want to be responsible for a decision about another man's life. No matter how guilty he might be, I just wouldn't want to be part of the machinery that winds up punishing him.

"Everyone rise," the clerk said in a deep voice, and more than eighty people stood. A door to the right of the judge's desk opened. A short bald man in a black robe rushed into the courtroom and quickly climbed the several steps to his desk. "Please be seated," he said, and banged a gavel.

Everyone sat.

"Good morning, ladies and gentlemen."

"Good morning," a number of people answered.

"My name is Judge Harlan Whitaker. Welcome to my courtroom. We are about to begin a criminal trial. You will participate in this trial in the crucial role of jurors."

The judge spoke quickly, and Maureen, squinting, tried to focus on the judge's lips.

"The first phase will be the voir dire, which is the jury selection process in which the lawyers and I get a chance to meet you. The words *voir* and *dire* are French and mean 'to see' and 'to speak,' and that's just what will happen," the judge said with a smile. "We'll all see and speak."

Judge Whitaker was mistaken, though the mistake he made was common. Voir dire means "true talk," the word *voir* being a corruption of the Latin *verus,* meaning "true." The voir dire is not just an opportunity for a meeting, but serves to expose prejudice in jurors and to eliminate those with extreme views. To some extent the voir dire is also used to motivate and/or indoctrinate juries as a group, to discover friendly jurors, to cause jurors to face their own prejudices, to introduce the lawyers and let them begin developing personalized relationships with the jurors.

"In a criminal trial," the judge went on, "a prosecutor or defense lawyer may, by what is called a 'challenge for cause,' object to the seating of a potential juror on the grounds that certain facts about the person raise a legitimate suspicion that he or she may not be fair in this particular case."

Judge Whitaker would not have time to explain all the technical grounds that disqualify citizens from sitting in judgment on their fellow citizens, but all are based on common sense: a juror is disqualified if he is related to the defendant, a witness, or one of the lawyers; if he has a special interest in the subject matter; if he has served in a related case or on the grand jury that indicted the defendant; or if he has a mind-set that will prevent him from acting with impartiality.

"In addition to challenges for cause," Judge Whitaker continued, "a certain number of potential jurors may be excused for no expressed reason other than the lawyer's subjective preference that the person not serve. These are called 'peremptory challenges.'"

The law assumes that challenges for cause are not enough to guarantee juries that are free from prejudice. Some jurors will refuse to reveal their true feelings or certain facts about themselves that would constitute grounds for a challenge for cause. Others may not actually realize how their prejudices affect their objectivity, or they may honestly but mistakenly believe that they can put their prejudices aside.

"If you are excused," Judge Whitaker continued, "you should not take it personally. It doesn't mean you're a bad person. It only means that for one reason or another, you were not considered right for this particular trial.

"Okay. Before we start the jury selection process, I want to tell you that even though one of the charges in this case is murder, the death penalty does not apply to this case. The death penalty statute recently adopted by the state legislature would only apply to murders which occurred after the enactment of that statute. The crime alleged in this case occurred before the new legislation. So those of you who may have reservations about the death penalty need not feel anxious or reluctant to serve as jurors in this case.

"I should also say that the legal principles and procedure are the same for all criminal trials, and your involvement as jurors would be the same regardless of the charge, but this case involves a particularly brutal crime. There will be descriptions of a sexual assault leading to the violent death of a thirty-six-year-old woman.

"I want to emphasize that the charges against the defendant are no more than that, merely charges. If any of you will be so upset by hearing details of these crimes that you feel you would be incapable of listening objectively to the evidence and rendering a fair verdict based solely on that evidence, you will have an opportunity to bring your reservations to my attention if your name is called."

A man directly in front of Laura raised his hand. "My daughter," he said, slowly rising to his feet. "She was raped last year. I couldn't . . . the memory of her tears is never out of my thoughts."

"If your name is called, I'll listen to your excuse," the judge said.

Several people in the front rows turned to look at the man who had spoken. Their faces revealed both sympathy and curiosity. Julius felt embarrassed for the man and looked away.

"The court officer will call the names of fourteen jurors who will take their seats in the jury box," Judge Whitaker said. "Fourteen are being called because two of you will be alternate jurors who will participate in the deliberations in the event that one or two of the regular jurors become sick or for some reason have to withdraw before the conclusion of the trial."

Mike Bernstein turned around in his seat at counsel table. He looked at the crowd of people who filled the courtroom. He had seen so many similar crowds in similar courtrooms. There did not seem to be anything unusual about this group.

"Okay. Call the first juror," the judge said.

As the court officer spun a small wooden drum resting on the clerk's desk, Bernstein studied his client sitting rigidly in the chair next to him. Bernstein knew that different people would, of course, have different first impressions of Leander Rafshoon. The navy blue suit didn't fit Rafshoon very well. During his twelve months waiting in jail he must have lost more than fifteen pounds. F. Lee Bailey had had Patty Hearst wear a dress that was too large for her in order to make her appear more frail and vulnerable to the jury. Bernstein knew there were few similarities between Patty and Leander, and anyway, Bailey had lost Patty's case.

Rafshoon was looking defiantly around the courtroom, glowering at everyone who met his eye. Bernstein suspected that this apparent hostility was merely the expression of the man's fear, but Bernstein believed that in close cases that could go either way: the unattractiveness of a defendant can affect the jurors' view of his credibility, making them less inclined to give him the benefit of a doubt. In the case of Rafshoon, with his scarred face, broken nose, and large, powerful body, most of the jurors would probably regard him as dangerous, if not terrifying.

The court officer placed his hand on the revolving drum, stopping it instantly. He turned it another half revolution to find the little door. A key hung on the end of a string attached to one of the supporting posts of the drum. He inserted the key. Lifting back the door, he reached down into the belly of the container. With his arm inserted up to his elbow, his hand found the thin slips of paper in the cavity of the drum. His fingers pinched one of the slips. Without thinking, without a reason, he let go of the slip and grabbed another. He pulled his arm out of the drum, delicately holding the pink slip of paper between his thumb and index finger, fanning out his remaining fingers.

Julius prayed that his name would not be called.

"D one-twenty-four, Mr. Julius Solars," the court officer called.

Julius stood and, stepping sideways, made his way awkwardly over the knees of strangers to the center aisle.

From his place at counsel table, in the seat closest to the jury where prosecutors always sat, Leslie Ryan studied the first juror: it was an older man, glasses, his gray hair brushed back without a part.

"For the benefit of Court and counsel," the clerk said loudly, "please answer 'here' when your name is called."

"Here," Julius said in a tight voice. He coughed to clear his throat. "Here," he said again. Ryan thought he seemed frightened. He liked that. This was the kind of juror who'd be respectful of law enforcement officers and of him, the representative of the state.

"One," the court officer by the drum said.

"Take the first seat, dear," the woman court officer said, pointing to the chair at the end of the front row.

"I four-ninety, John Turner," the court officer called out after removing another pink slip.

"Here." In the front row a black man in a blue blazer rose.

"Two," the court officer said.

Turner walked quickly and determinedly to the seat next to Julius Solars. Turner impressed Bernstein as a man who always knew his destination. He looked like someone who wasn't about to be intimidated by the judge or the prosecutor.

"D one-fifty-five, Andrew Pruitt."

There was silence in the courtroom.

"D one-fifty-five, Andrew Pruitt," the court officer said more loudly, scanning the rows of people.

Carl Copco looked around to see if someone would stand to the call for Andrew Pruitt. No one responded. Andrew Pruitt must have some connections, Carl thought to himself. My lawyer couldn't get me out of a paper bag.

"No answer," the clerk said.

The court officer laid aside the slip in his hand and reached again into the drum. "D one-twelve, Carrie Schultz."

"Yes." A young woman with short black hair stood. She marched smartly down the center aisle.

"Three."

The court officer continued to call out the numbers and the names, and Laura Sayres, four, Carl Copco, five, and Ann B. Davis, six, came forward. When D 121, Elliot Postom, was called, a man in a green polyester suit and a red bow tie shot his hand into the air and jumped to his feet. "That's me."

To Bernstein, who hardly took his eyes off the jurors to make notes, this Postom acted as if he had just won at bingo. The man strode forward in his white vinyl shoes with unmistakable zip. Bernstein nodded at Postom as he entered the well of the courtroom. He wanted him, each of them, to think they had a special relationship with him, and he tried to make a connection from the moment they stepped into the courtroom. So far, the only one who had nodded back was the first juror, the Jewish one, Julius Solars. But Solars looked so scared, he probably would have nodded at anything that had moved. But that's all right, Bernstein thought. It's good if they're scared—it means they'll take it all very seriously, including the judge's instructions on reasonable doubt and the presumption of innocence.

Bernstein found that about one out of five nodded back. Elliot Postom wasn't one of them. Bernstein did better with women. He knew he was good-looking for his height in a rumpled sort of way. A kind of flirtation was possible with women jurors, and he certainly wasn't above that. In his last case he had even been slightly coquettish with a juror he thought was gay.

Juror Number 4, Laura Sayres, the beautiful one, may be a distraction, Ryan thought. It was hard not to stare at her. She must get that all the time. So far, he had tried to avoid looking at her. He checked the jury list, which contained the names, towns, and professions of all members of the jury panel. The list said she was an advertising executive. Maybe she had a brain in spite of her looks. The case involved rape. She must have sensed that at times people were thinking about raping her. So maybe she'd be more sympathetic toward a rape victim than most people, Ryan thought.

Bernstein ran down the jury sheet to D 82. Merrill was a mechanical engineer. Bernstein liked that. An engineer had to use a slide rule, measuring quantities with precision. Perhaps he would measure the pieces of evidence as if they were bricks and find some shortage. The more disposed a juror was toward objectivity, the less room there was for him to get carried away by the viciousness of the charge against the defendant. Like most trial lawyers, Bernstein measured all the members of a jury including this engineer by the way he thought the engineer might measure the evidence.

Several more people were summoned to the jury box, and Alex Butler was called to fill the fourteenth seat.

Maureen Whalen, disappointed over not being called, studied the defendant. She could see only the back of his head, yet she could tell he was nervous from the way he'd pick up his pencil, scratch some note on the yellow pad in front of him, and replace the pencil in the middle of the pad. She could see the muscles of his neck bulging, his strong shoulders beneath the jacket. His black skin seemed to glisten against the collar of his white shirt. Even from the middle of the courtroom with his face turned away from her, Maureen could sense the power he exuded.

Leander's skin was in fact glistening from beads of perspiration caused by the overwhelming fear he felt.

"The questions I'm about to ask," the judge said, "are not intended to embarrass you or to pry into your personal lives. All we want to do is make sure, to the extent that we can by some brief questioning, that we get a fair and impartial jury.

"The first question is an easy one: have any of you ever

been a witness or defendant in a criminal case? If so, please raise your hand."

Carl Copco stared straight ahead. He could tell without turning his head that the woman sitting two seats to his left was raising her hand. He wasn't about to tell anyone about the court-martial. It was twenty years ago, and there was no way they would have his army record. Besides, what the hell he did with that Korean girl was nobody's business now.

After checking his list, the judge looked up. "Yes, Miss Schultz?"

"I testified in a criminal case fourteen years ago. An older man had exposed himself to me," the woman said.

"Well, in this case there will be evidence that the victim was raped before she was murdered," the judge said. "Let me ask, how old were you at the time of the . . . that incident?"

"I was ten at the time." There was something in her voice that Ryan liked, a clipped tone that suggested to him that she was still angry. The jury list said that she was a student. Most prosecutors didn't like having students on a jury because they are assumed to be more liberal.

"Would that experience fourteen years ago affect your ability to be a fair and impartial juror in this case?" asked the judge.

"No, sir."

"You wouldn't have any feelings for or against the defendant here, Mr. Leander Rafshoon? You would be able to decide this case solely on the evidence?"

"Yes, sir."

"Very well. Is there anyone else who has been a witness or defendant in a criminal case?"

"I vas," a woman in the back row in seat thirteen said with her hand raised.

The judge searched his list again. "Mrs. von Brundt?"

"Yes. Kathryn von Brundt. I vas. Last year, in an automobile accident, I vas a vitness, but there vas no trial."

"No, madam," the judge said. "I was asking about being a witness in a criminal case. An automobile accident case is a civil case, and if there was no trial, you were never actually a witness anyway."

Bernstein made a note on his chart: *Doesn't listen. German and dumb.* He didn't like either on his juries.

"Sorry," the woman said. Bernstein thought she looked as if she were pouting about having been reprimanded. Maybe she'd hold a grudge against the judge. That could only help his client. And as far as his reactions to her being German, that was a prejudice he should get over—a prejudice that, perhaps, cost his clients good German jurors.

Bernstein knew that superficial stereotypes could be misleading. Rather than feeling a special bond, a middle-class black, for example, might be embarrassed by the actions of a black narcotics dealer. An Italian banker might despise a person of his own nationality accused of involvement in "organized crime." On the other hand, he realized that sometimes he tended to overintellectualize, and as far as this German woman was concerned, fuck 'er. He'd find it too distracting having a possible Nazi staring at him from the jury box. It was bad enough having to deal with prosecutors.

"Anybody else?" the judge asked.

Ryan scanned the jury. He had a funny feeling about the fifth juror, the guy who didn't seem to blink. A check of the jury list showed "Carl Copco, pet store owner." Ryan didn't know what it was, maybe the way the guy sat with his head slightly tilted to the side. Maybe it was his imagination, but Ryan sensed something arrogant, something off about Copco. He couldn't put his finger on it. It was just a feeling. Although he knew that instincts were sometimes unreliable, Ryan also remembered what an experienced trial lawyer had once told him: "If you don't like a juror's face, chances are he

doesn't like yours either—and you'd better get rid of him."
Ryan tried to pick jurors who seemed as if they would like
him. He had to guess if the juror's personality, dress, or way
of speaking was compatible with his.

Ryan smiled at Laura Sayres, the attractive juror seated at
the center of the first row of the jury. Like most lawyers, he
was convinced that it was vital for him to establish a rapport
with the jurors. An attorney who seems aloof or arrogant will
probably not be liked by the jury, and this could be bad for
his case.

In a trial a few years before, Ryan had noticed that a juror
was wearing an expensive, hand-painted necktie. The next
day he himself wore a similar tie and focused his arguments
on the well-dressed juror. He won the case and always actually thought his choice of neckties had helped. One of the
intriguing aspects of the game of picking juries is that there is
no way to be sure that such things as similar neckties do not
actually help. Even if the juror denied the influence of such a
minor detail, he might not have realized its unconscious
effects.

"Have any of you been the victim of a crime?" the judge
asked.

Eight people raised their hands.

More than half the jury were victims of crime. "Welcome
to urban living," the judge said to himself. He'd seen similar
percentages from most juries in his courtroom. "Okay. Let's
start with Juror Number One, Mr. Solars," he said.

"My wallet . . . it was stolen," he said softly. "They just . . .
from my pocket. They pulled it away from me. Nothing. I
wasn't hurt or anything. I don't know." Julius sighed.

"Did they ever apprehend the people who did it?" the
judge asked.

"No. It happened so quickly."

Psychologists have studied speech patterns in an effort to
learn when a speaker may be lying. They have found that

unfinished sentences, breaking in with new thoughts, repetition of words, stuttering, saying "I don't know" not in answer to a question but in resignation or disgust, sighing or taking deep breaths, prolonged silences, inappropriate laughter, voice changes, questioning the interviewer, and unusual hesitation are often associated with deception.

Julius Solars, who had just answered the judge with many of the characteristics social scientists list as clues of deception, was simply nervous speaking in public, particularly to a judge.

Bernstein didn't want any juror who had been the victim of a crime, but it did not seem possible to find fourteen unvictimized people in Newark. There was a gentleness about this Solars fellow that he liked. And Bernstein hadn't noticed anything unusual about Solars's speech patterns.

The judge questioned the other seven jurors who had been crime victims: four had been victims of burglary, two of mugging, and one woman, Mrs. Ann B. Davis, raised her hand to ask if having a car stolen would count. Mrs. Davis and the rest of the victims of crimes said they wouldn't be prejudiced against Leander Rafshoon as a result of their experience.

"Have any of you served as grand or petit jurors?" the judge asked.

Three people raised their hands, and the judge called on them one at a time to explain when.

Elliot Postom had been on a jury that had considered an assault case. Another juror said that he had served about ten years earlier on an automobile accident case. The third juror had tried a murder case about seven years ago. All three of them said that their experience would not affect their decision in this case.

"Mr. Prosecutor, would you introduce yourself and tell the jury the names of the people who may testify or be mentioned in the course of this trial."

Ryan pushed back his chair from counsel table and stood.

"My name is Leslie Ryan. I am an assistant prosecutor with the Essex County Prosecutor's Office. Vincent Altieri is a detective in my office who will be working with me on this case. You will occasionally see him sitting next to me at counsel table. In fact that's Detective Altieri walking down the aisle toward me right now."

All the jurors turned to their right to watch the heavy man push open the low swinging door to the well of the courtroom. Ryan waited for him to take his seat, then read aloud a list of more than twenty names.

After Ryan had finished, Bernstein introduced himself. He gestured with his hand for the defendant to stand. "This is my client, Leander Rafshoon." Everyone in the courtroom looked at the defendant. Bernstein motioned to Rafshoon, and they both turned to the back of the courtroom so that the people in the rear could see them. Bernstein nodded to his client to sit down, and then announced the names of four people he intended to call as witnesses.

The judge asked if the jurors knew any of the people they had just met or who had just been mentioned. Occasionally trial judges allow friends of key witnesses or even friends of victims to serve as jurors. Appellate courts inevitably reverse the convictions in these cases.

No one raised his hand. The judge asked the prosecutor where and when the alleged offense took place.

"In Glen Ridge," Ryan said, getting to his feet. "On or about September fifth, 1982, Your Honor."

"Thank you," the judge said. He turned to address the jury. "Ladies and gentlemen, I understand there were newspaper articles about the alleged offense. Did any of you read or hear anything about this case prior to coming to court today?"

A woman in the back row raised her hand. "I did," she said.

"Would you come up to side-bar?" the judge said. He

pointed to a spot just to the left of his desk. "This is what we call side-bar."

The prosecutor and the defense counsel headed to the point indicated by the judge. The court reporter unscrewed her machine from its base and carried it to side-bar, laying it down on the judge's desk between the two lawyers. They all waited for the juror to join them.

Whenever a juror is asked a question that deals with his or her personal experiences or any exposure to pretrial publicity that might evoke a reply capable of prejudicing other jurors, the answer is supposed to be given out of the hearing of the rest of the panel.

"Yes, ma'am?" the judge said when the woman arrived.

"I'm from Glen Ridge, and there was nothing else people spoke about when it happened. There were articles in the local paper. We have a very nice local paper, and this case was on the front page for days, maybe more."

"Do you think your decision as a juror will be influenced by what you heard or read prior to coming to court?"

"Well, to be honest . . . I'm not so sure. Everyone was talking about it."

"I'll excuse you. Thank you." He turned to the court clerk. "Call the next name."

The woman left the courtroom, and another juror from the panel was called to the jury box. She said she had no affirmative answers to the questions the judge had asked so far. The judge allowed her to take her seat among the jurors.

"Do any of you have friends or relatives in law enforcement?" the judge asked the fourteen in the jury box. An older man in the back row raised his hand. The judge nodded to him: "Yes, Mr. Fitzgerald?"

"My kid brother's a cop in Newark," Mr. Fitzgerald said.

"Do you ever discuss police business with him?"

"Sometimes. Not so much anymore."

"Would your relationship with your brother and the fact

that you sometimes discuss police business influence you as a juror, or would you be able to decide this case solely on the evidence?"

"I could decide this case solely on the evidence."

Ryan liked Fitzgerald not only because he had a brother in law enforcement but also because he was Irish. He knew there were unconscious ways that religion, ethnicity, or personality could influence a juror's attitude to him and to his arguments as a lawyer.

"Very well," the judge said. He turned to a woman who had also raised her hand. "Now, Miss Bell?"

"My cousin is a town prosecutor in West Orange. But I'm not very close to him," the woman said.

"Would that have any influence on you as a juror in this case?"

"None whatsoever," she said adamantly—so adamantly that Ryan made a mental note that she probably didn't like the cousin or possibly what he did. The jury sheet showed that Miss Bell was an artist. Ryan didn't like artists. They were a little too eccentric for his blood. He didn't need any loners or free spirits on his jury. Bad enough that his wife was taking a sculpture class. Ms. Bell would have to go.

"Would any of you place more credibility or weight on the testimony of a police officer merely because he was a police officer?" the judge asked.

In all the trials Ryan and Bernstein had been involved with, neither had ever seen a juror raise his hand to that question. Perhaps the fact that a judge was asking whether people favor the testimony of policemen raised a suspicion in the jurors' minds that the police may not always tell the truth.

"Before I go any further," the judge said, "you have been told that this is a case of rape and murder. Is there anything in the nature of the case which would prevent any of you from trying this case impartially?"

A woman in the second row raised her hand. "I'd have a problem," the woman said.

"Would you come up to side-bar?" the judge said, with an edge in his voice. He seemed irritated at the idea that someone would want to avoid serving.

The prosecutor, the defense counsel, the court reporter, and the juror headed back to the judge's desk.

Julius Solars had wanted to raise his hand. He was afraid that the description of the murder might be too upsetting, but he didn't want to antagonize the judge.

"I'm not going to be able to deal with this," the woman said as soon as she arrived at the judge's side.

"Madam, none of us may like the responsibility of deciding if a person is guilty of a crime," the judge said, speaking loudly, and now angrily, "particularly if the crime is murder. But unless you have some compelling reason why you can't serve, I'm not going to excuse you. Now, why do you think you can't deal with it?"

The judge was not only trying to intimidate the woman who stood next to him. His loud and apparent anger was a deliberate effort to deter anyone else in the courtroom from claiming some excuse from jury duty. The judge knew that many people would prefer not to serve on juries, particularly on murder cases. But somebody had to serve, and he'd rather not waste the next few weeks finding a jury.

"Your Honor, I have two daughters of my own. It's going to be impossible for me to listen to how this terrible thing happened to this woman without me constantly thinking about my daughters."

"Are you telling me that if I instruct you to decide this case solely on the evidence that will be presented, you wouldn't be able to follow my instruction?"

"I would try, but I can't be sure I could do that."

"Challenge for cause," Bernstein said.

The prosecutor knew Bernstein wasn't going to allow this

woman to remain on the jury, but he wanted him to use up one of his twenty peremptory challenges rather than one of his unlimited challenges for cause. "May I put a question to the juror?" Ryan asked.

"Of course, but don't let the jury hear you," the judge said.

Ryan spoke quietly to the woman. "Madam, all of us, as human beings, have prejudices and fears, but all that the judge is asking for are jurors who would be able to put aside those prejudices and fears and judge this defendant on the evidence. You wouldn't want to convict an innocent man, would you?" By leading questions, the prosecutor was trying to get the juror to alter the impression she had already given that she would convict automatically.

"No, of course not. That would be awful," the woman said.

"And if the judge tells you this defendant is presumed innocent and if the state can't convince you beyond a reasonable doubt that the defendant was guilty, you would follow the judge's instruction and not convict an innocent man, wouldn't you?"

"Yes. Yes, I would."

"Your Honor, I would have to object to the challenge for cause," Ryan said, pleased with himself that he had gotten this woman to say she would be capable of voting against him and acquitting the defendant.

"Your Honor," Bernstein said, "may I?"

The judge gestured with his hand for Bernstein to proceed.

"Madam, you obviously love your daughters very much, and the thought of anything happening to them must be horrible for you. Is that right?"

"Yes, that's very true."

"You can't be sure that that enormous fear that you have won't affect your perception of the evidence, can you?"

"No, I really can't be sure."

"For cause, Your Honor," Bernstein said.

"May I, Your Honor?" Ryan asked.

"Let's not waste any more time." The judge was speaking loudly again for the benefit of all the other jurors in the courtroom. "I'm not going to excuse this woman for cause. Citizens must serve as jurors or we will have to resort to some alternative to the jury system. It is as simple as that. Take your seat, madam. Let's move on."

Judge Whitaker knew it was not as simple as that. Bernstein would have to have the woman excused by using one of his peremptory challenges.

Bernstein had sustained a minor defeat, one that in the end would probably not mean anything, but he knew that a lawyer has to fight all the battles, and there's no way of judging which smaller victories will influence the final verdict—and the final verdict is the only victory that counts.

"Anyone else?" the judge asked.

A man in the back row raised his hand, and the judge motioned to him to step up to side-bar.

"Your Honor," the man said, "I can't hear this case."

"And why not?" the judge asked gruffly.

"It has something to do with the bones," the man said.

"What are you talking about? You have some predilection in your bones?" the judge asked incredulously.

"I don't know what's wrong with them. Maybe it's the predilections, or whatever you call it, but it makes me hard of hearing."

The judge and the lawyers smiled.

"Well, why didn't you say that in the juror questionnaire you answered?" the judge asked.

"I didn't think I'd be called."

"How bad is your hearing? You seem to be hearing me all right."

"Pardon?"

"I'll excuse you," the judge said.

If a juror knows the right excuse and is willing to insist on it in the face of a judge's intimidation, it is easy to avoid serving on a jury. All a person has to say is that he can't hear or see well, or he has to be home to feed his kids, or that he hates criminals or that he loves them, and that juror can be off the case. But the approach of the juror with the two daughters—"I can't deal with this"—is usually not a successful way to get out of serving.

The court officer pulled another slip out of the wooden drum, and a moment later a black woman in her mid-thirties took her seat in the back row.

The judge asked the newest juror in the box if she had any affirmative answers to the questions he had asked so far. The woman said no.

The judge addressed the entire jury in the box. "Do any of you have any bias or prejudice against a person simply because he may be charged with a crime?"

No response.

"Will you apply the law as the court states it to be, without regard to your own personal feelings about it?"

No response.

"Do any of you know of any reason why you cannot be a fair and impartial juror in this case?"

The courtroom was quiet for a few moments. No one in the jury box raised a hand.

"Okay. Now I am going to ask each of you to stand and tell us your name, your occupation, whether you're married, and if you are, what your spouse does, if you have children, and the city or town where you live. Let's start with Juror Number One. Mr. Solars?"

"My name is Julius Solars. I'm a worker in a factory in Newark . . . just a worker. I have two grown children. And a few months ago we moved from Newark to Irvington."

"John Turner," Juror Number 2 said. "I'm a biochemical engineer. Single. I live in East Orange."

"I'm Carrie Schultz. I'm single. I'm presently living in

Newark, but I've just been accepted for training for the navy."

Bernstein checked the jury list. It said she was a student, but the information on that sheet was frequently incorrect. This Schultz woman had said she had been a victim of a crime, some guy having exposed himself to her. Rafshoon was accused of rape as well as murder. She had said she wasn't going to hold her experience against his client, but how could Bernstein be sure? Even if she didn't think she was holding any grudges, she certainly could be influenced unconsciously by the traumatic event earlier in her life.

"Single, short haircut, joining the navy," Ryan, leaning over to his detective, whispered. "I bet she's a dyke. If she sees how that Collins woman looks in the morgue shots, she's going to want to castrate Rafshoon."

Altieri raised his eyebrows: "You said it."

Another juror stood. "I'm a retired housewife," she said. Many people laughed. "I mean my husband is retired. I guess I'm not." More laughs.

The next juror presented himself with self-confidence as a salesman of diesel machinery. He reminded Ryan of his own father, before he'd had his stroke. Ryan had the feeling that nothing could change this man's mind once it was made up. This kind of personal reaction frequently influences a lawyer's choice of jurors.

Ryan was sure that it would be good for the prosecution to have a juror with a domineering personality if the juror believed the defendant was guilty. If he were the only holdout, he wouldn't be pressured into an acquittal by the other jurors, and maybe he'd be able to convince the others to go along with him. On the other hand, if a person like this voted for an acquittal, the best Ryan could probably wind up with would be a hung jury. A hung jury in a case like this would be a loss for Ryan. He knew if he hung on a retrial, he would have trouble getting approval from his supervisor for a third trial. Two hung juries would probably force him to dismiss the case, or at best offer a very light plea bargain. Ryan would not gamble on a hung jury with this strong-minded diesel salesman.

Both prosecutors and defense attorneys are anxious to avoid a "one-man" jury. An obviously intelligent juror is often excused because of a fear that he will control the jury, a risk that neither prosecutor nor defense lawyer is often willing to take. A jury's verdict should be the result of a joint decision of *twelve* people, not the dominating influence of one person, a negation of the very purpose of the jury trial.

Alex Butler, the last juror in the box, gave his profession as "writer." Several jurors in the front row turned around to look at him. I guess it does sound glamorous, Butler thought to himself. If they only knew.

Judge Whitaker looked over toward Ryan and Bernstein. "Do either of you have any questions you would like to put to the prospective jurors?"

Bernstein rose. "Thank you, Your Honor. I have a few," he said, walking toward the railing of the jury box. "Ladies and gentlemen, I find this question difficult to ask, but the case against my client is too serious for me to overlook it. Racial prejudice is an ugly fact of our society, and I am convinced that the large majority of Americans would agree that such prejudice has no place in our jury rooms. But I must ask: would you fairly try this case on the basis of the evidence and disregard the defendant's race? Do you have any prejudice against Negroes? Against black people? Would any of you be influenced by the use of the term 'black'?"

Bernstein was not expecting any of the jurors to admit to racial prejudice, but by trying to get a commitment from them at this stage of the trial, he was hoping to make it harder for anyone to be openly racist during the deliberations.

No one responded.

"Do counsel have any other questions?" Judge Whitaker asked.

"No, sir," Ryan and Bernstein answered.

Judge Whitaker told everyone to go to lunch and return in an hour to resume the jury selection.

Is it possible to create from brief personal interviews a screening process that finds fair jurors? Some judges believe that the voir dire merely gets at the most superficial information about a juror, and that only an in-depth examination extended over a period of months could offer even a chance of flushing out a potential juror's hidden antipathies. Others feel that as long as our society wishes a system of trial by jury, the voir dire is the only practical approach, and is therefore worth spending at least some time on.

Challenges for cause weed out a few potential jurors who are presumed biased by occasionally excluding those with membership in a narrowly defined social group. In 1881 the Supreme Court, for example, decided that because Mormons believe that polygamy was ordained by God, Mormons could be excluded from a jury in the trial of a Mormon accused of bigamy. Similarly, in a 1968 prosecution for the murder of a taxicab driver in Washington, D.C., taxicab drivers and those related to taxicab drivers were considered unqualified as jurors.

More typically, group affiliations have not disqualified jurors. Being a Catholic, for example, did not prevent a juror from serving in a case involving a bishop, or being a union textile worker did not automatically disqualify a juror in a prosecution growing out of a unionization struggle.

Some prosecutors and defense lawyers, unwilling to limit their information about jurors to answers at the voir dire, conduct investigations into the backgrounds of jurors prior to a trial. A lawyer may not keep jurors under surveillance or question them directly concerning their feelings about a case or send them questionnaires asking whether they are biased. But financial records can reveal buying patterns, social behavior, reading habits, and membership in associations. Through records of gasoline purchases and airline tickets, a person's travel history can be known. Department store credit cards, mailing lists, and magazine and theater subscriptions can say a great deal about a juror. Some investigators have even checked out the lawns and the bumper stickers of prospective jurors. The main limitations are a lawyer's ingenuity and funds.

In 1977, Texas businessman T. Cullen Davis spent $2 million to win an acquittal on a charge of murdering his stepdaughter. Defense investigators interviewed neighbors and employers, and circulated a list of potential jurors among bankers, executives, and reporters they considered sympathetic to Davis. A photographer even took pictures of jurors' homes to give lawyers a sense of their life-styles. The lawyer who defended Davis found the work of his investigators valuable, and he has continued the practice of investigating jurors in subsequent cases.

The government, with its much greater access to records of one sort or another, represents a greater threat to privacy than the defense lawyers. Some local prosecutors keep records of past jury service and how jurors voted in prior criminal cases. This information allows prosecutors to excuse by peremptory challenges those jurors who have been members of a jury that acquitted in an earlier case.

Without new legislation to curb abuses, the access to all the business and personal records of individuals being considered for jury duty could constitute an improper surveillance system. Public awareness of these investigations in itself could deter public participation in jury duty. The knowledge of an FBI inquiry may also intimidate certain jurors and appreciably affect their deliberations.

The trial of Leander Rafshoon, serious as the charges were,

was typical of the great majority of cases in that the lawyers conducted no investigations of jurors. Most defendants cannot afford pretrial investigations, and most lawyers know very few facts about the jurors they select. Unless a juror volunteers the information during the voir dire, the lawyer may have no idea that the juror has a familiarity with the scene of the crime, is a friend or enemy of another juror, has a personal illness, harbors some misconception of the law, or has some other private reason making him less than an objective juror.

In the federal courts and in most state courts, potential jurors are questioned for the purpose of ascertaining their "states of mind," but the judge determines what questions are, or are not, germane to discovering that state of mind. A number of cases have held that general questions about racial prejudice, like the one Bernstein put to the jury, should be allowed only in cases directly involving racial overtones.

But should the defense lawyer be allowed to ask a prospective juror if the defendant's beard will affect that juror's judgment? Prosecutors in the sixties would regularly exclude prospective jurors who were wearing beards on the basis that such people were nonconformists and might, even in an open-and-shut case, hold out against the majority to hang a jury.

In 1973 the Supreme Court focused its attention on a case involving beards in *Ham* v. *South Carolina*. Gene Ham, charged with the possession of marijuana, was a young, bearded black who lived most of his life in Florence County, South Carolina. He was well known locally for his civil rights activities, and he claimed to have been framed on the drug charge because law enforcement officers were "out to get him" for his political involvement.

The trial judge denied the defendant's request to ask the jurors if they would be influenced by the fact that the defendant was black or wore a beard. Instead, the judge asked the usual general questions about whether the prospective jurors were conscious of any bias or prejudice for or against the defendant. The defendant was convicted and sentenced to eighteen months' confinement.

Because of the failure to inquire about racial bias, the Supreme Court reversed the conviction, but the Court made it clear that minimal inquiry about race would have been sufficient, and a reversal would not have been required solely for the failure to ask about facial hair. The majority of Justices felt that the jurors' attitudes toward beards were not important enough to warrant questioning.

Justice Douglas, disagreeing with the Court, felt that many people associated long hair and beards with drug use and rebellion against traditional values. "Nothing is more indicative of the importance currently being attached to hair growth by the general populace," Douglas wrote, "than the barrage of cases reaching the courts evidencing the attempt by one segment of society officially to control the plumage of another. On the issue of a student's right to wear long hair alone there are well over 50 reported cases. In addition, the issue of plumage has surfaced in the employment-discrimination context as well as the military area."

Douglas argued that hair was "symbolic to many of rebellion against traditional society and disapproval of the way the current power structure handles social problems. Taken as an affirmative declaration of an individual's commitment to a change in social values, non-conventional hair growth may become a very real personal threat to those who support the status quo. For those people, non-conventional hair growth symbolizes an undesirable lifestyle characterized by unreliability, dishonesty, lack of moral values, communal ('communist') tendencies, and the assumption of drug use. If the defendant, especially one being prosecuted for the illegal use of drugs, is not allowed even to make the most minimal inquiry to expose such prejudices, can it be expected that he will receive a fair trial?"

Shortly after the *Ham* decision, the Supreme Court heard a case involving two black defendants charged with robbing a white security guard. The Court concluded that questions about race had not been required because racial issues had not been "inextricably bound up" with the conduct of the trial. Similarly, trial courts have refused to question jurors about political affiliations or about encounters with union pickets in a prosecution of a union officer, or bias against homosexuals in a case where a car owner allegedly gave the defendants his car after they had threatened to expose his sexual advances.

If the judge is a fool and/or a tyrant, he can make a disaster out of a voir dire. *United States* v. *Dellinger*—the Chicago Seven case—is a striking example of this. The defendants had participated in demonstrations during the 1968 Democratic National Convention, and the judge refused to ask questions about the background and attitudes of the jurors, including questions probing the jurors' attitudes about Vietnam War protests, establishment and youth values, police and demonstrators, and pretrial publicity. The judge limited his investigation to general questions about whether the jurors thought they could be fair. The voir dire lasted only a little more than a day. After a long and terribly expensive trial, the court of appeals reversed the convictions on a number of grounds, one of which was insufficient pretrial questioning of jurors.

The right to ask questions about potential areas of prejudice can be made meaningless if the questions are not properly phrased. If Judge Whitaker had asked each juror individually an open-ended question such as "How do you feel about police officers?" or "How do you feel about blacks accused of crimes?" perhaps some useful information might have been elicited. "Can you be fair?" almost always gets an affirmative answer that tells nothing about the juror. Even Adolf Hitler would have answered that he would be fair, and perhaps he would have thought he was telling the truth.

Few jurors think of themselves as biased, and some who recognize bias in themselves will lie about it. The most common way that jurors deceive is by withholding relevant information, the way Carl Copco did in not responding to the judge's question about whether or not he had ever been a defendant. A researcher who did extensive studies on how juries function, Dale Broeder, found a juror in a narcotics case who had failed to mention she was married to a member of a local crime commission that was in the middle of an anti-dope campaign. A juror in a case involving car theft did not disclose that he had once been arrested for car theft. In another case a juror failed to mention that he worked for a company represented by the defense lawyer, whom he had actually dealt with on several occasions. Another juror was a close friend of the plaintiff's family. Yet another juror had been generously compensated by the defendant railroad in a negligence case for an unrelated incident.

But even if a juror believes he is telling the truth, a major problem with the voir dire is that it will often fail to disclose unconscious bias. Questions such as "Can you be impartial despite your earlier opinion?" encourage self-delusion on the part of jurors. Unfortunately the most prejudiced individuals are often the least able to recognize their prejudices and the least able to put them aside. Excusing those jurors who admit to some problems of being impartial can result in the elimination of those most sensitive to their own prejudices, most concerned with being fair, and most likely to speak their minds during jury deliberations.

Unlike the woman from Glen Ridge who had read about the Collins murder in the local newspaper, some jurors can be unaware that they hold prejudices about a case as a result of what they may have learned from the press. At times the fundamental right of a free press comes into conflict with the right of a defendant and society to have impartial jurors. To what degree do the courts have the right to curb the press to avoid the prejudicing of potential members of a jury?

Chief Justice John Marshall, sitting in 1807 as a trial judge in Aaron Burr's case, established the right of a judge to question jurors about the effects of pretrial publicity. Burr had assembled a small army in Kentucky, and Jefferson, who apparently didn't like Burr, especially after Burr had killed his good friend Alexander Hamilton in a duel, brought treason charges against him. The newspapers had described the Jefferson-Burr feud in great detail. Before the trial began, members of the public had already taken sides, raising serious difficulties in selecting an impartial jury.

Marshall ruled that jurors with fixed, preconceived notions about the case should be excused for cause, and that the jurors had to be questioned so that their attitudes could be discerned. Marshall compared the situation to that of a juror who was distantly related to a litigant: "The relationship may be remote; the person may never have seen the party; he may declare that he feels no prejudice in the case; and yet the law cautiously incapacitates him from serving on the jury because it suspects prejudice, because, in general, persons in a similar situation would feel prejudice."

A person with preconceived ideas about the matter, Marshall argued, "will listen with more favor to that testimony which confirms, than to that which would change his opinion; it is not to be expected that he will weigh evidence or argument as fairly as a man whose judgment is not made up in the case."

Marshall was sensitive to the risk that if a person was disqualified as a juror simply because he had formed an opinion prior to trial on any important fact involved in a case, intelligent people would be excluded. "Light impressions [as to guilt or innocence]," Marshall said, "that which can fairly be supposed to yield to testimony that may be offered which leave the mind open to a fair consideration of the testimony, constitute no sufficient objection to jurors; but those strong and deep impressions, which will close the mind against the testimony that may be offered in opposition to them, which will combat that testimony and will resist its force, do constitute a sufficient objection [to the seating of a juror]."

With the state of modern communications, it has become much more difficult to find jurors who haven't been bombarded with publicity in sensational cases. Pretrial tests nowadays consider the juror's testimony about his ability to treat fairly the evidence produced at trial, viewed against the nature and magnitude of the pretrial publicity.

In 1976 Joanne Chesimard was prosecuted in New Jersey for murdering a police officer, a case which, though now forgotten by most, received a great deal of media attention at the time. A survey conducted before the start of the trial disclosed that 71 percent of the New Jersey community eligible for jury service had fixed opinions about her guilt, but only 15 percent of the jurors admitted to any form of predisposition at the time of the voir dire. This disparity suggests that some jurors lie during the voir dire.

If the prejudicial publicity has been localized geographically, a fair trial may be achieved by moving the trial to another location where the jurors are less likely to have heard or read about the case. Postponing a trial may allow the effects of publicity to dissipate, but this requires the defendant to abandon his right to a speedy trial. Once a trial begins, judges can protect the jury from prejudicial publicity by sequestering them.

It has sometimes been suggested that a defendant who fears the effect of publicity should waive a trial by jury. This assumes that judges will find it easier than jurors to disregard the pretrial publicity. And it also would require the defendant to give up his constitutional right to a jury in his effort to gain a fair trial, which seems an unfair bargain.

If the Collins murder had produced a bombardment of publicity, both Ryan and Bernstein would have been likely to excuse a juror who had not heard anything about it. When Judge John Sirica asked the panel of prospective jurors summoned in the first Watergate indictments in January 1973 whether they had heard of the case, a handful indicated they hadn't. Sirica felt that those people were probably the least qualified to sit on the jury.

Judges usually accept jurors at their word when they swear they will be able to put aside what they may have heard of a case before trial. Sometimes publicity has been so intense that it is difficult to believe the jury could avoid being influenced by it. No matter how much reliance the courts may place on a juror's promise to judge a case solely on the evidence, in certain cases an individual's biases and pretrial opinions cannot be put aside, and they may affect the way he deals with evidence.

For the most part, courts have been reluctant to impose restrictions on media coverage of criminal trials. When restrictions have been imposed, they have generally taken the forms of excluding the public from the courtroom or prohibiting any publication or conversation about activities taking place in the courtroom. Each form of restriction represents a judicially imposed prior restraint on publication, preventing certain facts from being brought before the public for a period of time, and therefore, each presents a "free press versus fair trial" issue.

In a few celebrated cases, publication of inadmissible information such as an illegal confession, or evidence illegally seized, or an improperly conducted lineup has jeopardized a fair trial. In the 1950s the Ford Foundation sponsored the University of Chicago's Jury Project, a monumental study of more than three thousand trials. It did not turn up a single case in which the judge believed the jury had been influenced by improper press coverage.

In most cases pretrial publicity is not an issue because there is no pretrial publicity. In the few cases where there is press coverage, it usually has no adverse effect on the jurors; in most of those cases the press coverage is accurate and fair, and in the handful where it isn't, the jurors usually feel they know more about the facts of the case than any newspaper reporter.

CHAPTER

IV.

THE LUNCHEON RECESS WAS OVER and everyone had reassembled. Judge Whitaker turned to Leslie Ryan. "Mr. Prosecutor, it's for you to begin."

This was the stage of the trial at which irrevocable decisions had to be made. There was no way ever to know whether one juror would have been better than another, where one person would have made a difference in the outcome of the case. But peremptory challenges would allow Ryan and Bernstein to play their hunches about jurors whose answers did not satisfy grounds for a challenge for cause but who, each might feel, would be unfavorable to his side. And now was the time when choices had to be made.

Ryan studied the group. He hated having to make judgments about people on the basis of such a brief first meeting. Most people make such judgments all the time, but rarely is so much at stake: the lawyer must weigh almost every perceivable fact about a potential juror—how he lives, how he walks, how he works, how he prays—and in the end, like most people, he often does not know the reason why he "didn't like someone."

"I'll excuse Juror Number Twelve," Ryan announced, looking at the man who reminded him of his father.

Bernstein excused Mr. Fitzgerald, the brother of a Newark police officer. Police testimony was going to be an important part of the state's case, and Bernstein wanted to play what he felt were the percentages. It would be harder, he wagered, to convince a cop's relative that a cop's testimony was mistaken or untruthful.

"The jury as presently constituted," Ryan announced, "is perfectly satisfactory to the state."

Some lawyers feel that too few facts are known, or can be known, to predict who will make a "favorable" juror, and so they challenge few, if any, of the first fourteen people called to the jury box. A lawyer who challenges few jurors may hope that the jury will interpret his easy acceptance of them as confidence in his case, as if he were saying, "Mine is the kind of case in which anybody would decide in my client's favor."

But Ryan was not up to this kind of cynical or grandstand play. Bernstein knew from having tried other cases against him that Ryan was just playing a tactical game with him. After Bernstein challenged another juror, Ryan would excuse more jurors. By claiming to accept the jury as then constituted, Ryan was saving a peremptory challenge by making the defense counsel challenge twice in a row. Ryan ran the risk that Bernstein would also say the jury was satisfactory, which would end the jury selection at that point. But both of them knew Bernstein would not do that.

Prospective jurors frequently say they have no preconceived opinions about a set of facts, but Bernstein knew this was impossible. Jurors, like all human beings, are flawed with

at least some prejudices; some jurors simply have more prejudices than others. In any event, not all prejudices come into
play in a particular case.

Elliot Postom looked to Bernstein like a "law-and-order"
type. Maybe it was his polyester clothes. Maybe it was his
crew cut; Bernstein never trusted a man with gray hair kept
tight in a crew cut. But for the moment Bernstein decided to
let Postom remain, and instead focused on the other jurors. It
was clear that the woman who had said at side-bar that she
did not think she could be fair had to go. He excused her.

"Miss Bell," Ryan announced, getting rid of the young artist he had known from the beginning he would excuse.

Bernstein studied the middle-aged woman at the end of the
first row. She was the mother of three kids, an earnest and
responsible housewife with teen-agers. The victim was also a
housewife, and her fourteen-year-old son had discovered her
body. Maybe this was another juror who would have problems disassociating herself from the horror of the crime.
Maybe she would identify with the victim or feel so horrified
for the son that she would be incapable of being objective
about the evidence against Rafshoon.

"I'll excuse Juror Number Six," Bernstein said.

The mother looked at the juror to her left with a puzzled
expression on her face, unaware of any of the criteria lawyers
use in choosing or excusing jurors.

"You're excused, with thanks," the judge said, nodding to
the housewife. "Please step down."

The woman rose. As she walked out of the jury box, she
looked at Bernstein in a way that seemed to be asking, What
did I do wrong?

Bernstein looked away from her. He knew she felt rejected
personally, and there was nothing he could do about that.

Ryan felt uneasy with uneducated jurors. He knew his vocabulary in front of a jury was sometimes stiff. He consciously tried to avoid sounding pedantic, but when he got

careless or nervous, he would hear those professorial tones coming out of his mouth. So he was sure he was better off with a college-educated juror than with a high school dropout.

He excused the black janitor in the back row.

Bernstein watched Ryan twist his cat's-eye pinky ring as he sat at the other end of counsel table. He wanted to beat Ryan for the personal satisfaction of the contest almost as much as he wanted to win for his client's sake.

Bernstein scanned the jurors remaining in the box. Number 3 looked good to him. She was a social worker in Newark. She must have seen too many atrocities to be outraged by the crime that was going to be described. Bernstein knew social workers who had become so hardened to violent crime that they actually got angry at some victims for getting themselves into a position in which they could be targets for crime. Bernstein had sometimes felt that kind of impatience with his clients.

Leander Rafshoon, frightened, felt that all the prospective jurors looked bad. But to him the judge was the most terrifying person in the room. The way the judge scowled at him when their eyes met was enough to convince Rafshoon that the judge was just waiting for the chance to hit him with a long sentence.

As the afternoon wore on and the lawyers took turns excusing jurors and listening to the replacements, Judge Whitaker struggled to concentrate on the proceedings. He had been a lawyer for twenty-seven years, the last eight as a judge. After more than a thousand trials, he had come to believe that a lawyer's attitude toward jurors, his choices of whom to include or exclude from a jury, gave clear indications of his prejudices or his neuroses about people. To Judge Whitaker, most lawyers had an inflated notion that they could pick juries by making fundamental judgments about human nature on the basis of superficial information, and to him this attitude implied a contempt for the intelligence and independence of those they selected.

While skeptical of the ability of lawyers to pick "favorable" jurors, Judge Whitaker did appreciate one virtue of peremptory challenges: they allowed a judge to avoid being in the position of challenging the honesty of the prospective juror by leaving it to the lawyers to excuse that person peremptorily. Since the lawyers excuse these jurors without having to announce a reason, people are not called liars, and presumably they do not hate the judge or lose respect for the trial system.

Ryan considered keeping Turner, Juror Number 2. This could be the kind of educated black who was tougher on black defendants because they were making it worse for all members of his race. On the other hand, Ryan did not want to take the risk that this guy, assertive and proud as he seemed, might bend over backward to believe a black "brother."

Most prosecutors believe that jurors who identify with a defendant should be avoided. Rafshoon's case was more complicated for Ryan because he knew that some black jurors might identify with the two impressive black police officers who were going to testify for the state. A case involving an elderly mugging victim is easy; the prosecutor would want older jurors who could certainly imagine being mugged.

"I'll excuse Juror Number Two," Ryan said.

Bernstein jumped to his feet and threw his pencil down on the table, as he had thrown similar pencils in similar situations. "That's the fifth black juror the prosecutor has excused!" he said in practiced disgust.

"I'll see you both at side-bar," the judge said.

The lawyers marched up to the judge's bench on the side farthest from the jury. The court reporter picked up her machine and carried it around to where the lawyers were, placing it between them and the judge.

"Bernstein, you know better than that," the judge said with exasperation. "If you have that kind of objection to make, you know you're supposed to make it out of the hearing of the jury."

"I'm sorry, Judge. I guess I lost my head," Bernstein said.

"Sure you did," Ryan said.

"Lose your head again, and I'll hold you in contempt," Judge Whitaker said.

"I apologize. In any event, I would like to put my objection on the record."

"Of course," the judge said.

"Your Honor," Bernstein said, "the prosecutor has systematically excluded all blacks from this jury, and has thereby deprived my black client of his right to a trial by his peers, discriminating against him because of his race. I move for a mistrial because of the prosecutor's racist actions."

"I'd like to respond to this personal attack against me," Ryan said, his face flushed with anger.

"I didn't make a personal attack."

"You did so. You called me a racist."

"I did not. I said that your actions were racist."

"Enough," the judge said. "Mr. Bernstein, you know what the law is on this kind of objection. The Supreme Court has said that unless the defendant can prove a systematic pattern of discrimination over a period of time, a prosecutor may exercise his peremptory challenges any way he sees fit."

"But my client *is* entitled to a jury that is a fair cross section of the community," Bernstein argued.

"You know that that only refers to the jury pools," Judge Whitaker responded. "In a particular case a defendant has no right to a mirror image of the community. Your motion is denied."

Bernstein wasn't surprised by the judge's ruling. He returned to his place at counsel table. He scanned the jury as it was then composed. A black woman and a black man were still in the box. Maybe Ryan would now feel pressured into leaving them there.

Bernstein had at least managed to get across to the white jurors in the jury box that the D.A. was playing them for their prejudices. Maybe one of them would be angry about that, as can happen. And if he had also rattled Ryan, and maybe even goaded him into leaving the two blacks in the jury box or accepting another one if one were called out of the panel, things weren't going so badly.

Usually Bernstein liked to fill the jury box with blacks when he represented a black defendant. But in this case he was not so sure they would be the best jurors. Rafshoon had a criminal record, and he looked and acted like the tough street fighter he was. Middle-class blacks might very well consider him "a disgrace to their race" and convict him more readily than would whites.

Having blacks on the jury could, at least, have the positive effect of making any white bigots keep their prejudices to themselves. A diversity of jurors is intended to ensure that opposing prejudices cancel each other out. All Bernstein could do was try to keep the more obvious bigots off the jury. But bigots rarely announce themselves. They keep quiet about their prejudices until they have a chance to act on them.

Bernstein studied the group for aspects other than its racial makeup. Ten out of the fourteen jurors were men. He was relying on a feeling that it might be easier to convince men that the attractive young victim had provoked his client into seducing her. Bernstein thought that women would be more likely to identify with the victim. He also knew that some lawyers believed that men, out of a protective, chauvinistic impulse, were more likely to convict when the victim was a woman, and that some women might be more prodefense in a case like this one because rather than identifying with Mrs. Collins, they might feel jealous of her wealth and beauty. Obviously he couldn't exclude both men *and* women from the jury. And he didn't want to excuse the black woman.

Bernstein excused the woman who had been subjected to a flasher when she was a child. The last thing I need is a juror with psychic scars, he thought. He simply couldn't take any chances having her on the jury.

Another name was called; a bald, middle-aged male took his seat in the jury box.

Ryan excused the Jewish woman who had said her husband had been falsely accused of a robbery. Just as Bernstein did not want jurors with possible grudges against men, Ryan did not want a juror with a real or imagined grievance against law enforcement authorities. Most lawyers believe Jews are more liberal, more concerned about people being falsely accused of crimes. Ryan did not believe anyone would mistake Leander for Dreyfus, but he did feel that Jews, particularly immigrant Jews, are, as a general matter, more prone to take the side of the defendant. But in the case of Solars, Ryan liked the fact that he had lived in Newark and had just moved out; many Jews who had moved out were fed up with all the crime in Newark.

Bernstein studied Solars. He sensed a kind of openness in the man, which might mean he would be willing to give Rafshoon the benefit of the doubt. But then again, that openness might leave Solars terribly shocked by the crime. Since he was sitting in the first seat in the jury box, Solars would be the foreman who would preside over the deliberations. Bernstein liked having a foreman who was not going to dominate his fellow jurors in the jury room. An extended discussion during deliberation should increase the chances of different opinions, and that could increase the chances of a hung jury if not an outright acquittal. At least that and the fact that Solars was Jewish were Bernstein's reasons for deciding, on balance, to leave him on the jury.

Bernstein looked at each juror, one at a time, trying to

make eye contact with every one of them. He stared for as long as the person could tolerate it. If one of them held his gaze in a defiant way, Bernstein would excuse him. In making this sort of contact he was hoping to establish a kind of agreement—that he was going to trust them and rely on them, and perhaps they would feel some obligation to repay his trust.

Bernstein was right to give some importance to eye contact with the jurors. People tend to look at and talk longer with people toward whom they have positive feelings. The way a prospective juror looks at a lawyer or the length of time he takes to answer his questions can reveal which side the juror is more comfortable with. After responding to a question, some jurors will look unconsciously to the prosecutor or the judge for approval or reassurance. The defense lawyer should excuse such a person.

Bernstein was not happy with the woman in the middle of the back row. He didn't like the way she was sitting with her arms folded across her stomach. He was more troubled by an intuition he had about her than any particular answers she had given.

Bernstein took a deep breath. "The jury is satis . . . no, I'll excuse Juror Number Nine," he said.

The woman in the back row gave Bernstein an angry look, unfolded her arms, and walked out of the jury box.

Bernstein looked over at Ryan, who seemed unhappy at losing the woman. The prosecutor's reaction was reassuring to Bernstein.

The court officer called the next juror. It was Maureen Whalen. She told the judge that she was single and worked as a supervisor at the telephone company, and she knew of no reason why she could not be a fair juror.

Ryan looked over the group assembled in the jury box. He thought Bernstein had made a mistake in keeping Elliot Postom because of Postom's experience on the jury in the assault case. A person who had watched an ordinary criminal trial involving a more typical charge like robbery, drug possession, or assault, with the minimal amount of preparation that goes into such cases by a prosecutor, was more likely to be impressed if not overwhelmed by the prosecutor's preparation for a murder case.

Ryan was right about the degree of preparation for a murder trial. The most experienced detectives are assigned to investigate homicide cases. A battery of experts is often involved. The scene of the murder is usually studied with care. Experts test for fingerprints, hair, or blood samples that might identify the killer. A medical examiner studies the body for what it may tell about how the murder was done and what kind of person could have done it. Teams of police will chase down leads, talking to dozens of people, checking business or police records, tracing the ownership of documents, personal property, or cars.

Ryan's principle about prior jury experience worked both ways. If a prospective juror had previously sat on a murder case and now was being considered as a juror on an assault charge, the defense lawyer, aware that he'd be expecting an impressive array of state's witnesses, should be inclined to take him as a juror. He'd be much less easily persuaded to convict. The shoddiness and inadequacy of police work for the more common crimes is often appalling.

"The jury is satisfactory to the state," Ryan said.

Two blacks remained on the jury. Bernstein believed that his protest about racism had inhibited Ryan from excusing the remaining blacks. After the trial Ryan told people that his decision to leave the blacks had had nothing to do with Bernstein. At that point of the voir dire, Ryan had only one peremptory left and Bernstein had three. If Ryan had used his last one, he would have had to accept whoever was called afterward, and Bernstein could have knocked three more off without running the risk of Ryan finding the replacements unacceptable. Ryan felt that the jury he had accepted was

"fairly bright," and he liked that. If Rafshoon was going to
be convicted, the jury would have to understand some very
complicated scientific evidence.

Bernstein also felt that the fourteen who sat in the box
were "fairly bright," and he, too, liked that. He knew that the
state was going to use a lot of scientific evidence, and he
wanted jurors who would not be overly impressed by the expert witnesses, and who would realize that the scientific evidence was far from conclusive.

Most attorneys believe that the circumstances of a particular case override general principles about types of jurors.
As a general principle, a lawyer believing he has a strong case
will want intelligent jurors, while with a weaker case he will
seek jurors expected to be sympathetic on emotional grounds
rather than because of a rational array of facts.

Bernstein wanted jurors who could consider the case
against Rafshoon without getting emotionally overwrought
by the gruesome details of the crime. Bernstein's intuition
told him he'd be better off with educated jurors: the more
educated they were, he felt, the more objective, the more cere-
bral and less swayed by emotions they would be.

Bernstein realized that his view of educated people might
be elitist and a reflection of his own prejudices. He had recently begun to see himself as detached from his feelings, too
little involved with "natural" emotions. His wife had accused
him of having turned into some cold observer about everything, including their relationship. That wasn't at all the kind
of person he wanted to be, but it was precisely the kind of
person he wanted on his jury.

"The jury is satisfactory to the defendant," Bernstein said.

"Swear the jury," the judge said. Ryan thought he sounded
like a submarine captain in an old movie ordering the crew to
"take her down."

"Please rise," the clerk said.

Two court officers approached the jury and handed out

black Bibles. There were only five Bibles, so the guards arranged the jurors in groups of twos and threes to share them.

"You, and each of you, do swear in the presence of Almighty God," the clerk intoned, reading from a dog-eared three-by-five card, "that you will well and truly try this matter in dispute between the State of New Jersey and Leander Rafshoon, the defendant, and a true verdict give according to the evidence."

The clerk looked up at the jury.

"I do," everyone on the jury answered.

"Please be seated," the clerk said.

The judge looked out at the ten people seated at different spots in the back of the courtroom. "All those in the jury panel who have not been selected for this jury may return to the jury control room on the fourth floor."

The judge waited for the unselected jurors to leave, and then turned to the jurors in the box. "You are now the sworn jury who will decide this case. We'll adjourn for the day. Be back at nine o'clock tomorrow morning. You should assemble in the room behind the jury box. That's the jury room. And when we're ready, you'll be called out, and we'll begin our trial."

Most successful lawyers develop their own criteria for their choices of jurors. Law professors, experienced lawyers, and a number of technical books suggest general rules to help select favorable jurors. The rules are frequently contradictory, making jury selection sound more like a parlor game than the serious business of deciding who should determine a defendant's fate.

Although each person may have his own reasons for not being totally objective about someone accused of a crime, verdicts are usually based on more than one prejudice. People are more complicated than the ways we often generalize about them. Statistics and studies can be helpful in describing how trials work or in understanding how jurors behave, but a lawyer must deal with a specific defendant like Leander Rafshoon facing twelve specific individuals like the people who were chosen to decide his fate. And each juror comes, of course, with his own complicated constellation of attributes.

Both Ryan and Bernstein would agree with a study of thirty-nine trial lawyers that found 50 percent of all their peremptory challenges were based on the occupation of the potential juror. Race, religion, or nationality were the other attributes most frequently cited. A feeling of lack of rapport between attorney and prospective juror was also mentioned.

Some defense lawyers feel that certain groups have to be avoided in certain cases—for example, religious people in obscenity trials; wage earners in income tax prosecutions; West Indian blacks who feel superior to American blacks accused of involvement in the drug trade; and young, idealistic jurors in political corruption cases. Some defense lawyers excuse butchers because "the necessary forbearance or compassion for blood or pain could not be expected of them." It was for this very reason that they were ineligible under Jewish law to serve as jurors.

Some well-known criminal lawyers have expressed views about jurors that are idiosyncratic if not absurd. Percy Forman, one of the most successful, is leery of Germans, Russians, and others with a strong sense of law, order, and "tribal tradition." Louis Nizer has said he is suspicious of prospective jurors with beards or bow ties: "They're usually individualists who will try to win a jury over to their view." Melvin Belli was quoted as saying that he prefers men to women jurors because "women jurors are too brutal."

In an interview, Clarence Darrow said that he would be inclined to keep an Englishman on a jury because Englishmen come from a long tradition and do not fear to stand alone. An Irishman, he felt, would be emotional, kindly, forgiving: "His imagination will place him in the dark, where he will be simultaneously trying himself and thinking of reasons for letting himself off."

The more common stereotypes relied on by prosecutors include men, Republicans, the prosperous, bankers, engineers, and accountants; defense lawyers generally favor women, Democrats, poorer people, social scientists, and minorities.

Attorneys for both sides are eager to remove those who are believed to hold extreme views. "Essentially what we are trying to do in these cases," Richard Christie, a social scientist who has advised defense lawyers on jury selection, said, "is to get rid of the kooks, the overrigid, irrationally law-and-order people. We are looking for fair-minded jurors willing to listen to the evidence." An assistant district attorney in Albuquerque, New Mexico, said that in order to avoid having a hung jury caused by one juror holding out for acquittal in the face of eleven other jurors, he had to question the jurors "to get the flaky weirdos off."

Some lawyers regard the voir dire, at least in some of their cases, as unlikely to affect the verdict regardless of who is on the jury. Bernstein knew a defense lawyer who once excused a businessman because the government had an airtight case and the defense lawyer wanted to have an attractive woman to look at in the jury box.

Lawyers often try to reach beyond the common stereotypes to find their own "types" with whom they feel most comfortable. In the same way that Bernstein felt a sympathy for Julius Solars, a trial lawyer is accustomed to looking for a person he considers open rather than closed, warm rather than cold. "If I see a juror who draws his mouth together very tightly," Louis Nizer has said, "I'm inclined to think he's a very severe fellow, too severe."

When Bernstein excused the woman who had sat with her arms folded, he was responding to what he intuitively thought the woman's body was saying. Similarly, a man who wears loafers may be thought of as more easygoing, more relaxed, and more liberal. A few lawyers have hired experts in body language to sit next to them at counsel table and interpret what they see in the prospective jurors. Other lawyers have used handwriting analysts to study the signatures of prospective jurors. In a few extreme cases, lawyers have had astrologers in the courtroom to tell them which jurors were sending out the best "vibes."

Facial cues can sometimes be more effective in communicating a person's attitudes than voice or speech. Social scientists have concluded that the face can reveal what emotion the individual is feeling, and body language can show the intensity of that emotion. But, they caution, the face is also the site most under an individual's control, so a person could fairly easily display false emotions there. Body postures and movements are not as easily controlled, and if they contradict signals given by the face, the juror may be lying.

Increases in body movements or a tense, still body posture can reveal anxiety or deception. Finger-tapping, wringing one's hands, and manipulating various parts of the body with the hands can indicate that the juror feels uncomfortable with a particular attorney or that he feels anxious because he is being deceitful. When a person is relaxed in answering questions, he is more likely to be telling the truth; but this is not always a reliable indicator and could lead lawyers to excuse nervous but otherwise capable jurors like Julius Solars.

In the 1972 trial of Angela Davis for kidnapping and murder, her lawyer had three psychologists assess her personality and appearance in order to anticipate her courtroom performance and its effect on jurors. After identifying beauty, determination, and friendliness as her three most positive personality and physical traits, the psychologists set out to find twelve jurors who would react to Ms. Davis on a "rational-human level" rather than on a "prejudicial-emotional level." Jurors were finally selected after their backgrounds, political views, handwriting, and "body language" were considered. By the time the jury was picked, the attorney for Davis was confident that the worst he could expect was a hung jury. Ten of the jurors attended her victory party after the acquittal.

Neither Bernstein nor Ryan used the variety of experts employed in the Davis case, nor did they use the statistical and demographic analysis that has become fashionable in recent years. In a small but growing number of cases, lawyers have enlisted social science experts to help select favorable jurors. Underlying such use is the premise that a person's demographic characteristics are indicative of how he has been "socialized" and will probably reveal his perception and attitudes.

Scientific jury selection was first recognized as important in 1971 when a team of experts helped pick jurors for the Berrigan brothers when they were charged with conspiring to kidnap Henry Kissinger. Over eight hundred phone interviews of potential jurors were conducted to determine the demographic characteristics of the jury pool. The defense team learned from the interviews that the pool underrepresented the young and used this fact, among others, to persuade the trial judge to order a new panel of jurors.

The Berrigan interviews revealed information about the jurors' contact with the media, their knowledge of the defendants and their case, and specific facts about their lives: their spare-time activities, their trust in government, their children's ages and activities, and their memberships in organizations. The potential jurors were also asked about their attitudes toward private property, religion, the police and the use of force to maintain public order, and the degree of antiwar activities they would find acceptable, the presumption of innocence, and whom they regarded as the greatest Americans during the past fifteen years.

The social scientists conducting the interviews expected to find that college-educated jurors would have the most positive attitude toward the antiwar defendants, but the studies showed that college graduates in Harrisburg, Pennsylvania, where the trial took place, tended to be less liberal than those who had only finished high school. Apparently many of the college-educated liberals had left Harrisburg.

It was determined that the best juror for the defense in the Berrigan trial was under thirty, black, possessing elements of a "counterculture" life-style, with a son or close male relative at or near draft age, and who opposed the Vietnam War. Being an Episcopalian, Presbyterian, Methodist, or Fundamentalist was found to be an unfavorable characteristic. Higher education and extensive exposure to metropolitan news media appeared to correlate with conservativism and was less likely to favor the defendants.

After the success of the Berrigan case, "scientific" jury selection was used in the trials of Joan Little, Russell Means and Dennis Banks (the leaders of the Indian takeover of Wounded Knee), the Attica inmates, John Mitchell and Maurice Stans, and the Vietnam Veterans Against the War in Gainesville, Florida. And the defendants won in every case.

The cost of jury surveys ranges widely depending on the sample size, the length and manner of the questioning, and the number of volunteer workers. The Berrigan survey cost $450, the Attica survey $400, and the Joan Little survey $38,992. The Little survey found twenty-three different demographic variables including age, education, neighborhood, politics, and reading habits to be significant indicators of attitude.

Some people feel that using social scientists or experts in body language threatens the very idea of a random selection of jurors by stacking the deck. Supporters point out that the use of experts to observe the demeanor of prospective jurors is little more than what lawyers have always done but with more discipline. Surveys merely allow lawyers to know the makeup of the community from which jurors will be drawn so that prejudice can be ferreted out. Social scientists recognize that there is nothing certain about their work, and that they are dealing in probabilities subject to varying margins of error. They understand that jury verdicts are much more than the sum total of individual attitudes, the crucial determinant being the evidence in the case.

The use of social science consultants opens up a number of difficult issues. If the work of the social scientist is really effective, those who can afford them have a major advantage over those who cannot. After Joan Little was acquitted of murder in 1975, her defense attorney, who had used a large defense fund to finance an extensive jury selection program, was quoted as saying that he had "bought" the verdict.

It may become necessary to limit the use of surveys or to require that their results be shared with the other side. The Department of Justice has proposed reducing the number of peremptory challenges, arguing that the availability of privately funded juror studies for wealthy defendants will cause indigent defendants to demand them at the taxpayers' expense. The continued use of juror studies will force U.S. Attorneys to undertake them.

The problem of evaluating the usefulness of "scientific" jury selection stems from the inability to demonstrate that it makes any difference. Scientific methodology requires comparison, and no case has been tried before both a normally selected jury and a group "scientifically" selected. Jury experts have been used primarily in political conspiracy trials, and it is possible that convictions in such trials are low probabilities anyway. The Chicago Seven and Panther 21 cases involved major political issues, and in each case the defense won without using social scientists. Lastly, the work of the social scientists is mostly intuitive, and their effectiveness in predicting human behavior, even in simple situations, let alone in a complex jury trial, seems highly suspect.

In the trial of John Mitchell and Maurice Stans in 1975, the jury reached its verdict of acquittal because one man—the only person opposite from the profile of the "best" juror imagined by the defendants' expert on jury selection—turned around a majority of his fellow jurors, who had voted on the first ballot for conviction.

To some defense lawyers, like Edward Bennett Williams, the use of modern marketing techniques and applied social science is "bunk." To others, it smacks of sinister manipulation, a subversion of the ideal of a randomly selected group of community representatives.

Philip H. Corboy, one of the country's most successful personal injury lawyers, has used sophisticated market research studies to select his juries. He regards such studies as helpful tools. He also dismisses jurors who wear toupees. "It's a personal idiosyncrasy with me," he said. "I don't want a man on my jury who is so vain as to wear a toupee." Corboy apparently believes a vain juror would be less sympathetic to his clients.

Melvin Belli used market research when he defended Jack Ruby on charges of having murdered Lee Harvey Oswald. After Ruby was convicted, Belli was quoted as saying, "I got a jury of bums."

Some studies and many lawyers believe that with or without scientific help, the voir dire is an ineffective screening mechanism. The way many lawyers conduct a voir dire certainly does make it perfunctory, boring, and brief. Often it takes only half an hour because lawyers do not wish to irritate unnecessarily judges or jurors who may have a psychological time limit beyond which they will get hostile.

An ingenious study by Hans Zeisel and Shari Diamond published in 1978 seems to support the proposition that some lawyers can select "favorable" jurors by relying on a sensitivity and intuition about people that they have developed over time and experience. Jurors in thirteen criminal cases who had been excused by peremptory challenges were asked to remain in the courtroom to watch the trial they would have sat on. Care was taken to prevent the excused jurors from learning whether the prosecutor or the defense lawyer had been the one to remove them from their jury. At the end of the trial these "shadow jurors" were asked how they would have voted in the case.

Those jurors excused by the defense lawyers were more inclined to vote for conviction; those excused by the prosecutors were more likely to acquit. By combining this information with posttrial interviews of the real jurors, a vote was reconstructed of those who would have been the first twelve jurors had peremptory challenges not been used. The reconstructed jury's vote was compared with what the real jury actually did, thereby measuring the effect of peremptory challenges on the jury's verdict.

This experiment used an important insight learned from an earlier study of jury decisions: nearly 95 percent of all jury verdicts coincide with the way the majority voted on the first ballot. Using the initial votes of the reconstructed juries to indicate how those juries would have ultimately decided, the new study concluded that in four of the thirteen cases involved in the new study, the likelihood of a guilty verdict was substantially reduced as a result of the defendant's use of peremptory challenges. In one of the cases, the real jury acquitted, while the "jury without challenges" would have almost certainly convicted.

Several explanations were offered for this propensity to convict: the voir dire process may impress upon the jurors the importance of their task and enhance their awareness of their duty to decide the case fairly and impartially; the shadow jurors were aware that the defendant's liberty was not really in their hands, which may have increased the amount of doubt needed to justify acquittal.

This study concluded that a lawyer who does a better job of challenging hostile jurors than his opponent can seriously affect, if not determine, a jury verdict. Lawyers, as they often boast, apparently do win some of their cases by their choices of jurors. The study could not tell how often the lawyers' choices are the result of superior skill or luck, but it cannot all be luck. Ironically, such victories by astute lawyers are defeats for the adversary system, which is based on the assumption of equal adversaries.

The use of peremptory challenges to excuse jurors on the basis of race or other group affiliation is considered by many to be a virtue of the system. The assumption is that occasionally there is a "core of truth" in some stereotypes. The case of *Swain* v. *Alabama* used by Judge Whitaker to allow the prosecutor to eliminate blacks has had an enormous impact on the profile of juries, going a long way toward making all the rules about a "fair cross section of the community" a sham, and wasting much of the money and time spent on trying to obtain representative jury panels.

This apparent twist in the law has had important consequences. In the original case, Robert Swain, a nineteen-year-old black, had received a death sentence for raping a white woman in Alabama. All six blacks who had been called to the jury box at his trial had been peremptorily challenged by the prosecution. Swain showed that while 26 percent of the population of his county was black, no black had served on a petit jury during the previous decade. Neither the trial court nor the Alabama Supreme Court found anything improper in this pattern of discrimination.

The United States Supreme Court found the trial record in the Swain case insufficient to prove a purposeful pattern of racial discrimination over a period of time. Jurors in a particular case, the Court reasoned, are not always to be judged solely as individuals for the purpose of exercising peremptory challenges. Rather, they are chosen or excused in light of the limited knowledge counsel has of them—which may include their group affiliations—in the context of the case to be tried.

Justice Arthur Goldberg, in a dissenting opinion, felt that the record in *Swain* had demonstrated the prosecutor's discriminatory intent, and the history of that Alabama county should have been enough to shift the burden to the state to prove, if it could, that the exclusion was for other than racially discriminatory reasons.

Both the majority and the dissenting opinions in *Swain* agreed that a court could not infer discrimination from the prosecutor's challenges in any one case, since the prosecutor might legitimately feel that all the blacks on a particular panel would not give the government a fair trial. The Supreme Court Justices were disagreeing only about whether the prosecutor or the defense should have the burden of proving that the elimination of blacks from a particular jury was part of a pattern of discrimination.

A defense lawyer almost never has the statistics to prove a pattern of discrimination, and the state under the *Swain* decision is not required to keep them. Even if those statistics had been collected, enough juries have been selected in most jurisdictions with at least some blacks on them to rebut a claim of systematic exclusion.

Most of the time when a prosecutor excludes people because they are members of a group, it is not only morally outrageous, it is also stupid. For example, the victims of urban crime are usually black, and there is probably no group more eager to punish the guilty than urban blacks. White jurors unfamiliar with ghetto language or ghetto ways are more likely to be taken in by a black defendant who is "jiving" them. And finally, many members of a group that is discriminated against would be capable of putting aside their sympathy for the defendant, or do not have any to begin with, or do not even identify with or "represent" their group anyway.

But the problem is more complicated than most liberals admit. Legal ethics obligate an attorney to represent his client zealously within the bounds of the law. A lawyer is not primarily interested in society's problems in general: he is concerned about his client's rights in particular. While all racism is of course repugnant, a lawyer's prejudices are sometimes correct. With very little specific information about a juror's background, a lawyer often relies on hunches based on stereotypical prejudices, and people's race, religion, or national origin can, in certain cases, turn out to have a bearing on the way jurors respond to the evidence or the characters in a case.

Prosecutors are correct in believing that some black jurors will be less likely to return a conviction against a black defendant because of a feeling of brotherhood. In a country that kept blacks as slaves for its first 250 years and has discriminated against them in a variety of "legal" ways since then, including in the selection of juries, some blacks might well be suspicious of their government. This suspicion can focus on a policeman who is a key witness for the government, or promote a sympathetic hearing for a black defendant's claim of a coerced confession or police brutality.

Some liberals might even find discrimination acceptable in certain cases. If a Nazi is accused of desecrating a synagogue, one can hardly blame the Nazi's lawyer for preferring a jury free of Jews. A prosecutor may honestly and, in terms of probabilities, correctly believe that he would have a better chance at convicting a Mexican charged with violating American immigration laws if there were no Mexican-Americans on the jury.

The dilemma becomes clearer in the trial of a white racist charged with lynching a black: a defense lawyer who eliminates all blacks or a prosecutor who gets rid of all whites will almost certainly leave one of the lawyers convinced that an unfavorable verdict was colored by the racial composition of the jury. An integrated jury would probably increase the chance of a hung jury. A jury of twelve Koreans flown in for the trial might offer the greatest possibility of rendering a verdict uninfected by prejudice.

The problem of jury discrimination has been made worse in the South by the reluctance of local lawyers to challenge the systematic exclusion of blacks. Those lawyers who do attack the system can and do suffer serious personal sacrifices in their communities; the loss of a law practice and social ostracism are not farfetched risks. Or the lawyer may fear that his objection, whether successful or not, will only serve to inflame racial feelings against his client and do him more harm than good.

More is at stake at a trial than the right of the defendant and the victim to have a particular jury accurately decide the question of guilt or innocence. Trials are supposed to settle violent disputes peacefully in a way that inspires confidence in diverse elements of our society. When an all-white jury convicts a black defendant, the black community may well be suspicious; racial incidents, if not race riots, have been triggered by more trivial happenings. The problem was demonstrated in the incidents in Miami in 1984 when four police officers were acquitted of killing blacks by all-white juries, and the verdicts were met with days of riots.

Society has a right to a criminal justice system that works *and appears to work* fairly. Obviously, a pattern of systematic discrimination against particular groups can only undermine the public's confidence in the fairness of verdicts. One of the underlying causes of the anger and alienation of many ghetto blacks, which may be one contributing cause of vicious crime against whites, has been the accurate perception of being officially discriminated against. Only when the black community believes that our courts treat blacks equally can black citizens be expected to cooperate fully with law enforcement in fighting crime. And it is only with the cooperation of citizens that the crime rate will significantly drop.

A pattern of discrimination over a period of time is inde-
fensible, but racism in jury selection will be eliminated only
when racism in our society is eliminated. In the meantime,
what are we to do about those cases in which common sense
suggests that race may be a relevant issue in selecting un-
biased jurors? In rare instances a defense lawyer or prosecutor should have the right to "discriminate" in a particular
case.

So far, the press has missed this story. Out of ignorance,
indifference, or incompetence, journalists have failed to inform the public about discrimination in jury selection. Perhaps most members of the press are only partly aware of it,
but if any of them cared to investigate the matter, they would
discover the enormity of the problem, how the discrimination
is usually needless or counterproductive, and how, in those
few cases, it does seem rational. Part of the problem is that
the "typical" criminal case is not followed by reporters, and
in the sensational case, the problem doesn't crop up because
the prosecutor knows he is being watched and is more careful. One thing is clear: taxpayers should not be paying prosecutors to exacerbate our race problems or to furnish
defendants with the excuse of a "prejudiced" jury. On the
other hand, prosecutors should do everything they can to
convict those guilty of terrible crimes.

One solution to the problem presented by the *Swain* case
would be to require that blacks be more fairly represented in
the jury pools. The Supreme Court and an American Bar Association committee have recommended limiting the number
of peremptory challenges allowed to both sides, reasoning
that if the number were limited to fewer than five or eliminated altogether, it would become difficult or impossible to
eliminate all blacks from juries.

Several state supreme courts have disagreed with the *Swain*
decision and ruled that if blacks are excused from a jury, the

prosecutor must prove that racial discrimination was not the reason. In April 1985 the Supreme Court agreed to confront the issue again and consider whether to reverse its twenty-year-old *Swain* ruling. Given the conservative bent of the Burger Court as compared with the Warren Court that decided *Swain*, a change in *Swain* seems unlikely.

PART
THREE

THE
TRIAL

CHAPTER

THE MORNING AFTER THEY WERE SWORN IN, thirteen of the fourteen jurors assembled in the small jury room. Two rectangular conference tables had been pushed together along their lengths to form a square. Twelve chairs in black leatherette surrounded the tables, and a half-dozen additional chairs were backed up against the walls, barely leaving a path wide enough for a person to walk around the room.

A fat bottle of water squatted in a beige water cooler stationed in a corner of the room. A large clock with arabic numerals and a long second hand staggering around it hung on a wall.

The doors to the men's and women's rest rooms were next to each other at the far end of the room. No paintings, no photographs, nothing adorned the green walls. There were no windows. Fluorescent lights glared and hummed down from the white, scarred masonite ceiling.

Unlike some of his writer friends, Alex Butler needed to be in a room with a window that allowed a view and some natural light. It was important for him to be able to look up once in a while to refocus his eyes on some objects at a distance and be reminded that there was a world outside that was carrying on with its usual business. The small enclosure of the jury room was a nightmare for him.

With so many people in so small a space, it was impossible to walk around the room without constantly bumping into someone. Most of the people took seats around the table and sat quietly—and waited.

The only juror missing from the jury room was Maureen Whalen. Maureen had arrived early, visibly upset, and had told the court officer that she would like to speak to the judge in private. She was ushered into the judge's chambers. She told him that the night before, she had received "at least half a dozen telephone calls." She was sure that the caller was trying to scare her about the trial.

"What did the caller say?" Judge Whitaker asked.

"Nothing. He didn't say anything. There was just this silence at the other end and then a click when he hung up."

"What makes you think that the phone calls have anything to do with this trial, Miss Whalen?" the judge asked.

"Well, this has never happened before. The only thing that is different is that I'm involved in this trial."

"This is a very difficult situation. I'm afraid there isn't very much I can do. If it happens again, I'll order police protection for you, and we can have your phone monitored. But it seems likely to me that it's just a crank caller who has nothing to do with this case."

The judge called in the attorneys and the court reporter and repeated the conversation he had just had with Miss Whalen.

"Do either of you have any questions you'd like to ask Miss Whalen?" the judge asked the attorneys.

"I have one," Bernstein said. "Would you in any way hold these calls against my client, Leander Rafshoon?"

"No, not at all," Maureen said. "I think the judge must be right that this is just a coincidence, that it has nothing to do with the case. I hope so."

Bernstein nodded.

The judge asked Maureen to join the other jurors in the jury room. "And don't mention this to any of your fellow jurors," he said.

After she left the chambers, the judge asked Ryan and Bernstein if they had any objections to Maureen Whalen's continuing in the case. Bernstein knew that there was no point in making an objection because the judge would not excuse her. But he also knew it was quite possible that this woman thought Rafshoon had something to do with the call; he was sure she wouldn't have thought anyone from law enforcement would call her. This might make her think that Rafshoon was even more dangerous than he looked. On the other hand, it occurred to Bernstein that if she was going to interpret these calls as threatening, she might be a little more afraid to convict him.

When Maureen entered the jury room, several people greeted her, and no one mentioned her lateness. Maureen took an empty seat and waited with the others. She felt much better for having talked to the judge, and she was convinced that the caller had simply been a crank.

Threats to jurors happen very rarely, and it is much rarer still that any harm comes to a juror. Statistically, slipping in the shower represents a much higher risk of personal injury. But, not surprisingly, many jurors have expressed anxiety about their safety when sitting on cases involving charges of violence.

The whole system of justice in the United States depends on the jurors' being able to function without fear of personal harm. The courts have responded to this need in different ways. Judges have sequestered jurors for the length of a trial, or furnished police protection during the time they are out of the courtroom. On occasion a judge has prohibited the press from interviewing or writing about the personal lives of the jurors. In a few instances judges have revealed the jurors' identities to the lawyers only, specifically prohibiting them from divulging information to their clients. In the 1979 trial of a notorious New York drug dealer, Nicky Barnes, the judge stipulated that during the voir dire there could be no questions about the names and street addresses of potential jurors.

But these kinds of measures are rare. The sequestering of a jury is a source of great anxiety for jurors called to service. It also means they must sleep in hotels and be separated from their families for the length of the trial, which may last days or months. Furthermore, it is very costly for the state. Some groups of people may find it more of a hardship than others—older people, mothers, the poor—so it may alter the deliberation process itself or change the complexion of the jury by reducing the availability of members of those groups to serve. In the Rafshoon case, none of these extreme measures were used.

A court officer knocked on the jury room door and entered. "We're ready for you," he said.

"You were selected to be fair," said the judge as soon as the jurors had taken their seats in the courtroom. "That's all we ask. It is my duty as judge to see that the trial is conducted according to the rules of law, to decide points of trial procedure and evidence, to maintain order and decorum, and to instruct you on the law. Your responsibility is to be the sole judges of the facts, and your verdict should be based solely on the facts as you find them."

As Laura Sayres listened to the judge, she looked over at the defense lawyer. Bernstein was writing on a yellow legal pad, making notes, underlining certain words or phrases, slashing exclamation points, and in between all of that, he seemed to be doodling in the margins. He had long, curly hair, like Laura's younger brother, but the eyes of the man who sat at counsel table looked old and tense. His rumpled suit jacket suggested to her someone who didn't pay much attention to his appearance. On the other hand, the prosecutor looked fastidious, with his checked suit, striped tie, and stiff white collar. She studied his meticulously trimmed beard shaved in sharp corners. He probably lined up the paper clips in his office. She felt she knew the type.

Laura noticed that the defendant had suddenly shot his gaze over to her. His eyes, dark and bulging, locked onto hers. He looked to her like a cornered panther, crouched and capable of springing loose. She had no intuition about whether or not he was guilty, but she was sure he was capable of real violence. Laura suddenly realized they were staring at each other. Frightened, she felt an icy shiver pass up the center of her back. She turned her head away to look at the judge, and felt comforted by his fatherly presence.

". . . so I instruct you not to visit the scene of the alleged offense," Judge Whitaker said. "Do not talk to anyone including your families about the case while it is still going on, and do not read any newspaper articles or listen to any television accounts of the trial."

Many jurors cannot wait to get home at the end of a day of trial to tell their husband or wife the events of the day. But a surprising number actually wait until after the verdict to discuss the case with anyone.

"I expect that there will be media coverage of this trial, so you will have to be careful to skip over the articles about it, or turn off your TV sets if this case is discussed.

"We used to sequester juries for the duration of trials to ensure that a jury's verdict was not influenced by anything improper. Nowadays we rarely do that. Instead we rely on your word that you will obey the court's instructions.

"If any lawyer or witness or anyone else tries to talk to you about the case, you should immediately let me know.

"You should not discuss this case among yourselves until all the testimony has been completed and I have had an opportunity to give you your final instructions."

Theoretically this was an important instruction because some evidence might be admitted late in the trial that should be considered by the jury, and if the jurors had discussed the case at some earlier point, they might not be as open to the new evidence as they would otherwise have been. Also, in order to discuss the facts, the jurors needed to know how to interpret those facts, and to do that, they had to know what rules to apply. Such rules are given by the judge in his instructions at the end of the case.

It is one of the more absurd expectations made of jurors that they listen to all the evidence, evidence that is often presented in no logical order and sometimes over a period of months, and only at the end are they finally told what rules to apply in interpreting what they have heard. Some critics have noticed this absurdity and suggestd that judges inform juries at the outset as to what they are supposed to be looking for. Unfortunately, few states have taken any steps in this direction.

The judge continued with his lecture. Carl Copco watched the court reporter as she typed away silently. She was seated just below the judge, directly facing the jury, not more than five feet away. Her legs surrounded the slender pole of the tripod that supported her small gray machine, and one foot rested over the ankle of the other. Carl noticed that her legs were long and shapely. He could see almost halfway up her inner thighs. He was sure she deliberately let her skirt ride up like that. An attractive woman in her late twenties, she was stylishly dressed in a purple turtleneck sweater. A thick gold chain hung down between her ample breasts. She was wearing a diamond ring on her right hand and a wedding band on the other. Marriage had never stopped Carl before.

The court reporter's eyes wandered around the courtroom, coming to rest on various objects and people. She didn't seem to be listening to the judge, yet her fingers moved swiftly across the keys, silently pressing down hard, then moving to a new position as if the long fingers had an intelligence and a will of their own. Carl saw her make eye contact with the woman court officer and exchange a smile with her. He wished she would look at him for a moment so that he could smile at her too.

"We're ready for the prosecutor's opening statement. Mr. Ryan?"

Leslie Ryan, holding the indictment in his hand, rose from counsel table. He took several steps toward the jury box and planted his feet directly in front of the wooden rail, not more than an arm's length from Juror Number 4, Laura Sayres. He paused.

Ryan looked at each juror one at a time, making sure that he had his or her attention, allowing tension to build in the silence. They were all watching, waiting.

Leander Rafshoon sat nervously, his eyes darting from the judge to the court officer to the prosecutor and back to the judge. He turned to look at his wife and little boy seated in the first row. His mother had been too upset to attend. He looked terrified. He focused on the jury as he waited to hear what the prosecutor was going to say. Rafshoon knew his life was in the hands of those twelve people. They would decide.

Leslie Ryan, in a loud voice, began by reading the indictment: " 'The Grand Jurors of the State of New Jersey, for the County of Essex, upon their oath present that Leander Rafshoon on or about the fifth day of September, 1982, at the Town of Glen Ridge in the County of Essex aforesaid and within the jurisdiction of this Court, did commit an act of

homicide upon one Carolyn Collins, with deliberateness, premeditation, and malice aforethought, contrary to the provisions of the New Jersey Statutes and against the peace of this
State, the government and dignity of the same.'"

Most of the jurors didn't understand many of the words in
the indictment. "Malice aforethought," "jurisdiction," and
"premeditation" have technical meanings that would be explained to them only at the end of the trial. This procedure is
followed in most cases, but prosecutors frequently read the
indictment to a jury because the words sound so impressive,
rather like the Latin once used in some church proceedings.

Judges tell juries that the indictment is not evidence of
guilt, but many jurors—26 percent according to one study—
still assume that if a grand jury has returned an indictment,
the defendant must have done something: where there's
smoke, there's fire.

The big secret not told to the jurors but known by judges,
lawyers, and just about anyone connected with law enforcement is that most people who are indicted *are,* in fact, guilty.
Of the several hundred clients Bernstein had represented, virtually all of them had been guilty of something, though not
necessarily of the crime they were charged with in the indictment. But to Bernstein, the innocence of the jury was its single greatest virtue. Jurors would actually presume that a
defendant was innocent in ways that judges, those brutalized
souls who deal with the administration of justice on a daily
basis, were no longer capable of believing. A defendant
should be acquitted if the state has not proved its case beyond
a reasonable doubt. It is harder for a judge who knows most
defendants are guilty of something to prevent his assumption
of guilt from affecting his perception or evaluation of the
evidence.

Looking up for a moment from the paper in his hand, Ryan
searched out the eyes of each juror, then read on: "The sec-

ond count of the indictment states, 'The Grand Jurors of the State of New Jersey, for the County of . . .'"

As the prosecutor continued, Rafshoon watched the man at the end of the front row, Postom, who was listening to the prosecutor like a man in church hearing the gospel for the first time. The man was hearing the Word. But there was no doubt about it: as the prosecutor was talking of murder and rape with Rafshoon's life on the line, Postom was smiling.

"Ladies and gentlemen of the jury, as the representative of the people of this state," Ryan went on, "I will prove to you that Leander Rafshoon brutally and viciously raped and then murdered Carolyn Collins by stabbing her thirty-seven times and bashing her head in with a sledgehammer."

The young woman behind Carl Copco gasped.

"My primary purpose as an assistant prosecutor in dealing with the tragically large number of criminal cases that become my responsibility is not simply to win convictions against someone charged with a crime, but to do justice. That is my sworn oath as an assistant prosecutor. And justice in this case demands a conviction of rape and of murder in the first degree."

This kind of argument by prosecutors is all too common. Prosecutors pretend they are not merely advocates, but stand in some loftier, more objective position than defense lawyers, the implication being that defense lawyers, in contrast, are sleazy hired guns.

"The purpose of this opening statement," the prosecutor went on, "is to outline for you what the state intends to prove. A trial is a little like a puzzle. You will observe a number of pieces, one at a time. Obviously I can't put all the witnesses on at the same time, but by the end of the state's case the entire picture will become clear. This outline of an opening statement should help you understand where each piece of evidence fits."

The main purpose of Ryan's initial remarks was to begin to sell his case. Like many Madison Avenue salesmen, most lawyers operate on the assumption that repetition is helpful in convincing people. The jury would hear parts of the opening statement again during the trial and yet again at the end of the evidence when Ryan delivered his summation.

". . . replacing the sledgehammer in the toolshed," Ryan said as he concluded his version of how he thought the crime had been committed. "It's a terrible, tragic crime caused by this man's hatred and lust for a blond, blue-eyed, beautiful white woman. Listen with an open mind to the evidence as it unfolds, interpret that evidence with your good common sense and return a verdict of guilty of rape and of murder in the first degree. Thank you." Ryan turned and went back to his place at counsel table.

Once, as an experienced trial lawyer was nearing the end of an opening statement at the start of a sensational trial, one of the jurors leaned over the rail and yelled, "That's telling 'em." Such is the stuff that lawyers' dreams are made of.

"Mr. Bernstein," the judge said, raising an eyebrow.

Bernstein rose slowly and approached the jury. "The prosecutor has concealed from you virtually all the important facts of this case," he said. "He has nothing to build his case on but the flimsiest pieces of speculation and possibilities. One fact, one tragic fact is undeniable: Mrs. Collins was brutally murdered. That's not an issue in this case. What is at issue is whether my client, Leander Rafshoon, committed that murder. And that's what the prosecutor has to prove to you beyond a reasonable doubt. My client doesn't have to prove anything to you. The burden is on the state, and as the judge will tell you, that burden on the state never shifts.

"You will hear a number of things that will surprise you. None of these will have been mentioned by the prosecutor."

Bernstein could have argued that the prosecutor had already subtly appealed to the jurors' racial prejudices. There was no evidence of racial motivation to the crime, so Bernstein could have screamed that the speculation about the defendant's "hatred and lust" being aroused by a "blond, blue-eyed, beautiful *white* woman" was playing the jury for well-worn, stereotypical racial fears.

This would have been risky, however. Calling attention to the remark could heighten its importance and increase the chances that jurors with fears capable of being aroused by such a suggestion would act on them as they considered whether or not the defendant was guilty.

"You have heard Mr. Ryan read the indictment to you. Judge Whitaker has told you and will tell you again that the indictment is not evidence of guilt. Your importance as a trial jury—sometimes you are called the petit jury—is seen in contrast with the grand jury. Grand jurors only hear the evidence presented by the prosecutor. A defendant has no right even to be present at the proceedings, or to confront his accusers, or to present witnesses on his own behalf. There usually isn't even a judge presiding to make sure that the proceedings are fair. And an indictment is returned when a simple majority of the twenty-three grand jurors believes that the defendant *probably* did it, rather than a trial jury's unanimous verdict based on proof beyond a reasonable doubt.

"At this point," Bernstein said, "I only ask you to listen closely to the testimony. Please wait until I have had an opportunity to cross-examine all the witnesses and have presented our own witnesses before coming to any conclusions. I am confident that after you have heard all the evidence and applied the law as Judge Whitaker gives it to you, you will return a verdict of not guilty of the charges. Thank you."

Bernstein had not told the jury anything about his defense. He had considered opening to the jury with an attack on the character of the victim. Defendants have at times been treated more leniently when juries have felt that the victim had been at fault, or had in some way caused the defendant to commit the crime. If this were just a case of rape, Bernstein would certainly have mentioned Rafshoon's relationship with the Collins woman. Juries often weigh the woman's conduct in the history of an affair and treat a defendant more leniently when they feel there is contributory behavior on her part. But with the thirty-seven stab wounds, there was no way Bernstein could argue that the victim "got what she asked for."

Bernstein had decided to leave his options open and wait to see how the testimony of the state's witnesses went. By playing the opening statement close to the vest he had also avoided alerting the prosecutor to his overall strategy. He turned around in his chair at counsel table and looked the crowd over. A man in his mid-sixties with a crew cut and horn-rimmed glasses was one of the twenty spectators in the courtroom. He wore a laminated card pinned to the front of his sleeveless sweater that read MORRIS GINZBURG, OFFICIAL SPECTATOR. Next to these words was a color photograph of Morris, smiling. The criminal lawyers who had tried cases over the years in this courthouse knew Morris as a regular—a "buffalo" they called them—someone who moved with other regular spectators as if in a herd, from one sensational trial to another.

Bernstein nodded at Morris, who returned the nod. He and Morris were in this together.

Ryan stared at the jurors. He often felt let down after picking a jury. It wasn't so much that he had regrets about any of the selections; it had something to do with a feeling of having lost the power over those selections. Before he announces that a jury is satisfactory, a lawyer can dismiss any of the members without having to give an explanation. Up until this point, the prospective jurors have had to please *him*. After they have been sworn in, he has to please *them,* persuade *them.* Ryan's jurors had changed from a group of ordinary people who didn't know each other to a new entity with a separate existence and holding the ultimate power over Ryan's case and his reputation.

"Mr. Prosecutor, you may proceed," the judge said.

"The state calls Violet Gardner."

The court officer walked up the center aisle of the courtroom and pushed open the door. A moment later a woman in a beige suit with bright blond hair and a rich tan entered. She walked pigeon-toed toward the front of the courtroom. Her brown silk blouse had ruffles, and a gold chain swung around her neck. The courtroom was silent except for the sound of her stockinged legs rubbing against each other as she walked. She reached the witness box, and the court officer asked her to raise her left hand and place her right hand on the Bible.

"Do you solemnly swear to tell the truth, the whole truth, nothing but the truth?" the court officer asked.

She cleared her throat. "I do," she answered.

"State your full name and spell your last," the court officer said.

"Violet Gardner. G-a-r-d-n-e-r." She sighed, and took her seat in the witness box.

The prosecutor's detective entered the courtroom carrying a large box. He approached counsel table and placed the box on the floor to the left of the prosecutor, in plain view of the jury.

Bernstein watched as the detective sat down next to the prosecutor. Ryan whispered something to the detective, who smiled and, putting his arm around Ryan, said something in response.

Bernstein knew that almost everything that Ryan did in front of a jury was deliberate. That big box, for example. The jury would, of course, be curious about what was in the box in front of them. As the trial progressed and the prosecutor pulled pieces of evidence out of it, each object would have a

sensational impact on them. Bernstein also knew he was help-
less to do anything about it.

The prosecution has a number of tactical advantages over
the defense, subtle and imperceptible though they may be. In
almost every state, the prosecutor makes the first opening
statement to the jury; he also gets to make the last summation. Throughout the trial the prosecutor sits a few feet away
from the jury, which enables him to overhear remarks jurors
might make to each other that the defense counsel ten feet
away would have trouble hearing. But most important about
the prosecutor's proximity to the jury is the feeling of closeness, even intimacy, that can develop between them. Bernstein had tried cases against prosecutors who had actually
winked at jurors during the trial. Some prosecutors, Bernstein
felt, were shameless.

In response to Ryan's questions, the witness told the jury
she was the older sister of the victim, and had visited her
often at her house in Glen Ridge. "It was a beautiful house,
very expensive. She had everything, except luck," she said.
She took a deep breath.

Ryan reached into the large box at his feet and withdrew a
folder. He removed several eight-by-ten glossy color photographs from the folder. He walked over to the bulletin board
behind the witness and tacked up the photographs. He
handed a pointer to Mrs. Gardner.

She pointed to the photographs and identified the pool, the
rear garden, and the toolshed with the garage. She pointed to
other photographs showing the various rooms in the house.

"Excuse me," the judge interrupted. "I see that Juror Number Eight . . ." He searched through his list of jurors. "Yes,
Miss Whalen. Miss Whalen, I noticed that you are taking
notes. Is that correct?"

"Yes, Your Honor," Maureen said, pleased that the judge
had noticed her diligence.

"Perhaps I should have instructed you about note-taking in my initial remarks. You are not allowed to take notes."

"I'm sorry, Your Honor," Maureen said. She folded the piece of paper she'd been writing on and placed it in her pocketbook.

"That's all right," the judge said.

Maureen, like many jurors, was upset with the rule against note-taking. It is unfortunate that judges usually don't explain the reasons for such a rule, which for the most part make sense. A juror's job almost always requires the determination of whether a witness is lying. To do that, jurors must closely watch the witnesses, scrutinizing their demeanor to evaluate how forthright and open they are. If a juror is taking notes, he or she may be distracted just at the critical moment from observing a witness. Also, there is the danger that a juror with what might appear to be better notes could have more influence in the jury room during deliberations. Each juror is supposed to participate equally, relying on a collective recollection of the evidence to which every juror should have an equal opportunity to contribute. A number of studies have shown that collective recollection is astonishingly good without any recourse to notes. Several states have begun to allow jurors to take notes in long or complicated cases, though most courts still do not allow it.

"Okay. Let's go on. Put your next question, Mr. Prosecutor."

"On August thirty-first, 1982," Ryan asked, "did you receive a telephone call from your sister?"

"Yes, I did. She said—"

Bernstein leaped to his feet. "Objection. Anything the decedent said to her sister would be hearsay."

"I'm going to let her go on," the judge said. "What Mrs. Collins may have said will not be offered for the truth of those statements, but to elucidate the perceptions and behavior of the witness. So let's hear what she wants to tell us. Go on, Mrs. Gardner."

"She was panicky. She told me, 'This man is watching me. I can't stand it. He follows me from room to room.'"

"Did she tell you who she was talking about?"

"The black man her husband had hired to be a bodyguard. I asked her why she didn't just get rid of him. She said her husband made her have him around. She was afraid of him. He looked so big and dangerous."

"Your witness," the prosecutor said.

A small woman wearing thick glasses sat hunched over in the first row of the spectators' seats, cradling a stenographer's notebook in her lap. She was writing furiously, hardly looking up at the witness. Her glasses kept sliding down her nose, and she kept pushing them back with the palm of her hand. She was one of several reporters from local newspapers who were following the trial.

"Mrs. Gardner," Bernstein asked on cross-examination, "didn't your sister tell you in that telephone conversation that this bodyguard, this big black bodyguard, was also 'gorgeous'?"

"Yes, she did say that."

"You knew that your sister was angry at her husband, didn't you?"

"Yes, she told me that."

"Why was she so angry?"

"Objection," the prosecutor said.

"Sustained," the judge said.

"Was she so angry that she might do something to hurt her husband or get even with him?"

"Objection," Ryan said. "That question is asking for sheer speculation from this witness."

"Mr. Bernstein, I have to agree with the prosecution. Sustained."

"But I'm asking about when the victim told her that she

wanted to get even with her husband. That's not speculation."

"No, that would be sheer hearsay, and I'm not going to allow that, Mr. Bernstein."

"But you allowed the prosecutor to elicit hearsay testimony."

"Don't argue with me. I've made my ruling."

"Apparently. I was just hoping for some consistency."

"I'll hold you in contempt if you make any more remarks like that." The judge turned to the jury. "Ladies and gentlemen, please do not consider exchanges between counsel and me in your deliberation. What counsel say is not evidence. Sometimes lawyers get carried away on behalf of their clients. My job is to see that they don't get away with it." The judge smiled at the jury, and then turned back to Bernstein. He exchanged the smile on his face for ice in his voice and said, "Put your next question, Mr. Bernstein."

"I have no further questions," Bernstein said.

The judge called a recess for lunch. The jurors filed out, the lawyers looked over their notes in preparation for the next witnesses, and the defendant was led to his cell in the basement of the building for what the guards refer to as "feeding."

Strategies and techniques of lawyers in today's trials vary widely. By carefully repeating the points he considered most important, Ryan was acknowledging that a trial lawyer is a salesman trying to persuade the jury to buy his arguments. If the defense lawyer has evidence to show the innocence of his client, or if there are weaknesses in the state's case, it should be easier for him to sell his "product." A few lawyers who don't believe in their clients' innocence are less effective because their doubts are communicated to the jury; as a lawyer, Abraham Lincoln did not like defending guilty clients because he could not successfully mask his feelings from a jury—and those were the cases he lost. But most defense lawyers who do criminal work usually wind up sooner or later representing guilty clients; curiously, some of these lawyers feel less emotional pressure and are freer to take more risks with the jury when they believe their clients are guilty.

Many lawyers are tempted to attribute a victory at trial to a single brilliant stroke, an inspired moment that captured the jury's imagination. There are a number of colorful, if perhaps fanciful, stories of such courtroom triumphs.

In defending a group of striptease dancers charged with having gone too far, an experienced lawyer in San Francisco won acquittals by having the portly arresting officer demonstrate to the jury his idea of the difference between a clean bump-and-grind and a lascivious one.

A flamboyant Chicago lawyer supposedly won his case during his summation when he stood before a jury and, pointing to his attractive woman client, was heard to say, "I ask you, ladies and gentlemen of the jury, are these the legs of a murderess?"

During the summation of a lawyer defending a man charged with murder by poison, the lawyer picked up the half-empty bottle of the alleged poison and turned to the jury. "I will show you how certain I am that this is not poison," he said and gulped down the bottle's contents. While the jury was in the jury room deciding to acquit the defendant, the attorney was across the street from the courthouse having his stomach pumped of the slow-acting poison by the medical team he'd had waiting for him there.

Many people familiar with the case involving Jimmy Hoffa believe that Edward Bennett Williams swayed a predominantly black jury in a single stroke by arranging for boxing champion Joe Louis to walk into the courtroom and, in the full view of the jury, shake hands with Hoffa.

While stories of this kind may be true, such theatrics are uncommon. The more typical practice involves careful,

workmanlike preparation and execution, and most of the decisions made by juries are based not on the single, brilliant
stroke, but on the evidence introduced at trial.

Yet many people, including lawyers, believe that a smart
lawyer, superior to his adversary, is all that is needed to win a
case. The Chicago Jury Project studied this issue at great
length and made some fascinating discoveries. Judges rated
the performance of lawyers in three thousand cases and concluded that defense lawyers were superior to prosecutors in
11 percent of the cases, prosecutors were superior in 13 percent of the cases, and the strength of both of them was balanced in roughly 75 percent of the cases. A surprise finding
was that counsel representing poor and black defendants
were not to any significant degree inferior to counsel representing other defendants.

The Chicago Jury Project broke down its findings to determine imbalances of counsel according to the type of crime. It
found that in income tax and perjury cases defense counsel
were superior to prosecutors in 27 percent of the cases; in
auto theft and cases involving the carrying of a concealed
weapon, the prosecution was superior in approximately 20
percent of the cases; and in murder, rape, narcotics, and burglary cases the two sides were roughly even.

The principal criterion of judges determining superiority of
counsel was verbal persuasion: this or that lawyer had "delivered a brilliant argument" or offered "a very impassioned
plea"; or "experienced defense counsel was able to convince
the jury that beyond a reasonable doubt meant beyond all
possible doubt." Superiority of counsel was noted not only in
summations. Judges also described impressive demonstrations of skill during trials: one judge cited the effective way
defense counsel managed to introduce "highly prejudicial, irrelevant matter . . . by asking irrelevant questions, objections
to which were sustained by the court"; defense counsel "ob-
fuscated the jury by bringing in extraneous testimony attack-

ing complaining witness's credibility"; and a "skillful defense counsel demonstrated successfully that the two county detectives should have been out digging ditches."

Sometimes the judges attributed the superiority of a defense lawyer to his attractiveness or youth or sincerity rather than to outright skill. In a few cases reported from rural communities a defense lawyer was seen as effective with the jurors because they had clearly felt prior obligations to him. One judge in a case of drunken driving explained an acquittal on the basis that the defense lawyer had been practicing for thirty-five years in the area and some of the jurors were "under his influence."

There were times when the youth and inexperience of the lawyer were seen as working to advantage by stimulating sympathy in the jury. One judge was quoted as attributing an acquittal to the fact that the young lawyer had told the jury it was his first case.

In the large number of cases in which judges found the prosecution inferior to the defense counsel, comments were usually couched in general terms—the prosecutor gave a poor performance—but sometimes there were specific complaints about a prosecutor's sloppy presentation or hypertechnical approach, or how a prosecutor had not pursued a certain line of inquiry or failed to stress a particular point. In one case, for example, a prosecutor had failed to impeach the testimony of the defendant by demonstrating that the defendant had made statements about events that only the perpetrator of the crime could have known.

The Chicago Jury Project's ultimate conclusion about the importance of counsel is deflating to the sometimes overblown public image and self-image of the defense lawyer: only 1 percent of the more than three thousand cases studied were considered to have been won solely by the superiority of defense counsel.

Chief Justice Warren Burger, who, of course, does not preside over trials where trial lawyers perform, has offered his own opinion of the competence of counsel: "From one third to one half of the trial lawyers who appear in serious cases are not really qualified." Trial judges asked to rate the performances of the lawyers who appeared before them, however, came to a different conclusion. The judges gave a "competent" rating to 87 percent of the lawyers and "partially incompetent" to 11 percent of the lawyers. Another study found judges reporting only 8.6 percent of the lawyers as inadequate.

The positive statistics and favorable opinions of judges can't offer much relief to the defendant who winds up with an incompetent lawyer. A defendant looking on while his lawyer mangled his case would find little comfort in the knowledge that the large majority of defendants do not have the same problem.

In a brilliant portrait of the craft, H. L. Mencken summed up the role of counsel in an essay he wrote in 1928:

> The sad thing about lawyers is not that so many of them are stupid, but that so many of them are intelligent. The craft is a great devourer of good men; it sucks in and wastes almost as many as the monastic life consumed in the Middle Ages. . . . The law . . . has few rewards for a man of genuine ambition, with a yearning to leave his mark upon his time. How many American lawyers are remembered as lawyers? . . . If lawyers were generally dull men, like the overwhelming majority of the reverend clergy, or simply glorified bookkeepers and shopkeepers, like most bankers and businessmen, it would not be hard to understand their humble station in history, but I don't think it would be fair to put them into any of those categories. On the contrary, it must be manifest that their daily work, however useless it may be, demands intelligence of a high order, and that a numskull seldom if ever achieves any success at the bar, even of a police court. . . . It may take only the talents of a clerk in a lime and cement warehouse to draw up mortgages and insert

jokers into leases, but once a cause in law or equity comes to bar it calls for every resource in the human cerebrum. The lawyer standing there is exposed to a singularly searching and bitter whirlwind. He must know his facts, and he must think quickly and accurately. Those facts, perhaps, are quite new to him; he has engulfed them so recently as last night. But he must have them in order and at his command; he must be able to detect and make use of all the complicated relations between them; he must employ them as fluently as if they were ancient friends. And he must fit them, further-more, into the complex meshes of the law itself—an inor-dinately intricate fabric of false assumptions and irrational deductions, most of them having no sort of kinship with fact at all, and many of them deliberately designed to flout it and get rid of it. This double job of intellectual tight-rope walk-ing the lawyer must undertake. More, he must do it in the presence of an opponent who jogs and wiggles the rope, and to the satisfaction of an audience that is bored, hostile, and worse still, disunited. If, marshalling the facts adeptly, he attempts a logical conquest of the jury, and if, while he is attempting it, he manages to avoid offending the jurymen with a voice that grates upon them, or a bald head that excites their risibilities, or a necktie that violates their "pudeurs"—if, by the lavish flogging of his cortex he ac-complishes all this, then he is almost certain to grieve and antagonize the judge, to whom facts are loathsome and only the ultra-violet rays of the law are real. And if, wallowing in those rays, he arouses the professional interest and libido of the judge, then he is pretty sure to convince the jury that he is a sciolist and a scoundrel. . . . It is the professional aim and function of the lawyers "not to get at the truth," but simply to carry on combats between ancient rules. The best court-room arguments that I have ever heard were not designed to unearth the truth; they were designed to conceal, maul and destroy the truth. I have heard two such arguments opposed to each other, and both driving at the same depressing end. And at their conclusion I have heard the learned judge round up and heave out what remained of the truth in an exposi-tion that surpassed both.

Mencken's jaundiced view of the role of lawyers took account of the wide-reaching power of the judge. A judge can influence a jury in a variety of ways. It is his task to instruct the jury about the law in the given case, and the way he phrases the principles of law can have a great impact on the jury. In some states the judge also has the power to comment on the evidence, offering his opinion of what facts warrant the consideration of the jury.

But a judge can "instruct" a jury with even greater force by a raised eyebrow, a grimace, an edge of sarcasm, an icy voice like the one Judge Whitaker used to chastise Bernstein, or by other indirect ways unnoticeable to a court of appeals reviewing the cold printed transcript of a trial. The judge's attitude toward a defense lawyer can greatly influence a juror's opinion of that lawyer and his client. Few judges if any can disguise their own impressions of lawyers, witnesses, or the evidence. Even if a judge makes no deliberate effort to convey his impressions, jurors will often sense them by means of the judge's unconscious indicators.

Social scientists have found that body language in one form or another constitutes well over half of a person's means of communication, and that for the most part, it is beyond the individual's control. Even untrained observers are often able to decode accurately a sender's nonverbal cues. The decoding process, like the sending of cues, is largely unconscious.

"I was very impressed by the judge's manner with the jury," Elliot Postom would say after the verdict. "He brought great dignity to the proceedings. It couldn't have been easy to control the decorum of the lawyers at times."

In the three thousand cases studied by the Chicago Jury Project, judges came to the same decisions as juries about 75 percent of the time, even when the juries were confronted with difficult evidentiary and legal issues. This high degree of agreement led the Jury Project to conclude that juries are more capable of understanding difficult cases than has often been thought. A conclusion not reached by the Jury Project, but a possible one in at least some of the cases, is that judges, perhaps subtly and unintentionally at times, convey to juries their feelings about guilt or innocence, and the juries can be influenced by these cues.

When Judge Whitaker had said, "My job is not to let a lawyer get away with anything," the message to the jurors was loud and clear: Bernstein is trying to pull a fast one. Bernstein certainly understood what the judge was up to—the judge could have called him to side-bar and spoken to him outside the hearing of the jury—but Bernstein also knew that he had to restrain himself from reacting or the judge could make him look even worse.

Most jurors arrive in a courtroom with great respect for the judge, whom they see as a fair-minded father figure interested only in the implementation of justice. Lawyers, on the other hand, are assumed by many to be bought for a price, paid to lie, finagle, do anything they can to get their clients off. What juries don't know is that many judges, like Judge Whitaker, were once prosecutors, and that such judges sometimes forget that it is no longer their duty simply to get convictions.

After the verdict in the Rafshoon case, none of the jurors would feel that the judge's attitude toward the lawyers had affected their decision. This view might well have been correct—but they might also have simply been unaware of how much they had been influenced by the judge. Several were to say they thought "the defense lawyer got on the judge's nerves." One juror would come to hate the prosecutor.

Just where these judges come from seems important. Judges up to the time of the Magna Carta were ecclesiastics. Lawyers were unknown in England until 1291, when Edward I authorized the licensing of forty lawyers, a number thought sufficient to deal with the legal work of the kingdom. Even in the two centuries following the appointment of the lawyers, judges were rarely lawyers.

In the Chicago Jury Project, a survey of 325 judges examining their prior experience found that 22 percent had been prosecutors, 14 percent had been criminal defense lawyers, and 64 percent had been neither or both. Those judges who had previously served only as defense lawyers presided over trials that acquitted almost twice as many defendants (22 percent) than those who had only been prosecutors (13 percent).

The early part of a trial is frequently a time for lawyers to test how far they can go with a judge. Many judges are particularly strict in this stage of the proceedings. Most judges and lawyers realize that what is really at stake is control over the trial.

Bernstein was indeed trying to see how far he could go with Judge Whitaker, and he actually did score a small point. When he said, "I'm asking about *when* the victim told her that she wanted to get even with her husband. That's not speculation," he was talking to the judge but was also cleverly addressing his remarks to the jury. In fact Bernstein had no evidence that the victim had been motivated by any desire to get even with her husband. The implication of his phrasing was that the desire for revenge was a given and that the only question was a matter of timing.

When the full range of the judge's power is taken into account, even such minor victories by a lawyer over an aggressive judge can seem like major triumphs. In addition to his indirect influence over the jury, a judge has a variety of specific powers in a criminal trial. If the judge finds that the state has not presented sufficient evidence for a jury to find a defendant guilty, he can dismiss the case without ever presenting it for the jury's deliberation. If a jury acquits a defendant, the judge must accept the verdict, but if it finds the defendant guilty, the judge can set aside the conviction on the grounds that there has been insufficient evidence to reach that conclusion. A judge can also grant a new trial if newly discovered evidence is presented to him after a jury has convicted.

The Jury Project found that judges had set aside 19 percent of the guilty verdicts involving serious charges, and 5 percent of minor charges in cases where they strongly disagreed with the juries' verdicts.

The judge also has the responsibility for determining the appropriate punishment for a defendant found guilty by a jury. When judges do not like a jury's verdict, they often impose the minimum penalty allowed by the law. Empowering the judge to reverse or mitigate the effect of an "unjust" decision of a jury is an important safeguard of the criminal justice system.

The judge also functions as a screening device to keep certain facts from the jury that, for reasons of fairness or because of constitutional requirements, are regarded as inappropriate for a jury to consider in their deliberations. For example, the judge will withhold information about plea negotiations, improperly obtained confessions or physical evidence, or in certain situations the criminal records of defendants.

In this way judges will often be aware of facts prejudicial to a defendant that a jury will not know. It would be difficult to believe that some of this tainted information would not color a judge's decision if it were up to him to render the verdict.

Charges against a defendant were not always resolved by means of a trial by jury. For centuries during the Dark Ages, disputes were settled by one of several ordeals. One method required the accused to carry a red-hot iron weighing from one to three pounds for a distance of nine paces or to walk barefoot and blindfolded over nine red-hot plowshares laid lengthwise at unequal distances. If the accused were burned, he was declared guilty. In another ordeal the accused was required to take a stone from a pail of boiling liquid; the stone rested at a depth equal to the length of his hand or forearm. If the accused were burned or, in a more sophisticated version, if the accused person's burn became infected over the next several days, his guilt was said to be confirmed.

In a variation of the boiling liquid ordeal, the accused, after swearing to his innocence, was lowered into a pool of cold water with his thumbs tied to his toes to keep him from cheating with his hands. If the accused floated, he was considered guilty, because it was believed that the "pure element of water would not receive into its bosom anyone stained with the crime of a false oath." If the accused sank, his accusers would try as best they could to save the "innocent" man from drowning.

There was also an ordeal of the "cornseed" or "consecrated morsel" in which the accused was required to swallow a piece of bread while people around him prayed that it might choke him if he were guilty. This ordeal was apparently the source of the once popular emphatic phrase, "If I'm not telling the truth, may this morsel be my last."

Ordeals were part of the early judicial procedure of practically all the nations and tribes of Europe and Asia. Basic to the ordeals was the conviction that God would intervene on behalf of the innocent, even to the point of overcoming the laws of nature. To ensure fairness, the trials were supervised by the clergy; in fact, in its early stages, trial by ordeal was encouraged by the clergy, as it strengthened their influence. In November 1215, Pope Innocent III prohibited the further involvement of the clergy in trials by ordeal. Without their participation, such trials no longer had the same impact, and they began to fall into disuse.

CHAPTER

VI.

RAFSHOON KNEW NOTHING OF THE TRIAL by ordeal as it was practiced in the eleventh century, but as he watched the jurors returning to their seats after lunch, his emotions may have been similar to those of a defendant in those earlier times. As for Bernstein, his own thoughts must have been distracted. The photographs of the Collins house taken after the murder were still tacked to the bulletin board. Bernstein knew that a defense lawyer should not let a prosecutor sear the image of a murder scene into the minds of the jurors, but he had simply forgotten to have Ryan remove the photographs.

The clerk called the roll. Each juror answered "Here," and the court officer counted out loud after each name until he reached fourteen.

"Good afternoon, ladies and gentlemen," the judge said.

"Good afternoon, Judge," the jurors answered in unison.

Ryan spent the rest of the day presenting witnesses to establish what the late Mrs. Collins had done on the day of her murder. The director of a nursery testified that Mrs. Collins had dropped off her two children at eight-thirty, as usual. The woman who gave Mrs. Collins her weekly massage remembered first seeing the victim at nine-thirty and completing the massage at around ten-thirty.

Bernstein had not asked the woman from the nursery any questions on cross-examination, but he did want to draw out some additional information from the masseuse in front of the jury. "When you gave her the massage," he asked the muscular woman from the fitness center, "was she naked?"

"Yes, of course. I always used oils and then finished her off with powder."

"Did you ever notice bruises on her body?"

"Objection," the prosecutor said. "Irrelevant and beyond the scope of the direct examination. This witness was presented solely for the purpose of establishing the time of death."

"That may have been the prosecutor's purpose," Bernstein retorted, "but the jury is entitled to hear the whole truth. Nothing should be hidden from them."

"I object to that," Ryan said. "I'm not trying to hide anything from the jury. Mr. Bernstein knows he can call this person as his own witness if he wants to bring out additional information." Both lawyers knew, though none of the jurors did, that if Bernstein had to call the witness as his own, he would not be allowed to ask leading questions and would therefore have much less control over the testimony.

"Gentlemen, calm down," the judge said. "I'm going to allow the witness to answer to speed things up."

Bernstein got the witness to say that she had seen bruises on the victim on the day of the murder as well as at other times during a two-month period prior to that. She remembered having seen bruises on her arms, and once on her face.

"Were the bruises fresh when you saw her that last time?" Bernstein asked.

"*If* she could tell," the prosecutor said. Ryan was trying to suggest to the witness that the only reasonable answer would be that she *couldn't* tell.

"They weren't there the week before," the woman said.

"What did the bruises look like?" Bernstein pressed further. He had already gotten more than he'd hoped to get, and he was like a dog running after a scent. "Did they look as if they'd been caused by someone hitting her with his fist?" Bernstein must have known this was an improper question— the witness was not a medical expert qualified to offer opinions about bruises—but he also knew that even if he wouldn't be allowed to get an answer, he would have managed to introduce the thought of beatings to the jurors' minds.

"Objection. This calls for sheer speculation on the part of the witness," Ryan said. "She's not a doctor."

"Sustained."

"I have no further questions."

A lanky, awkward eighteen-year-old named John Moore, Jr., followed the masseuse to the witness chair. As he sat with his legs crossed, one foot, which extended beyond the side of the witness box, shook nervously.

The young man said that he had worked during the summer of 1982 for the County Shade Tree Commission. On the day of the murder he'd been trimming trees with four others across the street from the Collins house on Ridgewood Avenue. He was at that location all day, from around nine o'clock until two-thirty. "I didn't even leave for lunch. My mother had packed a brown bag for me. I left for only about five minutes during the morning," he said.

He told the jury he had seen Mrs. Collins, driving a white Mercedes, arrive at the house at a little before eleven. He had seen only one other person enter or leave the premises, and that was at about one-thirty. "About an hour before we packed it in for the day, I saw a man leaving through the back. He ran past the pool and out the backyard."

"Could you describe the man?" Ryan asked.

"He was a big guy. Maybe thirty years old."

"Anything else?"

"Yeah. He was black."

"Now, this is very important, Mr. Moore. Do you see in court today the man you saw running out of the Collins house on that day? Look around the courtroom and tell us if you see that man in court."

The courtroom was deathly quiet. Fourteen jurors, a dozen spectators, the judge, the lawyers, the court personnel, all looked at the witness. Everyone in the room was waiting for the crucial identification as the witness looked around the courtroom.

Bernstein knew that Ryan would not have asked the question had he not been confident of the answer.

Rafshoon clenched his teeth, waiting with everyone else for the announcement.

"The man over there. That's the one."

Several jurors shifted in their seats. Rafshoon turned his gaze from the witness to the judge.

"Let the record reflect that the witness is pointing at the defendant, Leander Rafshoon," Ryan said. "No further questions."

"Did you see Mrs. Collins at any time after she arrived?" Bernstein asked as he rose from his seat.

"Yes. I saw her at the pool. She was sunning herself. It was around noon. She stayed out there about an hour and a half."

"Had you ever noticed her sunbathing at the pool before?"

"Yes, sir. Every day. Since we began that job—a week before."

"What made you notice her? What made you check to see if this woman was out there on that particular day?"

"Mrs. Collins was a beautiful woman."

"That's why you would notice her?"

"She was naked. She would sunbathe in the nude."

"Did you see the man you thought was the defendant arrive at the house?"

"No."

"So you wouldn't know how long he had been at the house. Is that correct?"

"Yes, sir."

"What was the man wearing?"

"I don't recall."

"Was he wearing a coat or a jacket?"

"I don't recall."

"Could you tell if he had scratches on his face or if he was bleeding?"

"I can't remember."

"You say you don't recall, but wouldn't it be more accurate to say that you couldn't make it out?"

"Yeah, maybe so."

"Because of the distance, right?"

"Right."

"How far away were you from the pool? How many feet?"

"Maybe fifty yards."

"So you couldn't tell if he had kinky hair or straight hair, could you?"

"No, I couldn't."

"Or if he had a straight nose and thin lips?"

"No."

"Nothing further."

The witness started to step down from the witness stand. "Just a second," the prosecutor said. "One last question, Mr. Moore. Are you sure the man you pointed to at counsel table was the man you saw running away from the house?"

"Yes, that's the man. I do remember he was running away,

so mostly I just saw his back, but at one point I remember he looked over his shoulder and that's when I saw his face."

"Nothing further," Ryan said.

The witness started to get up again. "Just a moment," Bernstein said. "When the man was running away, most of the time his back was toward you, right?"

"Yes, sir."

"So how long would you say you actually saw his face?"

"Maybe a few seconds."

"A few seconds, maybe. And when was the last time you saw the man you now think is the defendant?"

"On that day."

"You mean the day of the murder?"

"Right."

"So you only saw the man you think is the defendant for maybe a few seconds as he was running away from you at a distance of a hundred and fifty feet, and you haven't seen that person for more than a year now." Bernstein turned to the judge. "I have nothing further."

Bernstein should also have asked the witness how he had described the defendant to the police immediately after the murder. The police reports stated that at the time, Moore couldn't recall any details about the man running away from the house. Bernstein, who had seen the police reports, had intended to ask the question but had simply forgotten.

"You can step down," Ryan said.

The witness looked at the judge. "Can I really go now?"

The judge smiled. "Yes, you can really go."

Bernstein was dying to ask a crucial question: "Had you seen Leander Rafshoon's face before the day of the murder?" But he was afraid of the answer. The witness had said that he'd worked at the house across the street for a week prior to the murder. Rafshoon had been at the Collins house a number of times during that week. If the witness recognized him from earlier visits, the identification would be substantially stronger.

Bernstein turned over in his mind whether Ryan had failed to ask that question because he expected the witness to say he'd never seen him before, or because Ryan had simply forgotten to ask. The written statement the witness had given to the police was also silent on this point. Bernstein could have had an investigator ask the witness this question before the trial, but the witness might then have alerted the prosecutor to the lapse, if that was what it was. Bernstein decided to leave the question unasked. He would mention the absence of testimony at this point during his closing argument to the jury.

The first witness on the third day of the trial told the jury that he had gone to the Collins residence at two-thirty on the day of the murder, and that everything was quiet.

"I'm an exterminator," the witness said. "I went over that day for my regular servicing call. The back door was open three or four inches. I knocked on the door, but no one answered. I took a step inside and called, 'Hello.' Mrs. Collins was usually home when I made my calls. They had a problem with carpenter ants. Not unusual. And there was an old European housekeeper who was always there, but she wasn't there that day. So I did a little spraying on the outside and left."

On cross-examination Bernstein asked the witness if a dog had been in the backyard.

"Every time I came there, that dog would scare the daylights out of me," the exterminator said. "He was this big dog—I think they called it a mastiff. That dog would come running at me and throw his body against the wooden fence of the pen they kept him in. I mean like the whole fence would push forward."

"Did you see any cars there?" Bernstein asked.

"I think that dog would have ripped my heart out. I was really scared of that dog."

Bernstein made a large check on his yellow legal pad. "Exactly," he said. "Were there any cars there?"

"Mrs. Collins's white Mercedes was in the driveway. Everything was quiet. It looked ordinary to me, except no one was there. I mean it *seemed* no one was there. I had no idea when I was at the back door that Mrs. Collins was just a few feet away from me on the kitchen floor."

After the exterminator was excused, Ryan announced, "The next witness is Adam Collins."

The eyes of everyone in the courtroom fixed on the courtroom door. It slowly opened.

A tall, handsome teen-ager stepped forward. He looked straight ahead as he made his way down the center of the court. He was wearing a brown twill suit with a vest. His eyebrows were raised, leaving his forehead wrinkled.

After being sworn in, he took his seat on the witness stand. His fine light brown hair was parted down the center. He had a long, narrow nose, thin lips, and high cheekbones with chiseled hollows under them. His deep-set green eyes looked sad and made him seem older than his years.

Ryan had the boy tell the jury that he was fifteen years old, the son of Carolyn Collins, and that on the day of the murder, September 5, 1982, he was living at home with his mother, stepfather, and younger brother and sister.

"I was supposed to go to swimming practice after school, but for some reason I decided to go home instead. I guess I got home around a quarter to three, because school was over at two-thirty. Okay?"

"And then what happened?"

"I used the front door. I usually used the back door; that's the one my mother always wanted me to use. But I used the front door that day. Okay? So I went in and everything was real quiet. Then I saw a thick rope, the end of the rope, over by the other side of the center hall. I knew something was wrong. I went up to the rope and followed it down the hall into the kitchen. When I went into the kitchen, I saw my mother on the floor."

"What did you do?"

"I went hysterical."

"What do you mean 'hysterical'?"

"I started to kick things around. I picked up a chair and started to smash it into the wall. I broke the leg of the chair. I turned the table, the kitchen table, over. Okay?"

"Did you at some point call the police?"

"Yeah. That's right. I called the police first. As soon as I saw my mother, I called the police. It was after I called them that I went hysterical. Then I ran outside. I was crying. I waited for the police outside. I left my mother alone in the kitchen."

From two photographs, Adam identified the chair he had broken and the kitchen table he'd turned over.

"Let me show you this last photograph. Do you recognize what's in this one?"

Adam stared at the picture. He didn't say anything.

"Adam," Ryan spoke softly, "this is the last question. Do you recognize what's shown in this photograph?"

A few seconds passed. "My mother. That's the way I found her."

"I have nothing further."

Bernstein waited for about a minute for the drama of the moment to pass.

Patricia Stewart, from her seat in the second row, tried to imagine the terror that poor woman must have felt. Patricia never spent much time at home alone, but she'd often thought how vulnerable a person alone could be. If she ever saw someone like the defendant coming after her, she'd probably just faint. The image flashed across her mind of the scene in *Wait Until Dark,* a movie in which Audrey Hepburn played a blind woman alone in a house with a madman. When that crazed killer had leaped out of the darkness at Audrey, Patricia had nearly jumped out of her seat in the theater. It was frightening being a woman alone. You can't help feeling vulnerable, she thought.

"Adam," Bernstein finally began, "when did you first meet the defendant, Leander Rafshoon?"

"Two weeks before my mother's death," Adam said softly. "My stepfather had hired him to be a kind of bodyguard."

"Why was it necessary to hire a bodyguard?"

"My stepfather was having an affair with a woman, and some man had threatened to get him if he continued to see that woman."

"So what would the defendant do?"

"He'd follow my mother wherever she went. He never left her alone when he was over, and he'd go with her if she went shopping or visiting or something. Sometimes he would go off with my stepfather and spend the day with him."

"Did you see the defendant on the day of the killing?"

"No."

"And you never heard your mother complain that he had ever threatened her, did you?"

"No."

"Or had attacked her?"

"No."

"Who do you live with now?"

"Objection," Ryan called out. "That's irrelevant."

"Sustained," the judge said.

"You don't live with your stepfather, do you?"

"Objection," Ryan shouted.

"Sustained. Mr. Bernstein, I just ruled that that was irrelevant."

"Sorry, Your Honor. Okay. I have nothing further. Thank you, Adam."

Adam looked up at the judge, asking with his eyes if he was finished. The judge nodded. Adam stood and looked over at the jury, then he walked quickly out of the courtroom.

During the next several days, a series of police officers testified.

The first officer was Patrolman John Minton. He described how he had responded to a call on his car radio and had gone to the Collins home to find the boy yelling, "My mother's dead! My mother's dead!"

"I entered the house," Minton said, "and found the victim lying facedown on the kitchen floor in a pool of blood. The bottom of her bikini was lying about ten feet away from her on the kitchen floor. All she was wearing was the bikini top."

When Ryan was done, Bernstein asked one question: "Did you notice a photograph which had been torn in half and placed on the back of the victim's head?"

"Yes," Patrolman Minton said.

Bernstein knew that his question was unnecessary at this stage. He was going to introduce evidence about the torn photograph later in the trial. But he also knew there was going to be a great deal of emotional description about the killing itself, and to the extent that he could, he wanted to divert the jury's attention from the violence of the killing. He had to convey to the jury that his shock at the horrible nature of the crime was as great as theirs, while at the same time trying to focus their attention on the issue of whether or not it was Rafshoon who had done it. There was nothing in this police officer's testimony linking his client to the crime, and it would have been a mistake to give it more weight than necessary by lengthening his time on the witness stand. He indicated to the judge that he had finished with the witness.

The next witness called to the stand was the detective who had taken the photographs of the house and the victim. "You can see in the back of this picture," he said, pointing at the eight-by-ten in front of him, "that there's a thick black and white rope on the floor by the doorway. It runs the length of the corridor and leads into the next room, which is the kitchen. The next photograph shows the kitchen as you enter from the corridor in the previous picture. This next one shows the black and white rope leading up to the body of the victim, which is lying in the center of the kitchen floor."

The remaining pile of photos showed the scene in the kitchen from different angles, some with close-ups of the body. "You can see the arms outstretched on the floor. The blood was smeared all over her hair. Some of it had already dried. This one shows the body after it was turned over. You can't really make out the puncture wounds. This is a picture of the body being turned over—she's on her side here. This is a close-up of her face after she was turned over. You can see the right side of the head was bashed in. Here, her bikini top was opened and spread back to reveal her front. She wasn't wearing anything else. I mean she didn't have a bottom on."

Maureen Whalen and Julius Solars looked away. They didn't want to hear any more of the descriptions of the photographs.

"This one shows all the puncture wounds on her stomach and chest. This one shows the wounds on her neck. Here we had taken off her bikini top and turned her over to show the wounds in her back. There were only a few wounds in her back. Most were on the front."

Ryan reached into the carton on the floor next to his seat and pulled out a brown alligator pocketbook with a gold clasp at the top. He asked the witness if he could identify it.

"Yes. I found the pocketbook and its contents on the kitchen floor near the body. The contents had been dumped out on the floor around the body." The witness dumped the contents of the pocketbook on the table in front of him. "These are the objects that were in it—an American Express card in the name of Carolyn Collins, a checkbook, a card to Mountainside Hospital, a Visa card."

"Your Honor, I have nothing more of this witness, but I would like to move all the objects he has referred to into evidence."

The judge sent the jury to the jury room, anticipating an objection from Bernstein. He knew there was going to be an extended argument about the admissibility of the photographs. There is one in almost every murder case.

When the door to the jury room was closed, Bernstein argued that the photographs were so gruesome and inflammatory that they would prejudice the jury against the defendant.

"The state," Ryan responded, "is allowed to show a jury that a murder has taken place and the circumstances surrounding that murder. If it was a gruesome killing, and this was, it would be unfair to the state not to be allowed to show by the best evidence what really happened."

"But Judge," Bernstein interrupted, "there is no dispute in this case that the woman was murdered and that she was murdered brutally. These photographs are in color, and the ones showing the victim are so sensational, with all that blood smeared over her naked body, that any normal person seeing them would be incensed. What is at issue is whether my client committed the murder. Other people could have done it; Dr. Collins had a girl friend, and this woman had a lover who had threatened to kill Mrs. Collins. To inflame the jurors by the grotesqueness of the killing would only distract them from the relevant question: Was it my client or someone else who did it?"

The judge allowed the photographs into evidence, relying on a number of court opinions holding that the trial judge must exclude such pictures only if they are *inordinately* inflammatory.

The jury was brought back into the courtroom, and Ryan

asked if the photographs could be circulated among them. The judge assented, and a court officer handed the pile of photographs to the first juror, Julius Solars. He placed the pile on his lap and looked at the top one. His face registered no emotion, but his eyes squinted slightly. He quickly looked up at the judge, and then back at the photograph. A moment later he passed it to Leonard Klein, the juror to his left, and picked up the next photograph.

One at a time, the photographs wound their way across the front row of the jury and then behind and across the back row.

"God!" Matty Barnes, Juror Number 3, said on seeing the first photograph. She breathed deeply and took a mint out of her handbag.

Laura Sayres took the photographs from Matty Barnes. Laura had never seen anything like them, nothing so terrible. A beautiful woman on the floor, with blood all over her, now a dead body!

When Carl Copco first looked at the woman's face, his first thought was of his girl friend, Patty. He still hadn't heard from her. What if someone did something like that to her? He'd kill the guy. No question about that.

Elliot Postom muttered something under his breath and smiled nervously.

In the eighth seat of the jury box, Maureen Whalen touched the photograph with her index finger. "That's the rope," she said quietly. She handed the photographs one at a time to the court officer standing next to her.

Like most experienced criminal lawyers, Bernstein had been through this process dozens of times before, watching gruesome pictures being passed around a jury, waiting for them to make their way from one juror to the other. No matter what they may say, most prosecutors hope to disgust, if not enrage, jurors when they show them grisly photographs of a murder victim.

As the ritual of the passing of photographs continued, Ryan leaned over to his detective, Vince Altieri, and told him a story he'd heard about a trial in a molestation case. At one point the prosecutor had passed around a piece of evidence, a note written by the defendant. Each juror read the note and passed it to the juror at his elbow while the courtroom waited in silence. One of the jurors had fallen asleep, and the attractive woman juror next to him had to nudge him awake. He woke up and took the note. *Come to my house tonight for some kinky fun,* it said. He read the note and said loudly enough for the whole courtroom to hear, "Anything in the interests of justice." Lawyers like Ryan tend to become brutalized when they have been dealing with atrocities for too long.

Maureen handed the last photograph to the court officer. He gathered them together and bounced them on the wooden rail of the jury box to make a neat pile. He walked over to the court reporter and placed them on her desk.

The next police officer on the witness stand drew two plastic bags from his briefcase. "This bag contains samples of the victim's hair," the officer said. "At the autopsy I removed a suspected hair sample I found in the left hand of the victim and placed it in this other bag."

He reached again into his briefcase and withdrew ten small plastic tubes, lining them up on the rail of the witness box. He rearranged the order of the tubes and then looked up at the jury. "I also removed the fingernails from the body. These are the victim's fingernails."

The police officer next identified a bloodstained sledgehammer that had been found in the shed next to the garage, a pair of jeans found in the kitchen, a towel retrieved from the master bedroom, the black and white rope that had been around the victim's neck, and a sterile pad used to recover a sample of the defendant's saliva. It would be up to expert witnesses later in the trial to interpret the significance of the objects. The jury went home that day with one last image: the bloodied bikini top the victim had been wearing, which the witness held up daintily between his thumb and forefinger.

When the trial resumed the following day, Dr. Collins's medical assistant told the jury that she had been with the doctor in the office when he had gotten the call telling him that his wife was dead, and she had accompanied him to his house. She gave no other testimony.

The following witness, a nurse at St. Joseph's Hospital, had seen Leander Rafshoon as a patient on the day of the murder. She had been working as the triage nurse in the emergency room when the defendant walked in. The function of the triage nurse, she explained, was to make the initial decision as to the seriousness of the medical problem of patients entering the hospital. In the defendant's case she had determined that the wound in his eye and the cuts on his face were minor. He'd said he wanted to see Dr. Collins, but the doctor had already left the hospital, so the patient was treated by someone else.

The next witness was Officer Anthony Moreali, a member of the Glen Ridge Police Department, who testified that on the night of the murder he had interrogated the defendant at the Glen Ridge Police Station. Moreali had asked him how he'd gotten the scratches on his face.

"At first he said chips of wood had flown up in his face. I told him I didn't believe him. The eye was totally red. It looked terrible. It didn't seem possible that it could have come from a chip of wood. Then he told me a board had hit him in the face. I asked him how both cheeks but not his nose could have been injured by a single board. He had no explanation for that. Then we asked him to remove his shirt. He had marks on his body. He said he had been in some bushes a week earlier, but the scratches were obviously fresh."

Alex Butler raised his hand.

Judge Whitaker checked the jury list. "Mr. Butler?"

"Can we ask a question?"

"No, I'm afraid not. We can't allow that. You'll have to rely on what the prosecutor and the defense counsel ask and base your decision on the evidence that is brought out."

Both Bernstein and Ryan would have given a great deal to know what the juror's question had been. It might have revealed what he considered important and where his sympathies were thus far. As it happened, Alex had merely wanted to know if the witness had ever seen the defendant before.

Georgia is the only state that has categorically ruled out juror-questioning of witnesses, but where it is allowed, it is at the discretion of the judges whether or not to permit it, and they rarely do so. In 1981 the Georgia Supreme Court noted that "the practice of permitting jurors to directly question witnesses is a dangerous one. Jurors are not schooled in the rules of evidence which govern the posing of questions in a trial and are likely to be personally offended if their questions are objected to."

There is another and better reason for denying juror-questioning. A juror who asks a question may have a certain emotional investment in the answer, and to this degree he loses the detachment of an outsider in evaluating what he hears. With the competing egos of the official participants in a trial, there are already quite enough problems without adding twelve more to the pot.

If Officer Moreali had arrested the defendant on a previous occasion, that fact would have been highly prejudicial and inadmissible. Lawyers know not to ask such questions; if Alex had been allowed to do so but had not been granted an answer, he and the other jurors might have drawn a correct but prejudicial inference.

On further questioning by Ryan, Moreali told the jury that the defendant had tried to run away while being escorted from the interrogation room to the holding pen at the Glen Ridge Police Station. "As I walked down the corridor with

the defendant, he bolted. I hadn't restrained him, and he just
started running. He was trying to get away."

"What did you do, Officer Moreali?" Ryan asked.

"I took off after him. I caught up to him by the front desk.
Several other officers assisted me in subduing him. There was
a scuffle, but we subdued him, and we got him into a cell."

"I have no further questions."

This kind of testimony about an effort to flee is allowed
even if the flight was not part of the crime and took place
sometime after the crime had been committed. Courts have
reasoned that flight might imply that a defendant knew he
had done something wrong, and he was trying to get away
for this reason. A defense lawyer would have the right to offer evidence that the defendant had not, in fact, tried to flee or
that there had been some other reason for the flight besides a
feeling of guilt.

"Isn't it a fact, Officer Moreali," Bernstein shouted, ap-
proaching the witness, "that while the defendant was hand-
cuffed, with his hands behind his back, you beat him to a
pulp?"

"That's a damned lie!"

"You testified there was a scuffle. Does that mean he struck
you?"

"Yes, sir, he did."

"Did you receive any medical attention for your wounds?"

"No, that wasn't necessary."

"Did you strike him?"

"Yes, I may have."

"What do you mean 'may have'? You don't even know for
sure if you hit someone?"

"Yes, I hit him as I defended myself."

"How many times?"

"I don't recall."

"It could have been a hundred times?"

"No, maybe a couple of times."

"Did you hit him in the face?"

"No, in the stomach."

"Was that so there wouldn't be bruises to support a claim of police brutality?"

"I was fighting to protect myself, that's all. I had nothing personal against the guy."

"How many blacks live in Glen Ridge?"

"None that I know of."

"I have nothing further of this witness," Bernstein said, glowering at Officer Moreali.

After Moreali was excused, Judge Whitaker again instructed the jury not to discuss the case among themselves or with anyone else, and he recessed the trial for the weekend.

Expert witnesses testify for the prosecution in a quarter of all cases, but the percentage varies significantly according to the crime. In 58 percent of the homicide cases, experts are used by the prosecution. The following Monday morning Ryan began with the first of his expert witnesses.

"I thought of a cat, but those kinds of scratches are usually deeper," the county medical examiner testified. "It couldn't have been thorns because of the absence of cross-patterns," he continued. "If the wounds had been caused by wood chips, they would have been deeper. I concluded they had come from fingernail scratches."

On cross-examination the medical examiner admitted that he had never examined the defendant. His testimony was based solely on a study of the photographs of the defendant, which showed wounds on his face.

Leonard Klein had frequently hired experts for various assignments at his company. He was rarely satisfied with their competence. Now at the trial, he was not about to be impressed, as other jurors might be, simply because a doctor was giving a so-called scientific opinion. Ryan, like many lawyers, was convinced that many of the jurors were apt to accept what they are told by "scientific experts" rather than use their own common sense.

After the medical examiner, a forensic chemist testified that there were four blood groups: A, B, O, and AB. Mrs. Collins's blood type was A, the defendant's was type O, and the rope that had been marked in evidence contained bloodstains of both types, A and O. The fingernail clippings of the victim had showed A and O as well. The stains on the sledgehammer, wallpaper, and bathing suit were determined to be blood, but the blood group tests on those samples were inconclusive.

The chemist admitted on cross-examination that about 40 percent of the general population have type A blood and 40 percent have type O.

The next witness was a specialist in trace evidence. "I identify items transferred from one place or one person to another," he testified. "I have a B.S. in chemistry, and I've done graduate work in forensic chemistry. I've testified at least a hundred times on hair."

The witness explained to the jury that each hair has its own color, texture, and width. Under a microscope one can see if the hair had been cut with a razor or scissors, or pulled out. A comparison microscope allows the examiner to view the two specimens at the same time, as in ballistics comparisons. Scales on the external part of the hair vary from person to person. The medulla is a canal that runs down the center of the hair, and the structure of the medulla varies from person to person.

"I compared hair specimens of the defendant and samples taken from several objects involved in this case. A hair found on the sledgehammer had the identical characteristics as the control specimen of the defendant. Human facial hair was removed from a towel and was found to be physically and microscopically the same as the defendant's. One hair was on the towel. A wood chip was also removed from the towel.

Several medium brown body hairs were found on the rope which were the same physically and microscopically as the sample from the defendant. One human medium-brown body hair was found in the bags which the police had placed around the victim's hands, and that hair was found to be the same physically and microscopically as that of the defendant. Chest and facial hairs compared in these tests," the witness said, "indicated that they were from the defendant. Comparisons with hair belonging to an Ira Kaplan and Dr. Collins were negative."

"Is there any indication from these tests," Bernstein asked on cross-examination, "as to when the hair got on the rope, the sledgehammer, or the towel?"

"No."

"Is it fair to say that hair analysis is not as reliable as fingerprint comparisons and blood analysis?"

"Yes, that's true."

On redirect examination, Ryan asked the witness if any other hairs had been recovered from the rope that, in his expert opinion, were not those of the defendant.

"No."

The last of the expert witnesses was Dr. Graciela Linares, who had performed the autopsy. She had received her medical training in Buenos Aires, Argentina, and was now an assistant state medical examiner for Essex County. "So what do I do?" She spoke with a thick Spanish accent, her voice rising and falling in a distinctive rhythm. "I perform autopsies and I come to court—sixty-five, seventy times I've come to court—to testify about it. With the victim in this case, I observed multiple stab wounds in the neck, chest, and back, and a fracture of the skull. The victim died of the stab wounds."

The doctor identified a series of photographs, including one showing the skull with the skin of the face pulled away, revealing the fracture and the hemorrhage. "This injury came after her other wounds. There were thirty-seven stab wounds.

Some of them punctured the heart, the lung, and the aorta. The five wounds on the neck were superficial. There was the imprint of a rope around the victim's neck. The wrist and left forearm had defense wounds. Bruises to the face could have been inflicted by hands striking her."

"What do you mean by defense wounds?"

"I mean like when someone is attacked with a knife, they often hold up their hands and try to protect themselves. When they do this, and the attacker persists, the victim receives lacerations on the forearm and wrist. And that's what happened in this case."

"Now, was there any evidence of rape?"

"Yes, rape and sodomy, rape and sodomy. Sperm was detected in the vagina. In addition, there were lacerations in the anus to indicate a forcible entry."

Ryan withdrew an awl from the carton on the floor. He handed the instrument to the witness. "Doctor, is this the kind of instrument that could have caused those stab wounds?"

"Yes. Death was not instantaneous, because the wounds were not that deep. I would say that death took about fifteen minutes and came from the internal bleeding. She was in shock for a time and lying down, because otherwise there would have been a different reaction in the brain. Because of the defense wounds, I believe she had had an argument. It was not the type of wound to spurt blood. She could have been dragged by the rope. The last wound she received was the blow to the head. That fractured the head. It was a massive blow to the brain."

On cross-examination, the witness admitted that the only evidence that there might have been a rape was the discovery of sperm.

"But isn't it just as likely," Bernstein pressed on, "that the sperm could have resulted from a voluntary intercourse sometime earlier than the killing?"

"That's possible, but there was no physical evidence of anything voluntary, so I would have no reason to conclude that."

"But if the intercourse *were* voluntary, it wouldn't have been a rape, isn't that true?"

"That's a legal question."

"No, that's a question for the jury. I have nothing further."

It had been eight days since the jury had been sworn in, and they were about to hear the last witness to testify for the state, Dr. William Collins. Chunky, about five-eight in height, Dr. Collins had a domelike bald head that was darkly tanned. His eyes were black discs set deep into his head, his nose was large and fleshy.

The doctor described how he had spent the day of his wife's death: he had gotten up early; he had breakfast with his family; he had dropped off his housekeeper at his office for her to do her weekly cleaning; and then he went on to the hospital to treat his patients and perform an operation. He reached his office in the early afternoon, and he was there when the terrible telephone call came in.

"I was threatened by Ira Kaplan that August over some misunderstanding with his girl friend," said Dr. Collins. "I employed the defendant to be a watchman. I spoke to Mr. Rafshoon on the day my wife was murdered. I own a store across the street from my office and I was having some remodeling work done before it opened. He was going to help out there. When I called him up from my house in the morning, I told him I would leave the keys to the store at my office. Later in the morning, when I was at the hospital, I called him at the store to ask him how things were going. He said everything was under control. Those were his words, 'under control.'

"I had gotten back to my office at around two-thirty, and a

couple of hours later the police called me to say my wife was dead. I went crazy.

"When I arrived, I saw a lot of police cars. I ran into the house, and I saw my wife lying in a pool of blood." He paused for a moment and put his fingers to his lips.

"Had anything been taken?" Ryan asked.

"Yes. Three thousand dollars in cash had been stolen from the secret closet in our bedroom, along with all her diamonds. She used to wear them all the time: earrings, rings, and a heart-shaped diamond necklace. We kept the closet locked, and on the day of the murder it had been broken into."

Ryan walked over to the witness and held up a photograph. "I show you what has been marked in evidence. Do you recognize what is depicted in it?"

"It's a photograph of my wife in a pool of blood."

"No further questions."

Before the sound of the prosecutor's last words faded, Bernstein asked from his seat at counsel table, "Doctor, you said a few moments ago that you owned a store across the street from your office. What did you want the defendant to do there?"

"I wanted him to build some cabinets and a counter. It was going to be a boutique. We were going to sell designer clothes, things like that."

"You're a doctor, and you're telling this jury that you were also getting into ladies' dresses?"

"*I* wasn't. I was just going to own the store. It was an investment."

"Who was going to run the store?"

"Rena Grey."

"Wasn't Rena Grey your mistress, Dr. Collins?"

"I had a relationship with Rena. She had other relationships."

"The man who threatened you—Ira Kaplan—wasn't he, in fact, your girl friend's lover?"

"He claimed to be. I don't know." Collins raised his chin and looked squarely at Bernstein.

"When did you first meet Ms. Grey?"

"I operated on her in 1980. Before becoming my patient, she was a tenant in an apartment I owned above the office. When I met my wife later that day that Kaplan threatened me, she told me she knew everything about the store, and about Rena and Kaplan. She was angry and upset. I told her I was sorry. I'd made a mistake, and I would try to make it up to her."

"How did your wife learn about your affair with Rena?"

"Kaplan told her. He told my wife he was going to kill me. On August twenty-fourth Rena left a message on my answering service. When I called her back, he answered. He told me Rena was going to have nothing more to do with me. The next day my wife called me and said she was meeting with Kaplan. I sent Mr. Rafshoon to watch him."

"So you sent Rafshoon to watch them?" Bernstein said.

"I didn't say *them.* I said *him.* Don't twist my words, Counselor. You're dealing with a very intelligent individual, maybe as intelligent as you."

"Dr. Collins," the judge said, "just answer the questions."

"What did your wife tell you of her meeting with Kaplan?" Bernstein continued.

"She believed Kaplan was a drug addict. She said he was shaky. She said he had told her he would leave me alone if I left Rena alone. I was determined to call the police if he didn't stay out of my life and the life of my family."

"But you didn't call the police then, did you?"

"No, but I—"

"I didn't ask you for an explanation," Bernstein interrupted. "You didn't call the police then, did you?"

"No."

"Did you go with your wife and Mr. Rafshoon to your store sometime in September?"

"Yes, on Labor Day. Mr. Rafshoon came over to my home and told me he had seen Kaplan and a black man in front of the store."

"Did your wife find a photograph of Rena in the store?"

"Yes."

"What did she do with it?"

"She tore it up and put it in her pocketbook."

"Did you tell the police that your former wife, Elizabeth, wanted to kill Carolyn?"

"Sustained," the judge said, indicating that in his view, the prosecutor should have objected.

"I thought the prosecutor was seated to my left, not on the bench."

"What do you mean by that?" the judge shot back at Bernstein.

"The prosecutor didn't object to my question," Bernstein said. "You sustained your own objection."

"Mr. Bernstein, it's my obligation to see that the jury decides this case solely on admissible evidence. Your suggestion that in carrying out that function I am being a prosecutor is contemptuous, Mr. Bernstein."

"I don't mean to be contemptuous, Your Honor."

"Then consider yourself warned and put your next question."

Bernstein turned back to the witness. "Doctor, did you tell the police that you had purchased a weapon?"

"Objection," the prosecutor said.

"By the way," Bernstein pressed on, ignoring the prosecutor, "where is your housekeeper today? I'm talking about the woman that you took to your office on the day of the murder."

"She's in Germany. She went home."

"So she's not available to come to court to testify?"

"No. She retired. She was an old woman."

"Doctor, you had been married before, isn't that true?"

"Yes."

"Didn't you tell the police that your first wife offered someone five thousand dollars to kill your second wife?"

"Objection."

"Isn't it a fact that Kaplan threatened your wife?"

"Kaplan threatened me and no one else. No. I heard it was the defendant who went around boasting that he'd killed my wife," the witness said softly.

"May we approach the bench?" Bernstein asked.

The judge sent the jurors to the jury room.

"I feel compelled to move for a mistrial," Bernstein said. "The last statement of the witness, that my client boasted about murdering the victim, was highly prejudicial. The remark was totally unresponsive to my question. And no instruction from Your Honor could undo the damage it has done."

If the prosecution had had a witness who had actually heard the defendant make such a confession, Ryan could have gotten that witness to come to court and repeat what the defendant had said. Bernstein would have had an opportunity to cross-examine that witness to test his credibility, and the jury would have been able to determine whether or not the witness was lying. But Dr. Collins did not say that he himself had heard the defendant admit anything, only that he'd heard from others that he had done so.

"There is no reason to assume the jurors wouldn't abide by Your Honor's instruction to ignore the remark," Ryan said quietly. "I certainly don't intend to mention it again during the trial or in summation."

"Your Honor," Bernstein said, "a bell once rung can't be unrung. The jury heard it, and that's that. The damage has been done. Any instruction on your part would be like telling them not to think about a pink elephant that had walked through the courtroom."

"Mr. Bernstein, I'm not going to grant a mistrial. Do you want me to instruct them to ignore the statement?"

Bernstein knew that if a motion for a mistrial were made in the early stages of the proceedings, before a great deal of time and energy had been expended on the trial, the judge would be much more likely to grant it. At this late stage, he didn't expect to succeed. "I don't think anything short of a mistrial would be sufficient to safeguard my client's rights. But if you say anything, I would prefer that you not repeat the statement, and merely state that the last remark of the witness should be ignored."

When the jurors were brought back, the judge asked them to ignore Dr. Collins's last remark and the cross-examination continued.

Bernstein walked over to the court reporter, took the torn photograph from the top of her desk, and handed it to the witness. "Dr. Collins, I am showing you the torn photograph identified earlier as having been found on top of the victim's head. Do you recognize what is depicted in that photograph?"

"Yes," Dr. Collins said softly.

"Tell the jury what it's a photograph of."

"It's a photo of our two children."

"I have no further questions to put to this witness," Bernstein said.

Bernstein seemed to be trying to convey to the jury an image of a bizarre soap-opera life lived by the doctor and his wife, and into which Rafshoon had somehow been drawn. Some judges, lawyers, and social scientists believe that juries will occasionally apply different standards to different subcultures in society. In crimes of violence committed by blacks against blacks or Indians against Indians, juries are at times

more lenient because the defendant is viewed as not fully ac-
culturated and incapable of white standards of self-control.
Bernstein was hoping the jury would see the doctor's world
as being as different in its way as an Indian subculture.

Ryan stood and announced that the state rested its case.
The judge dismissed the jurors for the day and waited for
them to leave the courtroom before discussing the case with
Bernstein and Ryan. When the last juror had gone out and
the door was closed, Bernstein asked the judge to dismiss the
case on the grounds that there was insufficient credible evidence to allow the jury to return a guilty verdict. Such a
motion can be made only when the prosecutor's case is completed, and is always done outside the jury's hearing. If a jury
heard a defense lawyer argue that there was insufficient evidence to convict and then heard a judge disagree, it would be
difficult for the jury not to be influenced by the judge's opinion. If the judge does not agree with the defendant's motion,
the trial will continue. And that was what happened in this
case. Bernstein made his motion, and the judge denied it.

Judges almost always deny a motion to dismiss. Even in
cases in which a judge would have decided a case in favor of
the defendant, he will usually not dismiss the case. If there is a
factual dispute, the judge is supposed to leave it to the jury.
When trials come down to a decision about who is telling the
truth, the jury is supposed to make that decision. Judges are
reluctant to take the responsibility or the criticism for making
decisions of this kind themselves.

The witnesses Ryan had presented were of varying degrees
of usefulness to him in his effort to put his case to the jurors.
The closest he came to having an eyewitness was the young
man pruning the tree. Eyewitnesses wind up testifying on behalf of the prosecution in a quarter of all cases. A good eyewitness can be crucial to a prosecutor's case. On his cross-
examination, Bernstein asked the standard questions that

should be put to all eyewitnesses: What opportunity had the witness had to view the defendant at the time of the crime? What was the witness's degree of attention? What was the accuracy of his prior description of the person, the level of his certainty about the identification, and the length of time between the observation of the person and the identification made by the witness?

Eyewitness identifications made quickly under stressful conditions are not the most reliable evidence, and jurors are becoming increasingly more skeptical of such testimony. Some courts allow psychologists to testify about the specific capacities of witnesses, such as whether a witness can perceive color, sounds, or distances, but many courts have disallowed these kinds of experts because of the great impact they can have on a jury, and the way they can effectively replace the jury's function of determining the facts.

According to a study by Elizabeth F. Loftus published in the *Journal of Applied Psychology*, male eyewitnesses are more likely to remember men involved in crime and the objects that interest men, and female witnesses are likely to recall participants who are women and objects that may be of greater interest to women.

The Chicago Jury Project found that about three quarters of all trials involve police testimony as part of the prosecutor's evidence. The percentages vary according to the crime: 90 percent of all homicide and 60 percent of all rape cases contain police testimony. In several studies police testimony was named most often by jurors as the crucial element in their ultimate decisions.

Inexperienced lawyers often commit the common error of cross-examining every witness, even interrogating witnesses whose direct testimony has done no damage to their case. Eventually most lawyers learn to leave witnesses alone if there is nothing to be gained from them. Knowing when to stop asking questions is sometimes learned from painful lessons of having gone on too long. Lincoln was fond of telling the story of the young lawyer who had asked one question too many: "If you now admit not having seen the defendant bite the young man's ear, how can you tell this jury that he really did bit that ear off?" "Because," the witness answered, "I saw him spit it out."

Bernstein had been confronted with a very difficult task in dealing with Adam Collins, the young son of the victim. Cross-examining a sympathetic witness like a child, a handicapped person, or a vulnerable woman can be a mine field for a lawyer who is not careful. In Bernstein's dealing with Adam the risk was less great because Adam's testimony was not particularly damaging: he had not seen Leander Rafshoon on the day of the murder. But many juries have watched inexperienced or incompetent lawyers brutally and unnecessarily attack sympathetic witnesses. After watching such a spectacle, a jury is sometimes angry enough to want to convict not only the defendant but the lawyer as well. Bernstein had been careful with Adam. He had avoided even raising his voice, and during the heat of this emotional moment of the trial he never lost sight of the limited relevance of the testimony.

Sometimes because of the complexity of aspects of a case, a decision about how to treat a witness presents more complicated choices. In addition to the way social scientists have recently been employed to help select juries, applied social science and modern marketing techniques have even been resorted to for help during the course of a trial. A small number of lawyers have used "shadow juries," a group of twelve people demographically similar to the actual jury. The shadow jurors sit in the courtroom, hear all the evidence the jury hears, and nightly report their reactions to the lawyer. Sometimes the lawyer observes their discussions of the day's events through a two-way mirror and is able to learn the intensity of individual responses and ways in which the jurors' opinions may be changed by the interaction of competing perceptions.

Another new instrument devised to help lawyers divine the thinking of a jury is the "mock jury," a group of people with characteristics similar to those of the actual jury. The lawyer tries out on the mock jury various arguments, examines witnesses, and discusses tactics that he is considering for the real jury. As with shadow juries, the responses of the mock jury may determine a number of specific trial decisions. Perhaps a mock jury would have been a good place for Bernstein to try out his strategy of portraying Dr. Collins as the villain in a soap opera.

The use of such modern techniques has created great controversy. Critics claim that they threaten the independence of the jury by manipulating juror responses, making a trial indistinguishable from a toothpaste sales campaign. Defenders argue that since a client has a constitutional right to effective representation, these techniques simply allow the lawyer to be more effective in a scientific rather than an intuitive way. That only a wealthy client can afford them is not the fault of the wealthy client who is fighting for his life.

In any event, these new techniques, though their value is hotly debated, are presently used in a statistically insignificant number of cases. Jury experts and their studies are so expensive that, unless donated or financed by contributions, they are beyond the resources of all but the wealthiest criminal defendants. In 99 percent of the cases a lawyer today still approaches the witnesses in the same way they were approached in Lincoln's time.

CHAPTER

VII.

THE MORNING AFTER JUDGE WHITAKER DENIED Bernstein's motion to dismiss the case for insufficient evidence, he opened the proceedings by telling the jurors that an article with some incorrect and prejudicial statements about the case had appeared in a local newspaper. He asked if any of the jurors had seen the article. Only Elliot Postom raised his hand.

All the jurors were sent back to the jury room except Postom, who, on questioning by the judge, said he had glanced at the article but hadn't really read it.

"Why did you glance at it?" the judge asked angrily. "Didn't you hear my instruction not to read anything about the case?"

"Yes, sir, I did, but I didn't read it. I saw it was about the case, so I skipped it."

"Will anything you may have read affect your ability to be fair to both sides in this case?" Judge Whitaker asked.

"No, sir."

The judge sent Postom back into the jury room.

"Your Honor," Ryan said, "I move that Mr. Postom be excused. Even a glance would have had him read the headline 'Lover's Boyfriend Gave Death Threat,' and that would have been enough to prejudice a juror. We selected fourteen jurors so that we could afford to excuse one if, for some reason, he became unable or undeserving to be among the final twelve."

Bernstein gave some thought to joining with Ryan in his effort to get rid of Postom. He hadn't liked the way Postom had listened to the witnesses, and there was something disturbing in the way he frequently smiled at Rafshoon. There was also a chance that the judge's reprimand about the article might have activated Postom's timidity and made it difficult for him to stand up to the prosecutor's plea to uphold law and order by convicting the defendant. On the other side of the coin, Bernstein knew, Postom might just as likely feel alienated from the judge and the prosecutor by the way he had been treated a few moments ago. He also liked the fact that Postom had learned about the threats that Kaplan, Rena's boyfriend, had been making. Maybe Postom would even ignore the judge's instruction and tell some of the other jurors about the headline.

Bernstein finally turned to Judge Whitaker. "There has been absolutely no proof that the juror has been prejudiced by having read a headline," he said. "And we have his assurance that it will not affect his ability to be fair to both sides."

The judge denied Ryan's motion to get rid of Postom, and when the jury was brought back into the courtroom, he reminded them not to read any articles about the case.

It was the defense's turn. Now Bernstein faced the most

difficult and most crucial decision of the trial: should he put his client on the stand? Jurors often assume the worst if they don't hear a defendant swear to them that he didn't do it. That is why defendants testify in 82 percent of all cases. The problem was that Rafshoon, like defendants in about half of all cases, had a prior criminal record, and if he testified, Ryan would be able to bring out on cross-examination that Rafshoon had been convicted of an armed robbery six years earlier.

Bernstein knew there was sometimes more to lose than to gain by putting a client with a record on the stand; the jury might well conclude that he was a habitual miscreant who was known to have committed a crime before and was therefore very likely to have committed this one. The defense lawyer's decision in each case should take into account how bad the criminal record is, how old it is, what kind of impression the defendant might make on the jury, and how desperately his testimony is needed.

A further risk to Rafshoon was that Ryan's questions might make him look like a liar, or that Ryan might provoke him into losing his hairtrigger temper, which would be a disaster.

Bernstein looked over at his client, who was seated to his left. Rafshoon looked mean and tough, and his ghetto accent and vocabulary had the potential for scaring the daylights out of the jury. Instead of making him look more respectable, the black suit, pink-on-pink shirt, and blue tie he had put on for the trial now only made Rafshoon look like an ugly killer in a costume, but he would look that way whether he was going to testify or not.

A lawyer can ask the judge to instruct the jury not to form negative opinions of a defendant if he doesn't testify, but like most lawyers, Bernstein had the impression that jurors often disregarded such instructions.

Bernstein knew that if he called his client to the stand, it would be as the last witness. So the final decision could be postponed, at least for a while. In the meantime he would interrogate the other witnesses he had lined up. If their testimony seemed impressive enough, maybe it would seem unnecessary to call Rafshoon.

Bernstein brought Ira Kaplan on as the first witness for the defense. Kaplan admitted that around the middle of August he had contacted Carolyn Collins to talk to her about her husband. He wanted to discuss her husband's refusal to leave his girl friend, Rena Grey, alone. He met with Mrs. Collins at a French restaurant, La Grande Illusion, and told her that her husband was making a nuisance of himself.

"What did she say?" Bernstein asked his witness.

"Objection," Ryan said, getting to his feet. "This is pure hearsay."

"Your Honor," Bernstein responded, "the jury must understand Mrs. Collins's behavior in order to understand why my client responded to her as he did. Her statement to this witness is necessary to explain her subsequent actions."

Ryan saw the eyes of every juror staring at him as if he were trying to hide something. He couldn't think of how anything the victim had said could alter the facts about the killing. "I believe I have a valid objection here, Judge, but I don't want the jury to think I'm withholding anything, so I'll withdraw it. Even so, I do think the defense counsel is walking on thin ice."

"Answer the question, Mr. Kaplan," the judge instructed.

"She told me she would make sure the doctor didn't fool around anymore."

"Did she say how she was going to accomplish that?"

"No, but I imagined—"

"Objection." Ryan was back on his feet.

"I'll sustain the objection," the judge said. "We can't allow his speculation, Mr. Bernstein. The jury is supposed to make its decision on facts, not what witnesses imagine."

Bernstein nodded. "Did you ever speak to Dr. Collins?"

"Yeah. He called Rena once when I was there, and I answered the phone. I told him to leave her alone."

"Is that all you said to him?"

"That's right. That's all I said to him. But he sounded like he had a guilty conscience or something, all frightened and everything."

"I have no further questions," Bernstein said.

"Mr. Kaplan," Ryan asked, "did you at any time threaten to kill Dr. Collins?" Ryan knew the witness would, of course, deny any threats.

"No."

"And you didn't threaten Mrs. Collins either?"

"Absolutely not. I had nothing against her."

Ryan stared at Kaplan and watched his eye movements increase. Kaplan was blinking rapidly and at the same time seemed unable to continue looking at him. To Ryan these were all telling signs that the witness was lying.

"I have nothing more to ask this witness," Ryan said with a shrug.

Bernstein was surprised that Ryan hadn't asked Kaplan where he was on the day of the killing. If the jury heard him testify that he had been in Montreal, as he had stated to the police shortly after the murder, they would be more likely to be persuaded that he'd had nothing to do with the killing. Maybe the prosecutor was hiding something. Maybe Kaplan hadn't been in Canada. More likely, Ryan had simply forgotten to ask him. Bernstein was tempted to ask a few more questions on redirect examination about what kind of jerk the doctor was, but if he put any new questions to the witness, it would give Ryan another chance to ask about Montreal.

"Do you have anything more of this witness?" the judge asked.

"No, Your Honor," Bernstein said.

The next witness was the manager of a lumber store who identified two receipts showing two separate sales to Leander Rafshoon on the day of the murder. Rafshoon had bought lumber, nails, and a hammer from the store. The witness would have been more valuable had he been able to tell the time of day the merchandise had been picked up, but Bernstein knew he couldn't remember. For this reason he did not ask him that question in court.

Bernstein had called the manager to puff up his case by trying to give the jury the impression that there were witnesses who supported Rafshoon's claim of innocence. Ryan saw no point in cross-examining the witness. He hoped that his not bothering to do so would point up the fact that this witness had not helped the defendant.

Bernstein called his next witness, Elizabeth Collins, the first wife of Dr. Collins. Before he could ask his first question, Ryan objected. "The husband/wife privilege prevents this witness from testifying about anything that was said by the doctor during their marriage," he said.

"That privilege," Bernstein retorted, "only protects private communications between spouses uttered in the expectation that those communications will be kept confidential. I do not intend to elicit any such communication."

Judge Whitaker put his hand to the side of his face. "Okay, Counselor, put your questions, and I'll rule on them."

"Did Dr. Collins beat you?"

Judge Whitaker pounded his desk with his gavel. "I'll excuse the jury," he said angrily.

Alex Butler, Laura Sayres, and Leonard Klein sat next to the closed door of the jury room. They looked at each other as they heard snatches of the judge's shouted objections: "How dare you!" "Arrogance, contemptible arrogance . . ." "What Collins may have done years ago is not . . ." "I should hold you in contempt for . . ."

Bernstein didn't even try to justify what he had done. He

just said he was sorry, and that it wouldn't happen again. He knew he had risked being held in contempt of court for knowingly asking an improper question in front of the jury, but he had been willing to take that risk for the sake of his client.

When the jury was led back into the courtroom, the first Mrs. Collins was gone. "Ladies and gentlemen," Judge Whitaker said, "I want to remind you that the questions that an attorney asks of a witness are not evidence, and must not be considered by you in your deliberations. Let's move on. Anything else, Mr. Bernstein?" the judge asked without looking at him.

"Rena Grey," Bernstein announced.

Everyone in the courtroom stared at Rena, the woman who had been sexually involved with both Ira Kaplan and Dr. Collins, as she walked toward the witness stand. With her long, blond hair, green eyes, high cheekbones, milky-white skin, and stunning figure, she was astonishingly beautiful.

Carl Copco nodded. He finally understood what all the fuss was about.

Rena told the jury that she was a dress designer, twenty-four years old, and single. She had known Dr. Collins for two years before the death of his wife.

"Did there come a time," Bernstein asked, "when you and Dr. Collins became lovers?"

"The answer is yes," she said, "shortly after we met."

"Were you and Ira Kaplan also lovers?"

"He was my boyfriend."

"Wasn't that a problem for you? I mean having two boyfriends?"

"Dr. Collins didn't tell his wife," the witness said unresponsively.

"How often would you and the doctor get together?"

"Every day."

"Wasn't *that* a problem for you?"

"No. I don't know what he told his wife. I guess he told her he had a lot of emergencies."

Elliot Postom and several of the other jurors laughed.

"Did you have some interest in a store across the street from the building you were living in?"

"That was going to be my boutique. He had promised to turn that store into a boutique for me since we met. I was going to have a whole line of my own clothes. We were going to be partners."

"Did he promise you he was going to tell his wife about your affair?"

"We were supposed to be getting married. He told me all the time that he was about to get a divorce. He said their marriage had been dead for years, that all they did was fight."

"Did you believe him?"

"Yes, I believed him. He bought me presents all the time. He called me every minute."

"How did you support yourself?"

"He'd give me money."

"And not charge you rent for your apartment?"

"No, he charged me rent, but he'd give me the money to pay the rent. He said as a doctor he had to keep his tax records straight."

"When he kept promising to tell his wife and then not doing it, what did he give as the reason?"

"He told me he was afraid of his wife, afraid she would do something irrational. He said she was a violent person."

"Didn't there come a time when your boyfriend, Ira Kaplan, learned of your relationship with Dr. Collins?"

"Yes."

"When was that?"

"Around August."

"What was Mr. Kaplan's reaction?"

"He said he was going to kill him and his whole family."

"Your witness," Bernstein said.

"How did Kaplan find out about your relationship with Dr. Collins?" Ryan asked.

"I don't know."

"Isn't it a fact that you told him about it?"

"No. He told me about it."

"But you didn't deny it, did you?"

"No."

"Then you must have known this fellow Kaplan pretty well?"

"Of course. We were going together for about four years."

"Surely you wouldn't have admitted to having an affair with Dr. Collins if you thought Mr. Kaplan would really commit some act of violence, would you?"

"Of course not."

Ryan placed a check mark on his yellow legal pad. He was going through a series of questions that had occurred to him during Bernstein's direct examination a few minutes earlier. And the answers were coming just as he had expected. He knew that although much of the preparation for interrogating a witness must be done before trial, a good lawyer must be ready to take advantage of opportunities as they arise during a trial. "When he said he was going to kill the guy," Ryan pressed on, "you took it as a manner of speaking, right?"

"Exactly."

"You also said Dr. Collins explained his reluctance to tell his wife about your relationship by saying she had a violent temper."

Bernstein's heart jumped. He knew Ryan was about to step on the booby trap he had left for him. Bernstein had deliberately drawn Rena on until she seemed to be saying that Dr. Collins had not told his wife about the affair because he had been afraid of her reaction. Bernstein looked at the judge and waited.

"That's right," the witness said.

"In other words, he was telling you he was too timid to tell her, is that it?"

"No, he was telling me he was going to have her killed."

Judge Whitaker shot a look at Bernstein, who tried to suppress the involuntary smile that had appeared on his face at this piece of good fortune. The judge knew Bernstein had been waiting for this answer.

"No further questions," Ryan said, and sat down.

If Ryan had not asked the question, Bernstein would still have had his chance on redirect. But the witness's answer would have a much greater impact on the jury because Ryan had brought it out, especially since it was the last thing the jurors had heard before leaving for home that day.

The following morning, after all the jurors were reassembled in the jury box, Bernstein called out, "Leander Rafshoon." In the end, most criminal lawyers wind up putting their clients on the stand even if the accused has a prior criminal record. Defendants with a record reach the witness box 74 percent of the time.

With his chin tilted slightly upward, Leander rose and walked forward. He placed his hand on the Bible and stared at the judge as the clerk asked if he would tell the whole truth and nothing but the truth.

"I do," he answered.

Bernstein moved to the far end of the jury box, about twenty feet away from his client. "Leander, please remember to speak loudly enough for all the jurors to hear you." He stood behind the jury to force Rafshoon to keep his voice up and also to make him look at the jurors when he spoke to his lawyer.

Bernstein had Rafshoon tell the jury that he was thirty-four years old, a high school graduate, and a Vietnam veteran. "I'm married, and I have two children, a daughter, Saida— she's two—and Leander, Jr., age six." Rafshoon pointed to his wife, who was sitting with her arms around their daughter in the front row. Their son was sitting next to her, pressing up against her.

At Bernstein's prompting, Rafshoon said he had first met Dr. Collins about three years ago when his son was having a problem with his breathing. "I would bring Leander, Jr., back to him periodically for checkups. He's all right now." Rafshoon went on to explain that in the middle of the summer of 1982 he had taken his son for one of his regular examinations and the doctor had told him that "some guy was making trouble for him." The doctor had asked him to work for him "as a kind of driver and to sort of just watch out for him and his family." Since Rafshoon had been out of work for months, he had agreed to take the job. About two weeks after he started, the doctor asked him if he would do some carpentry work for him at his store. "He wanted me to put in a counter and some shelves and two closets and a lot of racks to hang clothes on. It was a good job. I would have done all right. I started it, but I never got a chance to finish with it."

"Why not?"

"I got arrested."

"What did you do during the first two weeks of your employment?"

"Whatever he told me to do. The first few days I was with the doctor. The first thing he wanted me to do was to follow him in my van, stay back maybe twenty yards or so, and see if anyone was following him. He told me some guy was threatening him. But there was nobody following him. Once he had me follow his wife to a meeting with this guy Kaplan, the guy who testified here the other day."

"Did his wife know you were following her?"

"Not at the time. I told her afterward when—"

"Just a second. We'll get to that. Where did you follow her to?"

"They met at some fancy French restaurant. I hung back at

the bar and watched them. I couldn't hear what they was saying, but I watched them. It looked like he was telling her something, and then she got angry and started pointing her finger at him like she was threatening him or something. The guy backed off. She stood up in the middle of the meal and threw her napkin in his face. She just threw her napkin and got up and left him."

"What did Mr. Kaplan do?"

"He sat there with his mouth open. He didn't do nothing. I was kind of hiding at the end of the bar, and after Mrs. Collins left, I left. I went to the doctor's office and told him what I saw."

"What did the doctor say after you told him what happened?"

"He sort of stared out the window and then he said, 'That bitch.' That's all he said."

"What happened next in terms of your work assignments?"

"After that, he had me staying with Mrs. Collins. I'd stay with her all day. He just told me to stay with her and watch her and make sure nothing happened to her. So I just did that for about two weeks."

"What kind of relationship did you have with her?"

"At first she seemed real angry at my hanging around. I thought she really hated me. I hardly spoke to her, and she didn't talk to me none either. I was there when she spoke to her sister on the phone complaining about me being around her all the time. I don't blame her. She was really spooked. One time she called the doctor and yelled at him that the only reason I was there wasn't to protect her, it was just to watch her, which wasn't wrong altogether either. The doctor did tell me to protect her, but then he'd also ask me like what she was doing, who she spoke to on the phone and things like that."

"So how would you spend your day with Mrs. Collins during this first week or so?"

"I'd go with her when she did errands, shopping, things like that. I'd drive her to get her massage, shopping, or whatever. But mostly she'd sit by the pool, and I'd sit in the kitchen having iced tea or something and watch her through the window. That's about it."

"Did there come a time when your relationship with Mrs. Collins changed?"

"Yeah, it changed. I don't know why. But one day, this was about a week after I was with her, and we hadn't hardly spoken at all, she called me out from the kitchen and asked me to come to the pool. So I went out there. She said, 'Leander, would you be a sweetheart and put some oil on my back?' So I put some oil on her back. She was lying on this puffy mat next to the pool. Then she says, 'You know, Leander, you got to rub it in for it to work.' So I like rubbed it in. And as I'm rubbing it in like some fool, she undoes her top, you know, the top to her bikini. She says that was so she could get an even tan. The rest of the week, this is the second week I was working there, she never wore no bathing trunks again."

"Leander, did there come a time when you and Mrs. Collins began to have an affair?"

"I wouldn't call it no affair," Leander said, looking at his wife. He looked back at Bernstein. "But after I rubbed in all that oil on her back, she asked me to rub the rest of her, her legs and so on. As I was working on her legs, she pulled the strings on the bottom to her bikini, and then I did her backside. And after a couple of minutes of that she like rolled over and said, 'Hey, nigger, now do the rest of me.'"

"Did you?"

"I did."

"Then what happened?"

"Then she put on her robe and went inside, and I followed her."

"Then what happened?"

"We got it on."

"You mean you had sexual intercourse with each other? Is that what you mean by 'getting it on'?" Bernstein said. He had been over this with Rafshoon dozens of times. Rafshoon was supposed to say "sexual intercourse" in the courtroom, not "get it on."

"Yes, I mean sexual intercourse."

"Where did you have sexual intercourse?"

"On the kitchen floor."

"Did this relationship continue over the next week?"

"It sure did, three, four times a day. I never met a woman like that before."

"How do you mean?"

"Like there was never enough. I never met a woman that was so hungry for it."

"Leander, tell the jury what happened on September fifth, 1982, the day of Mrs. Collins's murder."

"Dr. Collins had told me about how he wanted me to do the carpentry work the night before. I went to the lumber yard first thing in the morning. I bought me some lumber and a new hammer, some nails—things like that. I took everything over to the store and unloaded it. The German lady at the doctor's office gave me the key to get into the place. There was a telephone in the store, and as soon as I opened the front door, the phone was ringing. I answered it, and it was Mrs. Collins. This must have been around ten o'clock. She told me to meet her at the house."

"Was there anything particularly unusual about her calling you like that?"

"Yes, she never called me before. I would just go over to the house if I wasn't supposed to be doing something else."

"Did she tell you why she wanted you to come to the house?"

"She didn't tell me on the phone. She explained it to me later."

"Okay. So what happened?"

"So I went there like she told me. I got there around eleven. I walked into the kitchen from the back door. She—"

"Just a second. How did you get to the back door?"

"I just walked around to the back door. What do you mean how did I get to the back door?"

"I mean where did you park? Did you come from the backyard?"

"No. I parked on the street in front of the house."

"Okay. So what happened after you entered the house?"

"She was standing there waiting for me. She was naked as a new baby. She moved up to me and started to undress me. I said, 'Hey, what's going on?' She didn't say nothing. We made it on the kitchen floor. It was like she was going crazy, screaming and carrying on. She was really out of her mind. She dug her fingers into my back, and I was bleeding like a pig. When it was over, she told me she had told her husband about us. I said, 'Woman, you out of your mind.' And I slapped her. I did. But I didn't kill her, and I didn't really even hurt her."

"What did she do after you slapped her?"

"She hauled off and hit me in the face. I wasn't expecting that. And the next thing she did was scratch me in the face. So I grabbed her hands and threw her down."

"What did she do then?"

"She just laughed, a really scary laugh. *I* was the one that was hurt by the scratching and everything. At that point all I wanted to do was get the hell out of there. And that's what I did."

"Did she tell you why she wanted you to come to the house that morning?"

"Yes, she did. She told me that she knew her husband was mad as hell. Even with his woman and all, he was still mad as hell. And she wanted to tell me that if he caught us together, he was going to have me killed or something."

"Is that the reason you left her then?"

"No, I wasn't scared of him. I was scared of *her*. That woman was crazy. I really believe she could have done anything. And that laugh was scary."

"Did you kill her?" Bernstein asked, looking at the jury.

"No way. I didn't kill that woman."

"Your witness," Bernstein said.

The jurors were watching intensely, their faces straining to make out if the man accused of murder and rape was telling the truth.

Rafshoon was doing well. Bernstein felt reassured about his decision to put him on the stand. If he only holds up on cross, he thought.

"Mr. Ryan," the judge said.

"Your Honor, my cross-examination may take some time, and I see that it's getting on toward the lunch hour. Rather than interrupt my cross, could we recess now?"

"Of course, Mr. Ryan. I'll see you all back here at one." The judge tapped his gavel, and everyone found his way out of the courtroom.

An hour later, Ryan began the cross-examination. "Mr. Rafshoon," Ryan asked, speaking softly, arching his eyebrows, "you lied to the nurse at the hospital about how you received your wounds, right?"

"Yes, I did."

"And you lied to Officer Moreali, didn't you?"

"Yes, sir, I did. I was afraid."

"Of course you were. But aren't you afraid now?"

"Yes, sir, I am."

"But you lied to the nurse and the police officer because you wanted to save your skin, and you thought your lies would help you, right?"

"Yes, sir."

"And you testified today in the way you did because you

thought your version today would help you with the jury, isn't that true?"

"I told the truth."

"When, today or on those other occasions?"

"I told the truth today."

"So you say. Now, Mr. Rafshoon, you've been convicted of a crime before, haven't you?"

"Yes, sir."

"Armed robbery, wasn't it?"

"Yes, sir."

"And for that you were punished with a sentence of three years in prison, isn't that true?

"Yes, sir."

"What time did you leave the house of Mrs. Collins on the day of her murder, Mr. Rafshoon?"

"It was before twelve, I know that."

"Now, you were in court and heard the young fellow who testified say he was in a tree across the street and saw you leave the house sometime around two-thirty. Are you sure you didn't leave the house around that time?"

"Yes, sir. I'm absolutely sure."

"And you heard that young gentleman swear to this jury that he saw you running out the backyard. Isn't that the way you left the house"

"No, sir. Why would I do that? My car was parked in the front of the house."

"Where did you go after you left the house?"

"I was really shook up. I drove down to Newark and went to Weequahic Park. That's a park in Newark with a big lake."

"Why did you go there?"

"I don't know. Like I said, I was shook up. When I was a kid, if I was upset, I'd always go there and sit on a rock by the edge of the lake. And that's what I did this time."

"Did anyone see you?"

"I don't know. Not that I know of."

"How long did you sit there?"

"Maybe an hour—I don't know exactly. Then I drove back up to the store. I thought I'd be able to work some on the cabinets."

"Did anyone see you at the store, then?"

"Not that I know of."

"How long did you stay there?"

"Maybe it was an hour. I saw that I needed more lumber. And my eye was really hurting. So I went to the hospital to check my eye out. And then I went to the lumber store again."

"Didn't you ask to speak to Dr. Collins when you arrived at the hospital?"

"Yes, sir."

"You mean to say that you had just made passionate love with this man's wife and you had the nerve to want him to treat you for the scratches she gave you?"

"No, I didn't want him to treat me. I went to the hospital to talk to him. I actually didn't go to the hospital to be treated at all. I wanted to tell the guy I wasn't going to work for him no more, at least, not at his house. I didn't want nothing more to do with his wife. I'd finish the carpentry work if he wanted, but I wasn't going to be no more of a watchdog for him."

"When you were arrested that night, didn't you try to escape?"

"No, sir, I did not. The policeman beat me—that's the truth. How could I try to escape? The police was all over the place."

"How about that rope, that black and white rope that was found around her neck with your hair on it? Had you ever seen that before?"

"Objection," Bernstein called out. "It has certainly not been established that that rope had the defendant's hair on it.

All we have is a state's expert who said it could have been the defendant's or anyone else's."

"I'll withdraw the part of the question that offends Counsel. Mr. Rafshoon, had you ever seen that rope before?"

"Yes, sir, I seen it in the garage."

"Did you ever, as a matter of coincidence, happen to have touched that rope at any time?"

"No, sir. I can't think of the time I could have touched that rope."

"Did you ever use the sledgehammer that was in the shed?"

"Yes. There's a small wooden fence around the pool. A couple of posts were loose, and I banged them down. That was the first week I was at the place."

"Isn't it a fact that when Mrs. Collins told you that she had told her husband about your affair, you killed her?"

"No, sir. That's just not true. I slapped her."

"In fact she called you to tell you that she was not going to see you anymore, and you raped her and stabbed her."

"No. That's a lie."

"No further questions," Ryan said.

"The defense rests," Bernstein said.

The only sign that the testimony in the case was completed was the silence that filled the courtroom for a few moments.

That's it? Patricia Stewart, the actress sitting in the jury box, said to herself, surprised that there had been no surprise witnesses, no spectacular climaxes. It had been much different from what she had expected. She knew that television was not realistic, but she had expected at least a little drama.

A criminal trial in real life is different from what people are accustomed to seeing on television. Perry Mason is the only lawyer who has cases in which the real killer stands up to admit through his tears that he committed the murder for which the defendant was falsely accused. That level of theatrics simply never happens.

Laura Sayres felt a chill when she heard Bernstein say that

the defense rested. She realized that it was soon going to be up to her and the rest of the jurors to decide the defendant's fate. And there had been so little in the evidence that seemed certain, so little evidence either way to make such an enormous decision about a man's life.

All that was left for Laura, Patricia, and the others was to hear the summations of the attorneys and the charge from the judge. Then at last it would be the jury's turn to speak. Until this point none of the jurors had spoken even to each other about the case. No one knew what any of the others was thinking in response to the evidence.

Every jury is unique, and it is impossible to predict with certainty how a particular jury will decide a case. Studies have shown that in terms of probabilities a correlation can be made between certain sectors of society and the likelihood of their coming to certain kinds of decisions in particular cases. The conviction rate in an Oregon county, for example, dropped from 62 percent to 41 percent when women were added to previously all-male juries.

Anne Rankin Mahoney, a social scientist who studied sexism in the jury, found that women wanted convicted rapists sentenced to longer prison terms than men did, but were only slightly more likely to convict those charged with rape. In another study conducted by Ruth Simon, women jurors were found to be more sympathetic than men toward the plea of insanity when male defendants were charged with housebreaking; but when a plea of insanity was introduced to a charge of incest, women jurors were more likely than men to vote for conviction. In incest trials, housewives were more likely to vote "guilty" than working women. In fact, housewives were more likely to convict than any other group of jurors, including occupational, educational, ethnic, and racial categories.

When the percentage of blacks on juries was increased in

Baltimore from 30 percent to 46 per~ent, the rate of conviction dropped from 83 percent to below 70 percent. While cold statistics may be provocative, they become more useful with a closer look. The experience in Baltimore is a good example. Although the overall conviction rate dropped with the addition of more blacks to the jury lists, the conviction rate for burglary did not. The conviction rate dropped most, from 85 percent to 48 percent, in the trials for rape, the most emotionally freighted crime for a racially mixed community. A prosecutor in Baltimore with these statistics in his pocket would be more eager to eliminate blacks from the jury in a rape case than in a case where the charge was burglary.

The drop in Baltimore's conviction rate didn't necessarily mean that blacks were unwilling to convict. This would not make sense, since blacks in urban areas are most often the victims of crime. The explanation is more likely to be found in the suspicion and distrust many blacks have of the police. A survey in Detroit found 23 percent of the white jurors but only 10 percent of the black jurors saying they would accept the testimony of a police officer simply because he was a policeman with no reason to lie.

People in Baltimore attributed the drop in the conviction rate to the demand of black jurors for hard evidence. "What has always been legally sufficient to convict—police testimony, oral confessions, eyewitnesses—is no longer enough," a black state's attorney was quoted as saying. "The new juror wants to hold the weapon in his hand; he wants to see the diagrams of the scene; he wants to see the defendant's signature on the confession." Since more blacks were added to the jury lists, prosecutors began building stronger cases before going to court, explaining missing evidence to a jury, lining up more witnesses. And the conviction rate has slowly been rising.

Sex and race are not the only characteristics found to make a difference in the probability of conviction. Studies have shown that the greater the disparity in socioeconomic status between jurors and the accused, the greater the likelihood of conviction. This is interesting to criminal lawyers because those accused of crimes are more often from a lower socioeconomic status than the average jurors. Obviously a lawyer defending a poor client, if armed with this information, would try to choose poorer jurors.

Information has also been gathered about how jurors respond to certain kinds of defendants. Women defendants, for example, have fared better from a percentage standpoint than men, a difference that has been explained by the sympathy evoked in the jury merely because of the defendant's sex. The Chicago Jury Project found that in seventeen cases in which wives were accused of killing their husbands, juries acquitted 41 percent of the time; in the reverse situation, in twenty-seven cases of husbands accused of killing their wives, the husbands were acquitted only 7 percent of the time.

The Chicago Jury Project also found that judges occasionally felt that the jury had rendered a verdict of "not guilty" out of a feeling of sympathy toward the defendant. In one case in which a judge would have convicted a woman of murdering her husband, it took the jury nine minutes to acquit: the wife had been beaten by her heavy-drinking husband, and she had shot him with a rifle after he had come in from an all-night drinking session. The judge also noted that the wife was "exceptionally good-looking."

Similarly, a judge in another case believed that a woman defendant was acquitted not only because she was attractive, but also because she had claimed that she had tuberculosis, and wore a white breathing mask throughout the trial.

Other acquittals have been attributed to a defendant's visibly bad health, handicap, remorse, or heavy family responsibilities. If the defendant's family is silently suffering in court, or if the jury feels that punishing the defendant would punish the family, acquittals are considered more likely. The occupa-

tion of the defendant can also be relevant to the chances of
acquittal. If a defendant is a veteran or, better still, if he testifies in uniform, he does better with the jury. In some cases
judges have believed that juries have acquitted certain defendants primarily because they were students, public office
holders, policemen, or clergymen.

Although such examples of juries acquitting out of sympathy for the defendant do exist, the high percentage of agreement that the Chicago Jury Project found between judges and
juries on how they would render verdicts has definitively ex-
ploded the popular myth of the jury as gullible and easily
swayed by emotion. The Jury Project attributed a jury's verdict to sympathy toward a defendant in only 4 percent of all
cases.

In addition to the influence that the defendant's characteristics may have on a jury, the nature of the charges or the
behavior of the witnesses may also affect the chances of an
acquittal. Juries, for example, have frequently acquitted defendants as a means of protesting against what they believe to
have been improper behavior on the part of the police or
prosecution. Acquittals have resulted from a jury's reaction
to the fact that the police refused to allow the defendant to
see his wife or attorney, or had not advised the defendant of
his rights, or had entrapped him or, as Rafshoon was claiming, had beaten him. This kind of jury censure of the police is
an example of the way the jurors represent the conscience of
the community in giving the letter of the law a humanizing
flexibility.

Juries have acquitted in cases in which the defendant has
previously suffered hardship, or when the actions of the defendant seemed to spring more from negligence than from an
intention to commit a crime, as, for example, in vehicular
homicide cases. Jurors are reluctant to convict for crimes for
which, but for the grace of God, they could see themselves on
trial. They will also resist convictions if they feel the prosecu-

tion is picking on a particular defendant and thus violating evenhanded justice.

A recognition of the power juries have over law enforcement has affected legislators' decisons about what laws to adopt. In 1819 the bankers of England petitioned Parliament to remove the death penalty for forgery because it had become nearly impossible to get juries to return convictions for the crime. And it is still true that juries acquit when the punishment that could be imposed seems too severe to them. The need for the punishment to fit the crime has led some feminists, for example, to oppose stiffer punishments for rapists out of fear that they would cause juries to be more reluctant to convict.

Juries have often ignored the evidence and acquitted clearly guilty defendants when the jurors have felt that the wrong done was trivial. This kind of jury response applies to cases where, for example, "too little property" was stolen. The Jury Project quoted a judge who felt that one of his cases had resulted in a hung jury because the jurors "did not want to send a man to prison on a felony charge for taking one or two wieners."

Juries have been more lenient toward defendants charged with so-called victimless crimes, in which it is hard for juries to see any harm done by the criminal conduct, and when the government seems to be imposing its morality. For example, during Prohibition juries frequently refused to convict people for crimes related to the liquor laws. The same is true today in rural parts of the country where there are laws against hunting or fishing. In the larger cities, gambling laws are frequently not enforced by juries.

Defendants in tax or embezzlement cases have done better when juries have learned that restitution has been made. Verdicts are frequently favorable to defendants when it is known that the complaining witness is reluctant to prosecute: if the injured person doesn't want a conviction, so goes the reasoning, then the state should not be interested in prosecuting. Similarly, when a victim has resumed a relationship with the person accused of committing the crime, such as a spouse or business partner, juries have been reluctant to convict for the crime.

The independence of the jury was established in America when the role of the jury as conscience of the community was recognized. In 1734 John Peter Zenger, a New York City newspaper publisher, was tried for criminally libeling the royal governor. Zenger defended himself by claiming freedom of the press. The judge instructed the jury to decide only the admitted fact of whether the defendant published the articles in question; he, the judge, would decide if they were libelous. The jury defied the judge and returned a verdict of not guilty.

In refusing to enforce the strict letter of the law, juries represent a subtle distribution of political power, an arrangement of checks and balances by which discretion, equity, and flexibility are built into the legal system. Throughout American history, juries have served as critics of the law by refusing to convict people accused of violating certain laws considered unjust, such as those involving sedition, conscription, prohibition, the civil rights of blacks, welfare fraud, gambling, and others.

Before the Civil War, northern juries refused to convict people accused of aiding escaped slaves, and thereby effectively nullified the fugitive slave laws. After the Civil War, juries in the South were often composed of ex-Confederates who consistently returned verdicts against blacks in cases in which blacks were accused of crimes against whites or were the victims of crimes committed by whites.

A person's attitude toward decisions in which a jury has acted on its conscience usually depends on whether the person shares that jury's "conscience" or sentiments about the particular law. And "liberal" thinking may be selective. The same jury that might acquit someone charged with possessing marijuana could have a similarly relaxed attitude toward the law in other areas and mete out harsher treatment to a defendant who is a member of a group that is discriminated against by that community, as, for example, in cases in which blacks, gays, women, or Democrats may be tried, respectively, by racists, homophobes, sexists, or Republicans.

PART

FOUR

JUDGMENTS

CHAPTER

THE FOLLOWING MORNING there was a different feeling in the jury room as the fourteen jurors waited to be summoned to their places in the courtroom. There was small talk, but most of the jurors waited in silence, anxiously, seriously. The trial was entering a new phase. The testimony was over. All the evidence they would have on which to base their decision had been introduced. Today they were to hear the summations of the lawyers and the final instructions of the judge. When they finally took their seats in the jury box, even the atmosphere in the courtroom was slightly different from the day before. Everyone seemed ready for the final act.

Judge Whitaker nodded at the defense counsel.

Bernstein bounced the pages of notes in front of him into a neat pile. He reached over and touched Rafshoon's forearm in a gesture of reassurance. He then rose from his seat and approached the easel he had placed in front of the jury box.

He tacked a large white paper to a board resting on the easel. He turned and faced the jurors.

"The one unequivocal fact," Bernstein began, "is that Mrs. Collins was brutally murdered. The prosecutor has insisted on introducing dozens of photographs of the victim to drive that undeniable fact home. These are awful, terrible pictures that are capable of inflaming the coldest heart. But you have sworn an oath to decide this case on the evidence, and as Judge Whitaker will tell you, you must do this without being swayed by emotion—that means without being manipulated by the grotesque photographs submitted by the prosecutor."

Laura Sayres, Carl Copco, Leonard Klein, and the rest of the jurors focused their attention on the defense lawyer. Julius Solars nodded as he listened, and Elliot Postom gave his little smile.

"The issue in the case," Bernstein went on, "is not whether Mrs. Collins was brutally murdered, but whether my client, Leander Rafshoon, was the person who committed the murder. The prosecutor produced a large number of witnesses. He trotted them onto the stage of this witness box to try to overwhelm you by their number. But not one witness said that my client committed the murder, and that must leave you with a reasonable doubt."

Maureen Whalen had heard all the evidence; at least she thought she had. But it wasn't until Bernstein had put it in black and white that she fully realized that no eyewitness had testified to seeing the defendant commit the crime. She felt unsettled. What else haven't I put together? she wondered.

"Let's analyze it." Bernstein went to the easel. With a red crayon, he wrote the names of each of the state's witnesses. Each time he wrote a name he told the jury that that witness had given no evidence pointing to the defendant. Next to each name he put a zero. By the time he had finished, the large sheet of paper was filled with almost twenty red circles.

Bernstein's markings were not evidence, but he knew the image of red circles would be taken into the jury room.

Bernstein walked over to Ryan at his place at counsel table. He slapped the table with the palm of his hand. "Who saw or heard Leander Rafshoon kill that poor woman? Answer me that, Mr. Prosecutor. Didn't you call all those people to the stand just to impress the jury by the number of witnesses?"

Matty Barnes felt her adrenaline pumping as she watched Bernstein and Ryan stare at each other like two angry street fighters. As a black social worker on the streets of Newark, she had seen plenty of violence, but she was still afraid of it.

"When you strip away all the irrelevant testimony of the irrelevant witnesses," Bernstein said, making his way back to the jury rail, "you see that the state's case rests entirely on ambiguous expert testimony.

"Three kinds of forensic experts testified about blood, about hair, and about wounds. Let's take the statements one at a time.

"The blood expert told us that the blood found under the victim's nails matched the defendant's blood type. You heard the testimony: forty percent of the population has Type O blood. There's a forty-percent chance that the blood came from Leander Rafshoon. A forty-percent chance is not proof beyond a reasonable doubt. But in any case, Leander admitted to you that Mrs. Collins had scratched him. She scratched him when they made love on the day someone else killed her.

"Another expert stated his opinion that the hair found on the sledgehammer, the towel, and the rope belonged to the defendant. The sledgehammer and towel had been used previously by the defendant, so it's not surprising that some of his hair was found on them. The defendant candidly told you he couldn't remember if he had ever touched the rope. The awl has been identified only as the *kind* of instrument that could have been used. The prosecutor doesn't even contend this awl was used to stab the victim.

"I submit to you, ladies and gentlemen, that if the defendant wanted to lie to you, he could have said that he had also used the rope when he did chores around the house. But he said honestly that he can't remember. He probably did use that rope and has simply forgotten when. It is also possible that the expert is mistaken. He himself admitted that hair analysis is less reliable than blood or fingerprint analysis.

"The medical examiner testified about the wounds on Mrs. Collins's body, but nothing she saw indicated whether or not Leander caused those wounds. And there you have the three kinds of expert testimony. Each in its own way is irrelevant to the only issue of the case: has the state proved beyond a reasonable doubt that *Leander* did the killing.

"Which brings me to another point. The judge will instruct you that reasonable doubt may be found from the evidence that is presented to you"—he paused dramatically—"or from the *lack* of evidence. And in this case, much critical evidence is lacking. Where is the most reliable scientific evidence, fingerprint analysis? If Rafshoon really used that sledgehammer to kill Mrs. Collins, shouldn't we have seen evidence of his fingerprints on the sledgehammer? But the prosecutor failed to produce any evidence about fingerprints. And the burden is on the *state* to prove its case."

Bernstein was shrewdly playing on a popular misconception that fingerprint evidence is used more frequently and tellingly in trials than it actually is. It is often difficult to lift good fingerprint impressions from objects, and few fingerprint "experts" working in law enforcement know what they are doing.

"While the defendant has no burden of producing any witnesses or evidence, we *have* produced witnesses and evidence," Bernstein said. He went on to summarize the testimony of Ira Kaplan and Rena Grey. Then he pressed home his basic defense: "I don't know who committed the murder," Bernstein said, "but I do know it could just as likely have been Ira Kaplan, or Rena Grey, or the first Mrs. Collins, or even the good doctor himself, as my client.

"The only evidence of rape was the discovery of sperm in the victim's vagina. My client admitted that he'd had intercourse with her earlier that day, and there is no evidence to contradict his testimony.

"Finally," Bernstein continued, "Leander Rafshoon had a right not to testify. He knew that if he took the stand, the prosecutor was going to mention that prior conviction for armed robbery, but he chose to testify anyway. The judge will instruct you that you may consider that prior conviction only to weigh Leander Rafshoon's credibility as a witness, not as evidence that he was more likely to have committed this crime.

"So Leander testified and, I submit, told you a totally truthful account of what happened. It is up to you to determine if you believe him. In order to convict him, the law says you must be convinced beyond a reasonable doubt that he is lying.

"As jurors you have the incredible power to judge the guilt or innocence of your neighbor. You must somehow put aside your natural revulsion toward this crime; you must also put aside the eagerness all of us have to catch the monster responsible for such a crime. Somehow, in the face of this atrocity, you must manage to remain objective, and coolly weigh the evidence to determine if the state has proven its case against the man it has accused.

"Leander Rafshoon is charged with this most serious crime, with the most serious consequences to him if you find him guilty. I pray that you take your oaths as jurors seriously. And if you do, you must find the defendant, Leander Rafshoon, not guilty of all charges. Thank you."

The most serious possible consequence to Rafshoon if the

jury found him guilty of first-degree murder was the mandatory life sentence he would receive. In his weighty phrasing about "consequences," Bernstein had said as much as he was allowed to about the punishment the judge could impose. The law seeks to enable jurors to come to a decision about the facts of a case without being burdened by the consequences of their decision.

The judge nodded to the prosecutor.

Ryan had arranged the photographs into two stacks in front of him at counsel table. He had made six neat piles out of the pages of notes from his yellow legal pads. On top of his notes he had placed the awl with its long pointed spike. He had lined up the ten vials of the victim's fingernails in a row.

"When I spoke to you at the start of this trial," Ryan said as he walked toward the jury, "I told you that no one would be coming before you to say that he saw the defendant Rafshoon murder and rape this thirty-six-year-old woman.

"What is really at stake here is the way we know things and the way we make judgments. Some of you may have some mistaken notions about circumstantial evidence. The judge will instruct you that a conviction may be based solely on circumstantial evidence.

"Law enforcement officers rarely have a videotape of a crime. It would be nice if we did. Then we could just play it back for you. But when a crime takes place between the perpetrator and a victim who are alone in a house, there are no eyewitnesses except the victim. And in this case Mr. Rafshoon saw to it that the victim couldn't be here to testify against him.

"Mr. Bernstein's entire summation can be boiled down to the simple argument that his client should be acquitted because there were no eyewitnesses. Well, fortunately the law protects us better than that, and provides for the criminal who kills the only witness.

"Most of the things we believe in are based on circumstantial evidence. If we go to sleep and wake up to see snow on the ground when there was no snow the night before, we are convinced that it snowed during the night. That belief is based on circumstantial evidence. We didn't see the snow actually come down, but we can rely on our experience to be as sure that it snowed as if we had seen it coming down. Similarly, if we see a single set of footprints in the snow leading into the house, we can be convinced someone entered that house. And that's the kind of solid, believable evidence we have in this case.

"Mr. Bernstein very cleverly tries to distract you from the evidence by raising the possibility that other people may also have had motives to kill Mrs. Collins. This is ironic, because motive is the one thing the state doesn't have to prove in the conviction of a crime. The motivation for the evil that men do can flow from a million twisted sources. The law cares about a person's evil *behavior*. In short, we need not show why Leander Rafshoon killed Mrs. Collins.

"All these other people may have had motives, but there wasn't one shred of evidence that any of them, aside from her husband, had ever been in Mrs. Collins's house, much less dared to do her any harm. And you can well believe that Mr. Bernstein would have brought out any such evidence—if he'd had any.

"Let me point out that if you can actually believe that Rafshoon is not the killer, then someone else had to have done all those things to Mrs. Collins. Not only without leaving evidence, but without having removed the evidence of Leander Rafshoon's guilt. That's just too much of a coincidence.

"No, by asking you to speculate, without evidence, about the possibility that certain other people could have committed the murder, Mr. Bernstein is trying to divert your attention from the evidence that *is* in the case. And it is the accumulation of all these pieces of evidence that makes the state's case overwhelming.

"Perhaps no single piece of evidence standing alone would be enough to establish guilt beyond a reasonable doubt, but when you take all the evidence together, it is as certain as concluding that it has snowed when you see snow on the ground. Like footprints in the snow, there was only one set of tracks leading to the murder, and they all belonged to the defendant, Leander Rafshoon."

Ryan began a long and detailed review of the testimony of all the witnesses, then he began to bear down on the defendant's character. He reminded the jury about the defendant's prior conviction, and he restated the claim that Leander had tried to flee from the police, citing this as evidence of guilty knowledge.

"Officer Moreali is a law enforcement officer, sworn to uphold the law, not break it," Ryan said, raising his voice. "There was absolutely no reason for him to attack Rafshoon or to come into this court and commit the serious crime of perjury. It is a question of Moreali's word against Rafshoon's. And if you believe the law enforcement officer, Rafshoon, by trying to run away, was showing that he knew he was guilty and was trying to escape the day he would have to face you here in court.

"Ladies and gentlemen, don't be fooled by a clever defense lawyer. If something walks like a duck, looks like a duck, and talks like a duck, you can believe beyond a reasonable doubt that it is a duck. Mr. Leander Rafshoon walks like a murderer, looks like a murderer, and talks like a murderer because he *is* the murderer of Carolyn Collins."

Ryan walked over to the pile of photographs in front of his seat at counsel table. He took the top one and walked back to the jury rail. With his arm outstretched, holding the picture directly in front of the faces of the jurors, he slowly walked the length of the jury box. "This woman was raped. She was viciously, brutally stabbed thirty-seven times, and then he bashed her head in."

Still holding the photograph straight-armed in front of him, Ryan walked over to the defendant. Standing directly across from Rafshoon at the far end of the counsel table, holding the photograph out to Rafshoon, Ryan screamed, "Don't let this animal get away with it."

"Objection!" Bernstein shouted.

Patricia Stewart held her breath. This was the kind of dramatic confrontation she had been expecting since the beginning of the trial. She waited eagerly to see where it would lead.

"Sustained," Judge Whitaker said. He pounded his gavel, cutting off Bernstein before he had a chance to go on. "Mr. Ryan, that is wholly improper. I instruct the jury to ignore the last remark of the prosecutor. Sit down, Mr. Bernstein. Are you finished with your summation, Mr. Ryan?"

"Almost."

"Well, finish it without resorting to name-calling."

Ryan held his ground, still staring at the defendant. "Don't let this"—he paused, allowing the expression of disgust to remain on his face—"this *man* get away with this vicious crime."

He turned back to the jury. "I demand that this jury defend the rights of the victim, Mrs. Carolyn Collins. On her behalf and on behalf of the people of this state you must return verdicts of guilty of rape and murder in the first degree. Thank you."

The judge waited for Ryan to return to his seat. The only step left before the case was turned over for the jury's deliberation was for the judge to make his charge to the jury. The jurors shifted in their seats and waited for the judge's final remarks.

Judge Whitaker told the jury he would instruct them as

soon as they returned from lunch, and he recessed the trial until then.

When the jurors were again settled in their places in the courtroom, Judge Whitaker began his final instructions. First he explained to them that in order to find a defendant guilty, they must be convinced of every element of the charge beyond a reasonable doubt. "Reasonable doubt," he said, "is not a possible or imaginary doubt, for everything in human affairs, especially when dependent on oral testimony, is subject to some possible or imaginary doubt. Reasonable doubt is a reasonable uncertainty of the truth of the charge."

He then summarized the counts in the indictment and explained the various degrees of murder. "For purposes of this case," Judge Whitaker went on, "rape is defined as the carnal knowledge of a woman forcibly and against her will. 'Carnal knowledge' means sexual intercourse between a male and a female. To convict the defendant of rape, the jury must find that he had sexual intercourse with the female forcibly and against her will. To complete the crime of rape there must be penetration by the sexual organ of the male into the sexual organ of the female. The slightest penetration is sufficient.

"The essential elements of the crime of rape," Judge Whitaker plowed on, "are carnal knowledge by force by the male and nonconsent to it by the female. Consent, however reluctant, negates rape. If a woman assaulted is physically and mentally able to resist, is not terrified by threats, and is not in a place and position where resistance would be useless, it must be shown that she did, in fact, resist the assault. This resistance must be by acts and not mere words, and must be reasonably proportionate to the victim's strength and opportunity. It must be in good faith and without pretense, with an active determination to prevent the violation of her person, and must not be merely passive and perfunctory. Even here, the fact that a victim finally submits does not necessarily imply that she consented. Submission to a compelling force, or as a result of being put in fear, is not consent. It is only required that the female resist as much as she possibly can under the circumstances, and the circumstances and conditions surrounding the parties at the time of the alleged offense are to be considered in determining whether adequate resistance was offered."

The judge was reading a set of instructions called "pattern charges." These are prepared by judicial committees to apply to all criminal cases. The language is well balanced and approved by the upper courts, and anything objectionable has been dry-cleaned and pressed out.

After completing his discussion of rape, Judge Whitaker turned his attention to the question of intent. "Intent is a condition of the mind which cannot be seen, and can only be determined by inferences from a person's conduct, words, or acts. It is not necessary that witnesses be produced to testify that an accused said he had a certain intent when he engaged in a particular act. His intention may be gathered from his acts and conduct, and from all he said and did at the particular time and place, and from all of the surrounding circumstances. To find the defendant guilty, you must find that he intended to commit the acts for which he is charged.

"You were selected on the basis of our belief that each of you could, without fear, favor, prejudice, or sympathy, in sound judgment and clear conscience, render just verdicts on evidence presented in conformity with these instructions."

Julius Solars, from his position in the first seat in the jury box, was listening intently, trying to understand every word, nodding to confirm his understanding as the judge was speaking.

"The very object of our jury system is to secure a verdict by comparison of views and discussion among jurors themselves, provided this can be done reasonably and in a way that is consistent with the conscientious convictions of the several jurors.

"Each juror should listen, with a disposition to be convinced, to the opinions and arguments of the other jurors. It is not intended under the law that a juror should go into the jury room with a fixed determination that the verdict shall represent his opinion of the case at that particular moment. Nor is it intended that he should close his ears to the discussions and arguments of his fellow jurors who are assumed to be equally honest and intelligent. In coming to a conclusion about the facts in this case you should apply common sense gained from your life experience."

Finally he stopped reading. "Since this is a criminal case, your verdict, whether it is guilty or not guilty, must be unanimous. We will now draw two names of jurors who will be excused as alternates."

A court officer walked over to the wooden drum that had been used at the start of the trial. He placed the fourteen pink slips bearing the names of the jurors into the drum. He closed the small latch, turned the key, and spun the cylinder. When the cylinder stopped turning, he opened the door and removed two slips. "Juror Number Nine, Gordon Lofton. Juror Number Fourteen, Alex Butler. Would you please step down from the jury box and take a seat in the courtroom."

Gordon Lofton, a tall, middle-aged black, walked out of the jury box, leaving Matty Barnes as the only remaining black juror. Alex Butler could hardly bring himself to stand up. He'd been reluctant to participate in the first place, and now that he'd became totally swept up in the case and involved in his role in the decision-making process, it seemed cruel that he would only be able to watch from the spectators' seats in the courtroom and await a verdict from others. When he reached the spectators' section and sat down, he felt cheated and terribly frustrated.

"Ladies and gentlemen," the judge said, turning back to the members of the final jury, "the twelve of you may now retire to the jury room. As soon as counsel has reviewed the exhibits marked in evidence, a court officer will bring them in to you, and you may begin your deliberations."

Leander Rafshoon watched the people who would decide his fate slowly file out of the courtroom. "Please, please," he kept repeating in his head, hoping somehow they would hear him.

Bernstein's primary argument to the jury was that the state simply had not proved its case beyond a reasonable doubt. It does occasionally happen that a jury will feel that a defendant is guilty but that there has not been enough evidence to convict him. However, many lawyers and even some judges regard the general instructions that are read to the jurors, which contain such ponderous phrases as "reasonable doubt" and "presumption of innocence," as a kind of ritual chant that cannot be fully understood by most jurors. The jury is often thought of as having a different standard of reasonable doubt than a judge, a different threshold of proof requiring more for conviction than a judge would require.

In their book *The American Jury,* which summed up the Chicago Jury Project studies, Kalven and Zeisel called "reasonable doubt" an "almost heroic commitment to decency," a statement of values of a society that believes it would be better to let ten guilty people go free than convict one innocent man. The Chicago Jury Project concluded that in 11 percent of the instances in which a judge and jury disagreed about the verdict, the disagreement resulted from the jury's more generous view of what would constitute reasonable doubt.

During a summation a defense attorney is said to have told the jury, "In the next few seconds you will see the alleged murder victim walking into the courtroom." After every juror had turned to look in the direction of the door, the lawyer continued. "Although the victim has not appeared, I have proved that you must have a reasonable doubt in your minds that the victim is even dead, much less murdered. Otherwise you would not all have looked at the door of the courtroom."

When his turn came, the prosecutor responded to this argument by saying that the jurors might have had a reasonable doubt when they looked at the door in the hope of seeing the victim, "but I am sure no reasonable doubt as to the defendant's guilt exists at the present time, since the only person in the courtroom who did not turn his head in the direction of the courtroom door was the defendant himself."

The rape charge Judge Whitaker had read to the jury was identical with the charge he had read in his previous rape cases. Trial judges usually do not write specific instructions integrating the unique facts of a case with the legal principles that should be applied. The judges are afraid of risking reversal by an upper court on appeal by misstating the law or its applicability to the facts of the case. Writing individually tailored instructions requires real thought and effort, and some judges are simply too lazy or incompetent to do that.

A few states permit written instructions to be taken into the jury room. A judge in support of this practice said, "We somehow seem to think that jurors can get it on one shot and make monumental decisions on a person's freedom or property. It's crazy." Audiotapes, he also thought, could be helpful: perhaps jurors who had heard the instructions three or four times would then "tend to get it straight."

Jury instructions are often incomprehensible because they are drafted by lawyers and judges who do not realize how much of their "legalese" vocabulary and syntax was acquired in law school. The principles of criminal law are not complicated, but little effort is made to write clear and simple language for those not legally trained. Professional writers who are not lawyers should participate in the drafting of instructions, but they are rarely asked to.

In a disquieting finding in one study, juries that had received no instructions were making about the same number of misinterpretations of the law as juries that had received full instructions from the judge.

While the wording of instructions may be impenetrable to a layman, an occasional appellate court has treated the words very seriously. One defendant's conviction was reversed because a juror had consulted a dictionary as an aid to understanding the judge's instructions. After a day of deliberations on an assault charge, she went home and looked up the definitions of *reasonable, imaginary,* and *vague* in her dictionary. The juror discussed the definitions the next day with a fellow juror and they decided that their previous doubts about the defendant's guilt had not been "reasonable," and they therefore changed their minds and convicted. An appellate court reversed the conviction because the jury was bound to accept the court's definition of the legal concept of "reasonable doubt." If the juror needed clarification, said the court, she should have consulted the judge, not extraneous sources.

A study of the impact on the jury of different definitions of insanity as a defense found that the varying instructions made almost no difference. In one definition, insanity was related to whether or not the defendant knew the difference between right or wrong; in another, insanity was an allowable defense only if the defendant was irresistibly compelled to commit the act; and in the third definition, insanity could be cited only if the defendant's act resulted from a mental disease or defect. As it turned out, the supposedly harsh "right and wrong" test produced a few more acquittals than the supposedly more liberal "mental disease" or "mental defect" test.

Lawyers and judges cite contradictory evidence when arguing the question of whether or not the jury understands the law. Critics of present methods of jury instruction have argued that juries are bombarded with a mass of information, too much and too complicated to understand, often in no logical sequence, with no guidelines for evaluating it all.

Obviously if it is not possible for juries to understand the evidence in a trial, justice would be as well served by a group of monkeys making decisions of guilt or innocence. If jurors cannot understand, they should be replaced by a single expert, for example a judge, or by different jurors drawn from a more educated elite.

The Jury Project found that in 75 percent of the cases judges agreed with jury verdicts. This high percentage of agreement indicated that the juries' decisions were not arrived at by chance or arbitrary action. Judges interviewed in the study believed that only 2 percent of all cases were complicated, and that 86 percent were "easy to comprehend" and therefore unlikely to be misunderstood. Statistics also showed that juries deliberated longer on the more difficult and longer cases, which was seen as showing that the juries had understood the cases. Finally, judges did not disagree with juries any more often on difficult cases than on easier ones.

The Jury Project concluded that on the whole, juries follow the evidence and understand the cases; according to the judges reporting to the Jury Project, juries failed to understand the issues in fewer than 2 percent of the cases. While one juror may remember little, the total recall of the group of twelve is greater than the sum of its parts. "The net intelligence of the jury is miraculous," concluded Hans Zeisel, co-director of the Jury Project.

CHAPTER

THE TWELVE JURORS took their seats around the large conference table in the jury room. Julius Solars sat at the head of the table. "I suppose we should take a vote to see how we stand," he said.

"Good idea," Carl Copco said. "All those in favor of conviction, raise your hand."

"No," Julius said, "I think maybe we should take the vote by writing 'guilty' or 'not guilty' on pieces of paper."

Everyone seemed to agree with that.

And so the Rafshoon jury, like most juries, began their deliberations with a secret ballot. Julius gathered up the folded pieces of paper. As he looked at each one, he read aloud and made a mark on his yellow legal pad. "Not guilty." "Not guilty." "Guilty."

Everyone looked around the table to see if anyone was indicating agreement with the vote being read. "Not guilty."

"Guilty." No one showed signs of how he or she had voted, but most of the group seemed to be keeping score of the total vote on pads or loose pieces of paper. "Not guilty." "Guilty."

Julius tallied up the results: five votes for not guilty, six votes for guilty, and someone had written an O.

Elliot Postom thought that Rafshoon was guilty because no one else could have murdered the Collins woman without having left some evidence such as hair or blood at the scene of the crime.

Carl Copco was convinced that the defendant had been lying when he testified, so he wrote "guilty."

Patricia Stewart had voted to convict because of a strong feeling that in indicting Rafshoon, the grand jury had thought he was guilty. Many a juror assumes that where there's smoke, there's fire. According to one study, 36 percent of the jurors believed, after having been instructed otherwise by the judge, that it is the defendant's responsibility to prove innocence rather than the state's duty to prove guilt.

Leonard Klein and Laura Sayres had written "not guilty" not because they believed that Rafshoon was innocent but because they felt that the state had not proved its case, leaving substantial doubt about his guilt.

Julius Solars would have needed a confession in order to be able to vote to convict Rafshoon and perhaps any other defendant.

Matty Barnes had no doubt that the police were trying to pin the crime on someone, and she was certain that the officer had lied when he had claimed that Rafshoon had tried to flee. She had written "not guilty."

Feeling completely torn between the arguments of the prosecutor and those of the defense lawyer, Maureen Whalen had marked her ballot with an O. She knew, of course, that she could not agree with both sides, but she had simply been unable to make a decision at that point. She wanted to hear what the other people thought before she reached any final answer. She felt strongly that too much was at stake to rush into anything.

For a few moments after the vote was tallied, the room was silent. Everyone seemed to be waiting to see what would happen next.

"I guess it's important to go over the evidence," Julius finally said.

An outpouring of opinions and reactions and pent-up emotions filled the small jury room as the jurors felt free to talk to each other for the first time.

After twenty minutes of conversation in small groups, Leonard Klein spoke up loudly enough to attract everyone's attention: "Maybe Ira Kaplan murdered that poor woman."

"No," said Patricia Stewart, "Kaplan was a jealous lover. He was angry at the *doctor* and threatened *him*, remember?"

"I thought the prosecutor was a pompous ass," Matty Barnes said. "I wanted to throw him out the window."

Maureen Whalen furrowed her brow. "The doctor said Kaplan never threatened his wife."

"I just never believe bald men, particularly short bald men." Laura Sayres tried to lighten the atmosphere with a joke.

"How can we ever know what happened more than a year ago?" Julius asked with a sigh.

"We have to try," Elliot said.

For the next two and a half hours the discussion went back and forth over different aspects of the trial.

"Why else would he have had Leander spend two weeks with his wife, following her around and everything?"

"That's right. The doctor would have had Rafshoon with him if he had been the only person in danger."

"That poor son, finding his mother like that. Can you imagine?"

"The doctor had Rafshoon follow his wife to that meeting with Kaplan. Why did he do that?"

"Maybe it was so that Rafshoon would protect her."

"But why would he call her 'that bitch' when Rafshoon told him about it?"

"Maybe Rafshoon was lying and the doctor never said 'that bitch.'"

"I think there was a lot more going on than we heard."

"I felt so bad for his wife, the defendant's wife. She was there every day with those two beautiful little children. They're so young."

"That was a play for our sympathy, pure and simple. The kids didn't have to be there."

"Did you see how Rafshoon sat there for the whole trial with his hand clenched in a fist?"

"The doctor led that Rena Grey down a garden path. He convinced her he couldn't marry her because of his wife."

"That Grey woman was no innocent babe in the woods."

"I agree. I think Rena Grey could have murdered Mrs. Collins just as easily as Leander."

"Do you think we could get some coffee?"

"I don't think a woman would have had the strength to do it."

"That's ridiculous. Women are strong enough to stab someone. I remember once being with this woman . . ."

"Why did the prosecutor drag that exterminator into court? He went to the house and sprayed it for carpenter ants. What have carpenter ants got to do with the murder?"

"Even Dr. Collins had nothing to say, really. He wasn't there. He didn't see anything."

"I hope we don't have to stay overnight. They would send us home, wouldn't they?"

"I think it's very suspicious that that German housekeeper suddenly went back to Germany. I think she could have told us something."

"The doctor probably paid her to go away."

"Oh, come on. She probably didn't want to hang around

after the woman she'd been working for had been murdered."

"Of course. Would you want to work in the kitchen after all that blood was spilt there? Look at the photographs."

And so the discussions and the arguments continued. Sometimes emotions ran high, and voices were raised, but always the jurors struggled to resolve their differences of opinion. Details of what witnesses had said and what the judge had instructed came back as each juror added a little more from his own recollection and perception of the trial.

Three more ballots were taken on the first day of deliberations, but the results remained the same. The jurors, not being sequestered, were sent home in the evening, to return the next morning and resume the search for a decision.

Elliot Postom raised the first point of the new day's deliberations. "What about the three thousand dollars that was stolen from the closet?"

"There wasn't any evidence that Rafshoon took the money," said Leonard Klein.

"I'm not so sure any money was stolen," said Matty Barnes tartly. "You know about doctors, what they're like. He could get a tax deduction by claiming some money was stolen."

"Maybe he had insurance," piped up Julius Solars.

"Jesus! His wife was just murdered." Patricia Stewart looked shocked.

"Even so."

"You know, Rafshoon isn't even charged with stealing the money," Laura Sayres pointed out.

"I wonder why not," said Maureen Whalen to no one in particular.

"Probably even the prosecutor didn't think there was enough evidence to charge him with it."

"I bet it was the grand jury. They probably didn't believe that business over the money."

The first shift of opinion was recorded on the second ballot

near the end of the second day of deliberations. After Julius
Solars counted up the votes, he announced that the jury now
stood at seven for conviction and five for acquittal.

Maureen Whalen had decided that she would join those
who believed the defendant was guilty. Although she still did
not feel very confident about her decision, Maureen felt that
Rafshoon's lies to the nurse at the hospital and to the detective when he was being questioned could be proof of his guilt.

The debate continued.

"Why else would he have tried to run away from Officer
Moreali?" asked Elliot Postom.

"The cop was lying, simple as that," answered Matty
Barnes. "I don't trust the sons of bitches for a minute. I know
too many stories of how they beat up on blacks for no good
reason."

"Rafshoon *looks* guilty," said Carl Copco. "Did you look
at him? Don't you think he does?"

"Why? Because he's black?" asked Laura Sayres, looking
toward Matty Barnes for approval.

"Don't be ridiculous. He just looks like an ape, like a killer
ape." Carl Copco refused to give ground.

As the afternoon wore on toward the six o'clock deadline
fixed by the judge for the close of that day's deliberations, the
jurors began to analyze more closely the testimony of the individual witnesses.

"The young man in the tree saw the defendant running
from the house."

"He *thought* he saw Rafshoon. The only thing he was able
to tell was that the person was black."

"I think if he'd seen Rafshoon before, he would have recognized him. But he didn't say he'd ever seen him before, and
the kid was in the tree all week when Rafshoon was there."

"He admitted that he didn't see anyone go into the house,
not even the defendant. Someone must have gone into the

house to kill the woman. He could have just as easily missed the real murderer going in."

"Come to think of it, he did say no one came or left except Rafshoon."

"So?"

"So what about the exterminator?"

"Well, the kid should have seen the exterminator. There's no question the exterminator was there."

"You trying to say that the exterminator did it?"

"Of course not. There's no evidence of that. But if the kid in the tree didn't see the exterminator, he could just as easily have missed someone else, like the killer."

"Yes. That's a good point."

"That's right."

"Maybe the kid didn't mention the exterminator because he didn't think that was important."

"He flat out said he saw no one except the defendant."

"I think you're making a big deal out of nothing. He simply didn't see the exterminator. That's all."

"But the scratches—what about the scratches?"

"He explained that he was scratched by the woman, so what's the big deal that the blood matches?"

"Do you believe that? That it was some coincidence? And the rope had blood that matched his, that was a coincidence, too? Come on. How gullible can you be?"

"That expert said he found wood chips on the towel."

"Oh, come on. The defendant never got those wounds from wood chips."

"He admitted that when he testified," Julius said.

"But I don't understand why the prosecutor had all that testimony about wood chips if the defendant admitted that he didn't get his wounds from wood chips."

"Well, the prosecutor couldn't know if the defendant was going to testify."

"That defense lawyer was taking us for fools."

"The judge sure had it in for Bernstein. I mean he cut him off all the time."

"That's not true. He didn't cut him off. I liked the defense lawyer. He was just doing his job, and the judge was just doing his."

"Yeah. I bet they're friends. Probably go out drinking."

"I think the judge couldn't have been nicer."

"I thought the prosecutor was a jerk."

"Let's get back to the case. I really can't spend another day on this."

"You know, the doctor told his lover, Rena, that he was going to kill his wife."

"The judge told us not to consider that."

"Don't be so naïve."

"What's *that* supposed to mean?"

"Calm down."

"What happened to the photograph of Rena that Mrs. Collins found in the store?"

"What photograph? We have millions of photographs."

"The one that Mrs. Collins found in the store, that she ripped up. She put it in her pocketbook, but it wasn't found there."

"We have the torn photograph from her pocketbook."

"No, that one was different. That one was of her kids."

"That defense lawyer was very clever having Rafshoon admit to almost everything, everything except the killing."

"He swore he didn't do it. He didn't have to take the witness stand to do that."

"I must say, anyone who's capable of murdering is also capable of lying. He did lie to the nurse about his wounds, and he lied to the police detective."

"Remember, the judge said we should take into consideration the interest a witness had in the case. Well, Rafshoon sure has an interest in this case."

"I don't understand why the judge told us that. A defendant is presumed innocent, but if he testifies, we should consider his interest in the outcome of the case. Every defendant has an interest in his case. Why should we hold that against him when he testifies?"

"It means he testified to save his skin. That was the reason he lied to the nurse and the police officer those earlier times when he told different stories."

"I'm willing to go with him on his explanation of the blood under her fingernails, and his hair on the sledgehammer: he banged in some posts."

"If we believe Rafshoon is innocent, we have to believe that he was the victim of a hell of a lot of coincidences."

"If someone had seen him at Weequahic Park, that would have corroborated his having been somewhere else at the time of the murder. But if he didn't go to the park, that's the time that fits in perfectly with when the guy in the tree saw him running out of the house."

"The thing that bothers me is why he went to the hospital. I don't believe it was to treat his scratches."

"He said it was to see Dr. Collins."

"I know, but if he really had just stabbed that woman forty-seven times—"

"Thirty-seven."

"Thirty-seven times. What's the difference? If he had stabbed her thirty-seven times, how could he go see this woman's husband right after that?"

"Unless he was nuts."

"Well, we don't have evidence of that."

"The only thing that makes sense is what he said, that he was going to tell him he wasn't going to be her bodyguard anymore."

"Maybe he's such a cold-blooded killer he figured out a jury like us might believe he didn't do it if he went straight to see Dr. Collins."

"Whoever killed that woman sure had to be cold-blooded."

"But he doesn't seem that clever."

"He does have a criminal record. He committed a robbery."

"An armed robbery."

"We're going in circles. Let's take another vote, because at this rate I don't think we're ever going to reach a verdict."

The fourth and last ballot of the second day of deliberations showed the same division, seven for conviction and five for acquittal. Out of frustration and exhaustion everyone agreed that they should ask the judge if they could adjourn a little earlier that day. A note was sent to the judge with the jury's request, and Judge Whitaker sent everyone home.

The manner of deliberations varies from jury to jury. In rare instances a defendant's guilt has even been decided in a jury room by the flip of a coin or the roll of the dice. But those occasions have been rare, and they illustrate the difficulty of making a decision based on the reconstruction of events occurring months, sometimes years, earlier.

The central, fascinating question about juries is: how, in fact, do they arrive at their verdicts? To some extent, this question is unanswerable. No two juries are the same. Each juror may have his own special reason. The mix of jurors in each case interacts in a unique way. The evidence and the witnesses at every trial are always different. No two judges would preside over a trial in the same way. And all the other characteristics distinguishing one trial from another are unique to each particular case.

But by studying the behavior of enough juries, a few overall conclusions can be drawn. Men, for example, usually speak more in the jury room and are more active than women in keeping deliberations moving from one issue to another;

women, generally, play more passive roles and are more likely to say things that reduce tension and unify the jury.

Statistics have been collected that give a picture of how many juries have behaved. In studying 255 trials, the Chicago Jury Project found almost two out of ten of the juries unanimously voted on their first ballot for conviction and about one out of ten voted for acquittal. In other words, the deliberations ended after the first ballot in about three out of ten cases. This, of course, was not what happened in the Rafshoon trial.

The Jury Project also learned that the opinion of the majority on the first ballot ultimately prevailed in 95 percent of the verdicts, regardless of who comprised the minority—wealthy persons, the better educated, poor persons, men or women. The initial minority prevailed in only 5 percent of the cases, and then it was always a substantial minority—three or more jurors. In contrast to the popular impression created by such films as *Twelve Angry Men,* this information shows that the deliberations are usually unimportant: in more than nine out of ten cases, by the time jurors go into the jury room to deliberate, they have made up their minds. The verdicts are usually decided during the trial by the individual jurors themselves and not during the deliberations.

About 5 percent of all juries do not reach a verdict at all—they "hang"—meaning they are unable to come to the unanimous decision necessary for reaching a verdict. About two thirds of hung juries are caused by jurors holding out for acquittal. Contrary to popular belief, hung juries are not usually caused by a single stubborn juror, but by the closeness of the case itself, and by the moral support jurors feel when their minority view has several supporters.

Various studies have shown that for one or two jurors to hold out, they need to have companions who share their views at the beginning of the deliberations. Experiments to test group decision making showed that in an ambiguous situation, a member of a group will often doubt and ultimately disbelieve his own accurate observation if all the other members of the group claim that he must be mistaken. He must have at least one ally in order to maintain his original position, not only before others but even for himself. In the trials studied by the Jury Project, not a single jury hung with a minority of less than three; in fact it always took a first-vote minority of at least four to allow a permanent split in a jury.

The requirement of a unanimous decision affords great power to a minority opinion. A unanimity requirement affects the decision-making process by establishing that minority group members will have an equal voice in jury deliberations. It increases the chances that jurors will spell out the reason for their vote and respond to the views of others. The majority on a jury cannot simply disregard the positions of two or three members. If that minority viewpoint is held strongly enough, it will thwart the will of the majority. But if hung juries occurred too frequently, the system would break down.

In 1972 the Supreme Court decided that a unanimous verdict was not required in all jury trials for all crimes; the Court upheld convictions by verdicts of nine to three and ten to two in misdemeanor cases. Although the federal courts still operate under a unanimity rule, a majority verdict is allowed in Louisiana, Oregon, Idaho, Montana, Oklahoma, and Texas.

Recent studies have found that quorum juries appear to deliberate differently from unanimous juries. Very early on in the deliberations, disagreements in quorum juries dropped to almost half the level of those in unanimous juries. People were less contentious in quorum juries, more opinionated in unanimous juries. Since members of a quorum jury know that one or two people cannot prevent a verdict, there is more impetus to reach an agreement, and differences that tend to build into sharp oppositions are eliminated. Also, jurors who are in the minority in quorum juries do not insist on their views as much because they know they lack the power to hang the jury.

In 1980 the Supreme Court set limits on the use of quorum juries. Sensing a risk that the jury system as we know it could be lost, the Court held that nonunanimous verdicts threaten constitutional principles when a state has reduced the size of its juries to the minimum number of jurors permitted by the Constitution, which is six.

Whatever the dynamics of when and how a jury decides, the important question remains as to why a juror reaches his conclusion of guilt or innocence. Each juror's decision is often based on factors he is barely aware of himself. The Jury Project concluded that when members of a jury sense that the evidence is close, they feel liberated to do what they really want to do. The jury usually does not consciously or explicitly yield to sentiment, but there can be, as one judge reported to the Jury Project, "a deliberate hunt for doubt." Even if a juror should be aware of his motives, he may prefer not to disclose them to his fellow jurors, and instead couch his argument in the language of the judge rather than that of his private feelings.

CHAPTER

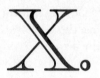

JUDGE WHITAKER WAS WAITING IN HIS CHAMBERS for the court officer to knock on his door and tell him that the jury had reached a verdict. He spent his time, as he usually did when a jury was deliberating, reading the most recent decisions of the New Jersey Supreme Court, but he was very much aware of the tension of the waiting period. His secretary and his law clerk spoke more quietly; the sergeant at arms and the court clerk talked about their vacation days and their accumulated sick days. Everyone was aware that the decision bringing the events of the last three weeks to a climax could be announced at any moment.

Mike Bernstein waited in his seat at counsel table in the empty courtroom. The jury was taking longer than he expected to come to a decision. The average jury deliberates for about half a day. As the third day of deliberations in the Rafshoon case got under way, Bernstein began to think that he would be satisfied with a hung jury. Too much was at stake. His stomach was churning. This was the last murder case, maybe the last criminal case he was going to handle. It simply took too much out of him. He was no longer physically and emotionally willing to deal with the strain.

Ryan was with Altieri on the third floor in the large office of the homicide squad. They were reminiscing about old cases they had worked on together, their usual way of dealing with the anxious time of waiting for the decision. Ryan believed that juries usually came up with the right verdict, but the averages did not mean much if you had an eccentric jury capable of going off in any direction—and there was no way of knowing whether a jury was eccentric until the trial was over. Ryan told his detective about a recent newspaper report he had read about a case in which a jury had returned after thirty minutes of deliberation not only with an acquittal for the defendant, but also with a $68 collection they had taken up for him.

While his wife and two children sat on a bench in the corridor outside the courtroom, Rafshoon paced back and forth in the holding pen on the other side of the door to the courtroom, replaying in his mind the testimony of the witnesses, particularly his own responses to the prosecutor's questions. He hadn't the slightest idea of whether or not the jury had believed him.

Although in the great majority of cases the decisions of jurors may be made before the deliberations, it would be a mistake to dismiss the importance of deliberations altogether. If a minority of jurors does turn the majority around during the deliberations in even one out of ten cases, that is still a significant number, particularly for the one out of ten defendants involved.

At the start of the third day of deliberations, the mood of the jurors was grim. One of them tried to make a joke, but no one laughed.

"Would someone like to start?" Julius asked.

"You know, I was thinking about it last night," Leonard Klein began. "Whoever was running out of the house was running west."

"So what? Why are you bringing up something irrelevant like that?" Carl Copco asked.

"Well, I made this kind of diagram," Leonard said, taking out a piece of paper and spreading it out on the table. "If the person was running into the sun, and the kid said it was around two-thirty, anyone looking at him, especially up in a tree at a distance of fifty yards, would be looking into the sun."

"Hey, that's right." Elliot Postom was excited. "And someone said it was a bright day."

"Of course it was bright," said Laura Sayres. "Mrs. Collins was sunbathing. It had to be bright."

"Big deal. All that would mean is that the kid could get a better view of him." Carl Copco looked impatient.

"No, just the opposite," Laura pressed on. "The sun was in his face, and when the man running away turned around, the sun was on the back of his head, not his face."

"Right! And it would have been right in the eyes of the kid in the tree." Matty Barnes looked pleased.

"That's true," Maureen Whalen acknowledged.

"What are we playing Sherlock Holmes for?" Carl Copco asked with irritation in his voice. "The defense lawyer never brought this out."

"Maybe he just didn't think of it," Leonard Klein said.

The discussion went on for another two hours. Finally Julius Solars said that he thought another vote should be taken.

"Let's do this one by an open ballot," suggested Leonard Klein. "I don't think that should pressure anyone, and I think it will give us a sense of whether we can reach a decision—

unless someone, anyone, has an objection. If anyone does, then it should be a closed ballot."

There was quiet in the jury room while everyone waited to see if an objection was going to be voiced.

"There doesn't seem to be anyone who wants a secret ballot," Julius said. "So let's vote. Matty?"

"Not guilty."

"Laura?"

"Not guilty."

Julius went around the table, looking at each person as he said the name, waiting to write down the vote. "Elliot?"

"Not guilty."

"Leonard?"

"Not guilty."

"Maureen?"

"Not guilty."

Everyone answered not guilty until it came to the twelfth juror, Carl Copco, the person who had been the most adamant for conviction when the deliberations had begun.

"Carl, what is your vote?"

Carl looked at the faces of his fellow jurors around the conference table. They were all waiting for him. "I have to say that I feel like I've completely changed my opinion. At the beginning I was sure the guy had done it, and I kept thinking so for a long time. But the more I listened to everybody, the more I began to think I was wrong and the rest of you were right."

"Then it's unanimous," Julius said.

"Couldn't have been easier," Leonard said.

Bernstein heard laughter coming from the jury room. He had heard laughter like that from other juries. He knew it was over, a decision had been reached. The laughter did not imply a conviction or an acquittal, just the release of tension. But to Bernstein that laughter was always chilling.

The small red light over the door to the jury room went on. Bernstein saw it immediately. One of the jurors had flipped the switch inside the jury room to signal to the court officer that the jury had come to a decision.

"We got a verdict," Bernstein said to the court officer.

Within minutes the courtroom was filled with spectators. Bernstein and Ryan were at their seats at counsel table. Leander Rafshoon was led in from the holding pen. His handcuffs were removed and he sat down next to his lawyer.

Judge Whitaker emerged from his chambers. Everyone stood as he climbed the three steps to his desk. He banged the gavel, and lawyers, defendant, court reporter, clerk, and spectators sat down.

"Bring in the jury," the judge said, looking over at the defendant.

Two court officers positioned themselves a few feet behind the defendant to guard against escape in the event of a guilty verdict.

Rafshoon stared straight ahead, showing no emotion.

One by one the jurors walked out of the jury room. They filed into the two rows of seats they had occupied for three weeks and sat down. Their faces looked grim, which to Bernstein usually meant bad news for the defendant. None of the jurors looked at the defendant. Another sign of a conviction.

"Ladies and gentlemen of the jury," the clerk intoned, "have you reached a verdict?"

Several jurors nodded.

"Will the foreman rise," said the clerk.

Julius Solars stood up.

"Is the verdict unanimous?" the clerk asked.

Julius cleared his throat. "It is."

"Will the defendant rise and face the jury as the clerk records the verdict," the judge said.

Bernstein stood up and prompted his client to do the same.

Rafshoon didn't seem to be aware of what was going on as he rose from his chair.

"Ladies and gentlemen of the jury," the judge said, "how say you through your foreman? Is the defendant, Leander Rafshoon, guilty or not guilty of the charge of murder in the first degree?"

Julius looked down at the piece of paper rattling in his shaking hand. Ryan held his fountain pen in his hand, as he always did when listening for a verdict.

"Your Honor," Julius spoke slowly, "we find the defendant not guilty of murder in the first degree. We find him not guilty of any of the charges."

Rafshoon began to cry. With tears rolling down his face, he turned to his lawyer. His body began to shake. He tried to say something, but no words came out of his mouth. He threw his arms around Bernstein. Rafshoon's wife, carrying their small daughter and pulling their son by the hand, rushed over to her husband.

The jury watched, and some of them began to cry.

Bernstein had been involved in about a dozen cases in which some of the jurors had cried after giving their verdict. He had great respect for the good sense of jurors, but what was even more impressive to him, even for one who had made a career out of trying to manipulate jurors, was the decency and desire to be fair evidenced by those tears.

"Does the state wish the jury polled?" Judge Whitaker asked.

"No, Your Honor," Ryan responded.

"Then the clerk will enter not guilty to all counts against the defendant," the judge said.

"Yes, sir," the clerk said.

Judge Whitaker turned to the jury. "Ladies and gentlemen, I want to thank you for your service on this case. Without people like you who are willing to serve, our system of justice would simply break down. You have judged your neighbor

fairly, and you should leave here and return to your more
normal lives with the satisfaction of knowing that you have
done your duty as citizens of this country. You may now go
home."

The twelve jurors rose and began to file out of the jury box
for the last time. As they walked to the low swinging door at
the center of the wooden rail, each juror, one at a time,
looked over to Leander Rafshoon. Some smiled at him. Others nodded. And a few said congratulations or good luck.

"Thank you," Rafshoon said to each person as he or she
passed.

After all the jurors had left the courtroom, and with the
defendant still standing before him, Judge Whitaker made his
final remarks: "The indictment will be dismissed, and after
the paperwork is completed at the jail today, the defendant
will be discharged. Good day, gentlemen." The judge rose
and headed toward his chambers.

"Thank you, Your Honor," Rafshoon said.

The judge looked back at Rafshoon, nodded, and left the
courtroom.

Rafshoon turned to his lawyer. "I don't know how to
thank you," he said and embraced Bernstein once more.

Bernstein was embarrassed. "It's okay. I'm glad it worked
out."

The guards led Rafshoon out of the courtroom. In a few
hours he would be a free man again.

"Congratulations," Leslie Ryan said to his adversary. They
shook hands. "I'll get you next time."

"We'll see," Mike Bernstein said. He knew that there probably would be another time, with another client who would
start out by being just a face to him but who would get
through to him eventually, and that they would all face another jury together. However cynical he might have become
after years of scrambling in the justice system, there was still

nothing like the excitement of winning. And he had to admit that it didn't feel so bad to be part of a process that, with all its imperfections, was based on the well-meaning efforts of ordinary people trying to be fair.

CHAPTER

XI.

"THE THING THAT STRUCK ME THE MOST about jury service," Laura Sayres said to her colleague on her first day back at work, "was the way twelve strangers were suddenly working together, each person adding a little bit, trying to figure out what happened, what was fair. In the business world we rarely get this kind of team effort."

"I'm not sure we did the right thing," Maureen Whalen said to her sister on the night the trial ended. "And there was a while there when I thought we should tell the judge that we couldn't reach a verdict and there should be another trial. But then I thought that any other jury would probably have the same trouble, and there had to be a decision one way or the other. I don't know. Maybe we made the wrong decision. If Leander Rafshoon didn't do it, I don't know who did. I would have felt a lot better if we had convicted the murderer. It was such a terrible crime."

"I think I'm never going to get the photographs of that poor woman out of my mind," Patricia Stewart wrote in her diary.

"A lot of things impressed me," Elliot Postom said to his wife. "That business about 'reasonable doubt,' for example. When you listen closely to the judge's definition, all it seemed to mean was that 'reasonable doubt' meant 'reasonable doubt.' I couldn't pin down what he was saying. But the funny thing was that when we reached the deliberations, we had the feeling there really was some quantity of evidence that had to be reached, like a vase that had to be filled to a certain mark before we could find the guy guilty."

"We did what the judge had told us. We didn't talk to each other about the case at all during the trial," Matty Barnes said to a close friend, a psychiatric social worker. "So when we first began talking in the jury room, I was really surprised. When some of them opened their mouths, I thought, Jesus, these people are nitwits. I kept asking myself, where do these people come from? Don't they know what it's really like out there?"

Julius Solars told his son that he had been determined that his decision about the defendant's guilt or innocence was not going to be swayed by the government's insistence—even if the judge joined in it. "The thought I kept having from the beginning of the trial to the end was that as long as there are juries made up of ordinary people, we'd be safe, I mean as a country. Any dictator would have to destroy the jury system because the twelve jurors would have the power over the dictator."

"I'm not sure how much the jury understood the judge's charge," Alex Butler said to his agent when they were discussing the possibility of his writing a book about the case. "But the seriousness, you could even say solemnity, of the presentation made it sound very important, and I think this really affected people's attitudes. It was like a morality play,

with all the different acts, all performed on the stage of the
courtroom with all the different players. And we the jurors
were part of the cast. But the judge's charge shook me into
realizing that this wasn't just a play. The Collins woman
really bled, and Rafshoon's life really was on the line. I'm
sorry I wasn't in on the deliberations."

On his first day back at work, Leonard Klein said to a
friend in the office, "It was not an easy decision to come to. I
honestly think the verdict could have gone either way. And
even if there was a little shouting, we all tried to listen to
what other people were saying. There were shifts of opinion,
but we tried not to pressure anyone."

"Twelve jurors are harder to bribe than one judge," Carl
Copco said to the bartender of his favorite pub. "That's why
I think the world of the jury. It's kind of a guarantee against
corruption. I'm no saint or anything, and I never gave much
thought to things like civic responsibilities, but I was surprised how I got so caught up in it. I didn't want to be there. I
hated wasting all that time waiting, and I didn't think I gave a
damn about whether this guy did it or not, but I wound up
really wanting us to do the right thing. Everybody did. After
it was over, we all said we'd be in touch, and maybe get together again. I guess that won't happen, but when we were
leaving the courtroom, we all said we'd try."

Carl Copco had experienced what has been called a "halo
effect," when average people, realizing the importance of
their responsibility on the jury, rise to the occasion and perform with such an astuteness and integrity that they surprise
even themselves.

In a national survey of trial court judges, 1,030 respondents gave their opinion of the jury system: only 3 percent of
the judges described juries as unsatisfactory. In those cases
studied by the Chicago Jury Project in which the judges disagreed with the verdicts of the jury, they were more prone

toward conviction than the juries. If all of the defendants in the cases studied had been tried by a judge without a jury, the number of acquittals would have been reduced almost in half to approximately 250 from the 500 acquittals that actually occurred; the jury was more severe in only 6 percent of the cases. In the cases where the juries were more lenient, the judges were usually grateful for the leniency, feeling that the juries were doing "justice" in some larger sense than they as judges would have been allowed under the letter of the law. In only 2 percent of the cases did the judges criticize the jury's verdict as improper or a miscarriage of justice.

It is far from clear how satisfied people would be with judges as replacements for juries. There has been little research into the way judges function as fact finders, but it would be fair to assume that they have many of the same human characteristics and flaws as jurors. Our commitment to juries was not made for efficiency, but out of a belief, based in part on faith, that we are all better protected from government by the good sense of our fellow citizens than by any institutional or intellectual elite—an astonishing transfer of power from the rich and few to the common man.

Whether it is a judge or a group of twelve jurors, whoever must bear the burden of judging an accused person will bring to that terrible task his own limitations of insight and generosity of spirit. Humbling as that undertaking might be, there is no perfect alternative. The best that can be hoped is that given the responsibility, we would judge others as we would want to be judged.

When Bernstein walked out of the courtroom, he was surprised to see Laura Sayres, Leonard Klein, and Julius Solars waiting at the elevator. Bernstein smiled at the three now ex-jurors, and he stood waiting for the elevator beside them. When the doors finally opened, the four of them stepped in.

"Do you handle many cases like this one?" Laura asked.

She felt odd now that the restriction against speaking directly had been lifted. They had all spent three intensive weeks together and had never had a "normal" conversation.

"I do find myself in court a lot," Bernstein said, trying to smile in such a way as to eliminate any impression of boasting.

"You hear a lot of things on television, in the newspapers, about how lawyers . . ." Laura hesitated. She seemed embarrassed to ask what was clearly troubling her. "I guess it's a lawyer's job to try to convince the jury his client is innocent even if he's guilty."

Bernstein realized that what she was asking him, and what Leonard and Julius were asking him by the expressions on their faces, was whether he had made fools of them, whether they, with all their earnestness, had been naïve about the innocence of his client.

"It was pathetic the way Mrs. Collins was murdered, but I honestly believe Leander didn't do it," Bernstein said. He knew that many jurors had no idea of how they were looked upon by judges, lawyers, and defendants. He couldn't deny that lawyers try to influence, if not manipulate, the jurors from the moment they step into the courtroom.

"Was there any evidence of guilt that was kept from us?" Leonard asked.

"No," Bernstein said. "You heard all there was. But I honestly think your verdict was the right one." He wanted to reassure them. They didn't need a lecture about how justice in America depends on juries, and he could have told them about other cases he'd tried where he thought the jury had arrived at the wrong verdict.

The elevator arrived at the ground floor. The four of them stepped into the corridor and walked out the front door of the courthouse.

Mike Bernstein had often said that he never got personally involved in his cases, but as he was about to head toward the lawyers' parking lot, he recognized a curious feeling that sometimes came over him at the end of a trial. As the three jurors waved good-bye and walked over to the jurors' parking lot, he felt what could only be described as a sense of loss. He'd lived with these people for three weeks. There was a way in which they knew almost all sides of him as a person. They'd seen him be angry and funny and clever; they'd watched him being rebuked by the judge and riled by Ryan. They'd witnessed his client's touching gratitude at the end. And in a strange way, even though he knew it was completely irrational, he couldn't help feeling that by their verdict they had somehow expressed their approval of him. And if he had a feeling that they knew him, it was also true that in some real way, he knew them. After his constant effort to read them and predict, interpret and influence their every reaction, from a smile or a grimace to a look of strained concentration, he had reached a point at which he had a real sense of each one of them. He felt that he knew them not only individually, but as a group.

Bernstein had noticed that from the moment a jury is sworn in, it takes on a unique identity; it becomes, in effect, a new creature, with its own life. It has been called into existence for a brief moment, for a particular and awesome task—to decide the fate of another human being. To a greater or lesser degree, everyone who is part of this new organism is changed by it.

Maybe Bernstein had been changed a little bit himself. He and the jurors had spent three weeks closeted together in an intense common effort. They would probably never see one another again. He began to understand that the strange sense of loss he was experiencing was linked to the fact that once again an organism with which he had been involved in this intimate way had just ceased to exist.

APPENDIX

The State of Jury Research

OVER THE YEARS, the jury has often been portrayed in popular American literature as a collection of ignorant members of society who allow their personal prejudices and lack of concern to affect their verdicts. Those who have written personal accounts of what it was like to be a juror have described either outrage at having to waste so much time waiting, or their moving experiences trying to "do right."

Films have portrayed juries in a variety of dramatic but unrealistic situations. No case like that of the lone dissenter who turns the jury around in *Twelve Angry Men* ever cropped up in a study of over two thousand juries. Although the southern jury has earned the reputation of never giving a black defendant a chance against the accusation of a white woman, *To Kill a Mockingbird* presented a small-town jury of neighbors overcoming their racial prejudices after a good performance by Gregory Peck, while the town's blacks watched from the courtroom balcony. Woody Allen has shown a jury passing around joints of marijuana in between naps.

Few serious books describing the history or present operation of the jury system have been written in England or the United States. Before the 1950s a number of articles were published in legal periodicals debating the value of the jury, but these dealt only with ways the Constitution or court cases had been, or should have been, interpreted. Aside from individual intuitions or impressions, very little was known about how the jury really worked.

In the 1930s and '40s a handful of studies were published in which researchers interviewed ex-jurors to learn if they had understood the cases and followed the judges' instructions. But these studies were not conducted in any disciplined way: the samples of jurors interviewed were small, the biases of the researchers were evident, and the results were not analyzed with any sophistication.

During World War II, social scientists expert in decision making, statistical analysis, and group dynamics studied human behavior so they could anticipate bombing targets, troop movements, and other strategic decisions of the enemy. When the war was over, a new body of social science knowledge and techniques existed, and a group of skilled experts was in need of a new outlet.

These experts and their progeny turned to the jury as a perfect subject of study. The twelve people on a jury formed a group of manageable size. The very function of the group was to make decisions, and since its members were from a cross section of the population, a variety of attributes influencing their decisions could be isolated and identified. The jury was an important American institution engaged in an important function, and although its worth was much debated, little was really known about juries. The jury was, indeed, an "interesting" target for their skills.

In August 1952 the Ford Foundation gave a $400,000 grant to finance the University of Chicago Jury Project. This study was to become, as its director, Professor Harry Kalven, Jr., predicted, "the most comprehensive study of the workings of the American jury ever undertaken."

By using social science techniques to study the impact of legal rules and institutions, a team composed of roughly equal numbers of lawyers and social scientists was to advance the state of knowledge in the law and behavioral sciences. Working with Professor Kalven in masterminding the project were two distinguished social scientists, Professor Hans Zeisel, former president of the American Statistical Society, and Professor Fred Strodtbeck, an expert on the behavior of small groups.

According to Edward Levi, then dean of the Chicago Law School, the purpose of the project was to "determine to what extent (a) the jury conceives of its functions the same way that the form of law conceives it; (b) the jury comprehends the judge's instructions; (c) the jury's criteria for a verdict are consistent with those laid down by the law; (d) the jury comprehends the evidence in the case; (e) the jury was moved by 'rational' or emotional factors rooted in personality, social background, and the social situation of the courtroom, the jury box, and the jury room discussions."

The project used a variety of investigative techniques: statistical analysis of court records, public opinion surveys, and questionnaires; interviews with jurors after they had served; experimental juries; and recordings of a limited number of actual jury deliberations, intended to provide a practical check of results of the more extensive experimental techniques.

In the fall of 1953 Judge Delmas C. Hill of the United States District Court for the District of Kansas was asked if he would assist in the study by allowing the recording of a limited number of jury deliberations in his court. The judge indicated his willingness provided the approval of the chief judge of his circuit court of appeals was obtained. The chief judge felt that he had no official power to approve the recordings, but he agreed to express his personal opinions concerning the project.

A proposed set of rules governing the procedures and safeguards was formulated: although the Jury Project would later go on to concentrate on the behavior of juries in criminal cases, in the stage when the recordings of deliberations was being planned, only civil cases would be involved; the trial judge's permission would be secured in each case as well as the permission of counsel for both parties including the approval of the U.S. Attorney in any case in which the federal government was a party; no one would be allowed to listen to the deliberations of the jury while they were taking place; the recordings would be kept under lock and key until the case had been decided; the names and identifying features of the jurors and of the case would be altered in the transcriptions so that the privacy of the jurors could be maintained. It was also agreed that a sufficient period of time would elapse before either judge or counsel would have an opportunity to hear the recording or see a transcript of it.

The chief judge felt that, in general, juries should be informed about the recordings, but he said he would not object if a limited number of recordings were made in which the jurors were not informed. Although there was no comparable precedent to the actual recording of jury deliberations, a study had been conducted in 1935 in which observers were planted in jury rooms to determine whether jurors could follow judges' instructions, and this study had provoked no criticism. In 1938 a commission in Pennsylvania had placed dozens of ex-jurors under oath and elicited testimony from them as to what had gone on during their jury deliberations; this, too, had provoked no major criticism.

In the spring of 1954 six civil cases in Wichita, Kansas, were selected for recording. Microphones were hidden behind the heating system in the jury room. For the first time in our country's history, actual jury deliberations were recorded.

In July of that year the solicitor general, an associate justice of the Supreme Court, and some two hundred other lawyers gathered at the annual Judicial Conference of the Tenth Judicial Circuit in Colorado. One of the jury tape recordings—which had been altered to protect the confidentiality of the participants—was played at the conference.

Those in the Jury Project responsible for the recording

naïvely underestimated how protective and sensitive many Americans were about the American jury system. They were also unrealistic about the degree of suspicion that could exist in connection with "academic types," or how much the Mc-Carthy hysteria terrorizing the country at the time could affect the perception of so well-intentioned a project. Since a number of the participants in the Jury Project were Jewish, a layer of anti-Semitism may have been underneath some of the vicious attacks that ensued.

Nothing happened until October, when a story about the recordings appeared in the *Los Angeles Times*. Within a few days articles about the "invasion into the jury room" appeared throughout the country. Virtually all of the stories vehemently condemned the "eavesdropping" on the jury.

On October 5, Attorney General Brownell issued a statement that "the Department of Justice will present for the Congress at the first opportunity a proposed bill to prevent such intrusions upon the privacy of the deliberations of both grand and petit juries of the Court of the United States by any persons whomsoever and by any means whatsoever."

Senator James O. Eastland of Mississippi called for an investigation to see if "the sanctity of the jury room was violated."

On October 12, Assistant Attorney General Warren E. Burger delivered a speech before the Northwest Regional Meeting of the American Bar Association in St. Paul, Minnesota, condemning the recording of the deliberations.

Participants in the Jury Project obtained the endorsements of twenty-seven distinguished lawyers and judges supporting the project. Typical of the endorsements was the statement of Dean Albert J. Harno of the University of Illinois: "I believe the study of the jury system is important and necessary to our understanding and improvement of the administration of justice. Such a study in my opinion necessarily involves a consideration of jury deliberations for the light they are certain to shed on instructions, rules of evidence and other rules of law. I think that a limited body of recordings of actual jury deliberations under the control of the court, with adequate safeguards as to anonymity of the persons and transactions concerned, and with the consent of counsel furnishes an important, useful and proper research tool."

On October 12 and 13 the Subcommittee on Internal Security of the Senate Committee on the Judiciary held an investigation into the "University of Chicago jury-bugging project," as *The New York Times* reported it. Ten witnesses were called including Dean Levi, Professor Kalven, and other participants in the project, as well as those U.S. Attorneys who had given their consent to the recording.

Dean Levi submitted a written statement that was entered into the Congressional Record: "The use of a limited number of actual jury deliberations can contribute to the better understanding of the jury and to the improvement in instructions. By serving to validate other means of study, it can serve to improve the administration of justice so far as the rules of evidence are concerned and the speed with which trials are secured or conducted. It can serve to maintain and to continue a great American institution. This is no doubt the reason that there are distinguished and able leaders of the bar who are in favor of such a study, including the use of a limited number of actual jury deliberations under proper safeguards."

"I'll guarantee that you'll not do any more 'bugging' after Congress has passed some legislation," Senator Eastland, chairman of the subcommittee, told Professor Kalven.

Irving Ferman, Washington director of the American Civil Liberties Union, told the subcommittee, "We plead today that the jury room remain tightly closed forever."

Senator Eastland and Senator William Jenner issued a joint statement at the conclusion of the hearing: "What was done in this Kansas City court constituted, in our separate judgments, flagrant abuse of authority, a violation of the Constitutional guarantee under the Seventh Amendment of the right of trial by jury, and a serious threat to such right for the future so long as there is no guarantee that incidents of this nature will not again take place."

The senators pledged themselves to promote legislation prohibiting eavesdropping on juries, and they referred to the House Judiciary Committee the conduct of the federal judges who had consented to the recordings. Shortly thereafter, federal legislation was passed making the recording of jury deliberations a federal crime. After that, some thirty states enacted similar criminal statutes.

Some twenty years after the Congressional outrage, Dean Levi had become Attorney General of the United States, and Assistant United States Attorney Warren E. Burger had become Chief Justice of the United States. No one I spoke with seemed to remember where the tapes were now located. I asked a former member of the Chicago Jury Project who had heard the actual tape recordings of the jury deliberations what they were like. He told me they were boring.

The Chicago Jury Project continued with its work after the Congressional hearings, but without recording any more deliberations. In 1955 the Ford Foundation gave an additional $1 million so that the Jury Project could continue for another four years. Dozens of important articles were published in legal periodicals using the information gathered from the project, and Kalven and Zeisel authored a seminal book published in 1966 titled *The American Jury,* which has been quoted and relied on by social science and legal scholars as well as by the Supreme Court in a variety of cases. Although *The American Jury* was extensively reviewed in popular magazines, the technical descriptions of its studies make it difficult reading for those untrained or not highly motivated, which explains why it has been largely unread by the general public. Its publisher informed me that only some four thousand copies had been sold.

Since the Chicago Jury Project concluded its work, sociologists and psychologists have studied the jury by conducting more than two hundred experiments and surveys. As a result of these studies, we know more about how the jury functions—how jurors are selected, who they are, and how they reach decisions—than at any time in our history. Most of the social science information in *Anatomy of a Jury* came from the Chicago Jury Project or the work done by its participants in the years after the project was completed.

NOTES

Preface

p. vii The fact that more than 1,200,000 people in America serve on juries every year was found in "Is Our Jury System Working?" by Warren E. Burger, Chief Justice of the United States, *Reader's Digest*, February 1981, p. 126. Obtaining reliable figures of the number of criminal jury trials each year in this country has been difficult. In their book, *The American Jury*, Little, Brown and Company (1966), Kalven and Zeisel estimated that in 1955 there were 2,290 criminal jury trials in federal district courts and 53,380 jury trials in state courts throughout the United States. According to the 1980 annual report of the director of the Administrative Office of the United States Courts, there were 15,649 criminal trials in the ninety-five federal district courts during the year ending June 30, 1980.

p. vii Over the years there have been different kinds of juries. Coroners' juries are summoned to investigate deaths. Sheriffs' juries render verdicts regarding ownership of personal property. Grand juries bring formal criminal charges to which individuals must respond. Statutes sometimes provide for juries in condemnation proceedings. There have even been juries brought together to inquire into the pregnancy of a woman. A jury of matrons was used on rare occasions in America, as they were employed in England at least until 1879, to determine the pregnancy of a woman condemned to death. In *Union P.R. Co. v. Botsford*, 141 U.S. 250, 253 (1890) the Supreme Court said, "The writ de ventre inspiciendo, to ascertain whether a woman convicted of a capital crime was quick with child, was allowed by the common law, in order to guard against the taking of a life of an unborn child for the crime of the mother." It was also used where a woman who married soon after the death of her husband asserted pregnancy by him as reason for withholding land from the next heir.

Surprisingly little is known with certainty about the history of the jury. When one considers all the possible different origins, the most likely conclusion is that the jury system as we know it probably developed from a variety of sources over a period of time.

The Supreme Court has avoided the disputes about the jury's origin by simply announcing that the facts have too often been told to need repeating. *Duncan* v. *Louisiana*, 391 U.S. 145, 151 (1968). The "facts" as they have been set out by historians are a mass of contradictions and implausible conjectures based on obscure sources.

One source of disagreement over the origin of the jury stems from the lack of agreement about what is meant by a jury. Some historians have taken the position that any group that decided the guilt of one accused of a crime was a jury.

Under this broadest definition, the Athenian Code made all citizens of ancient Greece eligible as jurors. Six thousand were annually chosen by lot and placed on a list from which as many as twelve hundred were drawn onto a panel and from which a jury of sorts was summoned. Socrates was tried by an assembly of five hundred who were judges of the law and the facts, and the verdict of the majority was all that was required.

In Rome under both the republic and the empire a permanent jury list of usually 850 names was compiled of senators or men owning a designated amount of property. A praetor (magistrate) would select between 51 and 75 to sit as a trial body, from which a majority would determine the verdict.

According to William Forsyth, a well-respected historian who wrote a history of the jury in 1852, a defining characteristic of the jury system was that it consisted of a body of men summoned from the community at large who, as distinct from law judges, were charged with the responsibility to find the truth of disputed facts in order that the law may be properly applied by the court. Under this definition there were modes of trial in use in England, but trial by jury was unknown to the Anglo-Saxons before William the Conqueror. W. Forsyth, *History of Trial by Jury* (1852).

It appears undisputed that William introduced to England the practice of the "inquisito," a prerogative of the Frankish kings since the ninth century, by which the king, at his pleasure, called together a group of men familiar with certain facts, and had them make declarations about ownership of land, taxes, the conduct of suspected royal officers, or of crimes or conspiracies against him or the public peace. An inquisito, under William's direction, compiled an extensive tax roll in 1086 called the "Doomsday Book," which was a collection of "dooms," or judgments, concerning the ownership of property. According to some historians, the Frankish inquisito "as expanded and developed in England by William and his northern successors, was the germ of the modern trial jury." F. X. Busch, *Law and Tactics in Jury Trials,* Encyclopedia Edition Vol. 1 (1959), p. 5.

On Friday, June 19, 1215, thirteen barons and twelve bishops confronted King John at Runnymede to compel, among other things, his assurances that the jurisdiction of his common law courts would not apply to them. Chapter 39 of the Magna Carta, after being translated from the Latin, reads:

> No freeman shall be arrested, or detained in prison, or deprived of his freehold, or outlawed, or banished, or in any way molested; and we will not set forth against him, nor send against him, unless by the lawful judgment of his peers and by the law of the land.

Pointing to the reference to peers, many writers over the years have mistakenly called the Magna Carta the fundamental document that codified the right of Englishmen to a jury trial (Albert Q. Maisel, "The Right to Trial by Jury," *Reader's Digest,* January 1963, p. 121), but later historians are convinced that that document had nothing to do with a jury. The common law judges, men of a lower status than peers of the barons, had been appointed and removed at the will of the king. Not surprisingly, the barons wanted to be judged in their own courts. The phrase in the Magna Carta about a judgment of peers did not grant a right of trial by jury to Englishmen. Rather than a guarantee of equality, the provision granted a special privilege to the barons that they be tried by men of their own order, their peers, and not merely by a king's justice. The nature of the trial to determine his rights was by ordeal (F. Frankfurter and T. Corcoran, "Petty Federal Offenses and Trial by Jury," 39 *Harvard Law Review* 917, 923 [1926]) or, in the more common manner, by battle (W. Clark, "Magna Carta and Trial by Jury," 58 *American Law Review* 23, 30 [1928]).

According to some writers the first jury trial as we now know it took place in England in the year 1351. Others claim that by the time of the reign of Henry VI (1422–1461), the jury trial had become the established method of disposing of civil and criminal disputes, replacing the nonrational alternatives such as trial by ordeal or battle. H. Kalven and H. Zeisel, "Jury," *Encyclopaedia Britannica.*

"To the Englishman of the 1500's it had already become an 'ancient prerogative' to have twelve laymen stand between him and the vengeance of the king in a criminal prosecution of any kind, whether the charge was tippling at the inn or murder." F. Frankfurter and T. Corcoran, "Petty Federal Offenses and Trial by Jury," 39 *Harvard Law Review* 917, 923 (1926).

p. vii "The lamp that shows that freedom lives": P. Devlin, *Trial by Jury* (1956), p. 164. "A palladium of liberty": W. Blackstone, 4 *Commentaries on the Laws of England,* 350 (Cooley ed., 1899). A "touchstone" ensuring our peace and safety: Thomas Jefferson quoted in "The Jury System on Trial," *Senior Scholastic,* March 20, 1964, p. 8. That some critics viewed the jury as "dolts" was recognized by Fletcher Knebel in a review of *The American Jury* in the August 23, 1966, issue of *Look* magazine, p. 75.

Part One: Who Shall Judge Me?

CHAPTER I

pp. 9–10 H. Kalven and H. Zeisel found that the insanity defense was raised in less than 2 percent of all criminal cases. *The American Jury* (1966), p. 330. Juries hear confessions at trial in about a fifth of all cases—almost half the homicide but virtually none of the narcotics cases. Kalven and Zeisel, *The American Jury,* p. 143. A 1982 National Institute of Justice study found that prosecutors in California rejected only 0.8 percent of 520,993 reported felony arrests because of potential search and seizure problems. T. Davies, *National Law Journal,* March 19, 1984, p. 12.

p. 12 Some 15 percent to 30 percent of the people who are sent questionnaires have died, moved, or otherwise do not respond. The percentage of those who do respond varies in different parts of the country, and what happens to those who do not respond varies widely. Dallas has no follow-up program, while Asheville, North Carolina, pursues all of its nonresponsive jurors. M. Graham and R. Pope, "One Day/One Trial or a One-Week Term of Jury Service: The Misleading Marketing of Modern Jury Management Systems," 45 *Missouri Law Review* 255, 266 (1980). Pittsburgh increased responses significantly by a widely publicized crackdown on a few nonresponsive jurors. Clerks sending follow-up letters to those in Honolulu who did not answer questionnaires raised the rate of completed questionnaires from approximately 80 percent to 96 percent. J. Van Dyke, *Jury Selection Procedures: Our Uncertain Commitment to Representative Panels,* Ballantine Publishing Company, Cambridge, Massachusetts (1977), pp. 133–34, and Graham and Pope, "One Day/One Trial or a One-Week Term of Jury Service: The Misleading Marketing of Modern Jury Management Systems," 45 *Missouri Law Review* 255, 269 (1980).

Since the percentage of returns from different groups varies, the profile of the jury pools is affected by the simple function of who returns the questionnaire. Because of feelings of alienation or intimidation, the poor, the less educated, and minorities respond at a significantly lower rate than others. Young people respond less than the general population because they are more mobile and less likely to have received the questionnaire in the first place. D. Zeigler, "Young Adults as a Cognizable Group in Jury Selection," 76 *Michigan Law Review* 1045, 1047 (1978).

Various studies of responses to questionnaires are reported in W. Macauley and E. Heubel, "Achieving Representative Juries: A System That Works," 65 *Judicature* 126 (1981), and H. Alker, Hasticka, and Mitchell, "Jury Selection as a Biased Social Process: The Case of Eastern Massachusetts," 9 *Law and Society* 41 (Fall 1976). The most interesting analysis was done by Hans Zeisel when he compared the way the state and federal courts in the Chicago area handled responses to questionnaires. H. Zeisel, "The American Jury," 7 Earl Warren Conference (1977).

p. 17 Some thirty-two states grant exemptions from jury service to those in certain professions: people working for the police, fire department, fish or game wardens, physicians, dentists, schoolteachers during the school year, those with custody of a minor child, telephone or telegraph operators, members of first-aid squads or the state legislature, or anyone employed in the administration of justice. In federal court, people over seventy, active ministers and the members of religious orders, men or women with daily care of a child under twelve, active lawyers, law students, physicians, dentists, and registered nurses can be excused permanently from jury duty if they wish.

The "class" exemptions from jury service are a reflection of the importance a state attaches to certain occupations. Other assumptions underlie other exemptions: people such as lawyers or police officers might wield a disproportionate influence on their fellow jurors; police officers and clergy might, simply because of their occupation, have a prejudice about a defendant's guilt or innocence.

Although the employment exemptions may have once reflected the peculiar needs of particular states, they now constitute anachronisms with little relevance to today's world. Allowing fish and game wardens to escape jury duty may have seemed plausible to the New Jersey legislators who enacted the exemption eighty years ago, but it is hard to jusify their continued exemption. Virginia tobacco farmers are exempted during harvest time; in Indiana ferryboat operators are excused. Until recently, stagecoach drivers were exempt by law from jury duty in Fairfax County, Virginia.

Exemptions and excuses can reduce the total percentage of qualified jurors substantially: the figures vary from 10 percent to 40 percent. Center for Jury Studies, *Methodology Manual for Jury Systems* 4–4 (1979). The number of people exempted would not be important in obtaining a fair cross section of the community if the reductions were in the same proportion for all groups. But they are not, and the representativeness of jury panels is distorted as a result. Until the early 1970s, women, for example, were exempt from jury duty in New York City unless they volunteered, and the result, according to a study by the New York Supreme Court, was that 88 percent of all jurors were men.

Excusing doctors, lawyers, teachers, and other professionals produces juries with fewer people with a postgraduate education than would have been produced from a random sample of the general population. Besides a lower level of education, the absence of professionals also implies a lower socioeconomic group of qualified jurors.

"Although the elimination of occupational exemptions might further weight the jury pool in favor of white, middle-aged, higher-income males, the elimination of all excuses except hardship should increase the proportion of blacks, women, blue-collar workers, the young, the old, and the poor on the jury list. Implicit in the idea of limiting excuses to hardship alone is the need to examine excuse requests closely. Where a request, even for hardship, really appears to focus on the inconvenience or imposition caused by a certain date, a postponement rather than excuse should be granted. A liberal postponement policy can accomplish the twin goals of enhancing community participation and increasing citizen satisfaction in the criminal justice system." H. Dogin and D. Tevelin, "Jury Selection in the Eighties: Toward a Fairer Cross Section and Increased Efficiency," 11 *University of Toledo Law Review* 939, 955 (1980).

The American Bar Association Committee on Jury Standards recommended the elimination of all exemptions for any class, and twenty states and a few localities have done so. Several other states provide for only a few exemptions such as for members of the legal profession or the armed services.

p. 22 Most states exclude felons from jury duty in the belief that most felons "might well harbor a continuing resentment against 'the system' that punished them or hold an equally unthinking bias in favor of the defendant on trial." *Rubio* v. *Superior Court of San Joaquin,* 24 Cal. 3d 93, 593 P.2d 595 (1979).

Some people have argued that people merely accused of committing a crime should be ineligible for jury duty on the same grounds as those who are convicted. In fact anyone with a pending criminal charge is disqualified from federal jury service. But since a person accused of a crime is presumed to be innocent, to disqualify him from jury service because of a pending prosecution is a denial of that presumption. The issue is more academic than real, because even if he is not disqualified by law, the lawyers, if they learn about the pending charge, will probably excuse him when the particular jury is selected.

Vague phrases about good character have been used, particularly in the South, to exclude blacks from the jury rolls. These subjective standards are like the literacy tests that were used to disenfranchise black voters. The Supreme Court, however, has not regarded such terms as unconstitutionally vague, but has required proof that they were used as a pretext to discriminate against a class of citizens. *Turner* v. *Fouche,* 396 U.S. 346 (1970). But according to Judge Irving R. Kaufman, the chairman of the federal judiciary's committee on the operation of the jury system, discrimination and arbitrariness can result even when the jury officials use these subjective standards in good faith.

Most people, particularly citizens, unquestioningly assume that jury duty should be the exclusive privilege and responsibility of citizens. But juries without aliens means that those juries do not entirely reflect a cross section of the community, especially in jurisdictions with large resident alien populations.

Nowadays, not only is citizenship essential, so is residence. The federal government and a number of states demand that a juror be a resident for one year, and some states such as New Jersey require two years.

The minimum residence requirement has been supported as ensuring a substantial connection between the juror and the community whose sense of justice the jury as a whole is expected to reflect. It seems clear, however, that people new to a community are just as much a part of that community as long-term residents, and they also have a valid point of view on its activities.

The residence requirement affects certain classes in our society more than others. While our society has generally become mobile, some groups, like the poor, the young, and blacks, are more mobile than others, and as a result of this mobility the jury selection process is less inclusive. A study in the eastern part of Massachusetts found 41 percent fewer blacks on juries than justified by their population, and attributed this discrepancy, at least in part, to the residency requirement in the voter registration lists and the higher mobility of blacks. Alker, Hasticka, and Mitchell, "Jury Selection as a Biased Social Process: The Case of Eastern Massachusetts," 9 *Law and Society* 41 (Fall 1976).

p. 25 Some states now allow the deaf or the blind to sit on a jury, and several blind persons and a deaf person assisted by a signer have served on civil juries in Seattle, Washington. *Trial,* "California Law Allows Deaf Jurors," November 1980, p. 14. Texas, Illinois, Maryland, Michigan, Florida, Kentucky, and Oregon have also permitted deaf people to serve as jurors. W. Barrett, "The Deaf Deserve to Serve," *The Village Voice,* May 29, 1984, p. 5. But it appears that most lawyers would excuse the handicapped. "Should Deaf, Blind Serve as Jurors?" 66 *American Bar Association Journal* 133 (1980).

In 1979 a woman who was a deaf-mute brought a lawsuit in Arkansas to try to be declared eligible for jury duty. A federal district judge rejected her application on the grounds that jury service was "primarily for the benefit of the litigant—not persons seeking service on the jury." "Should Deaf, Blind Serve as Jurors?" 66 *ABA Journal* 133 (1980).

The law is in a state of flux regarding the eligibility of the disabled. Nearly thirty states have laws specifically prohibiting the deaf and others not in possession of the "natural faculties" from serving on juries. The federal courts and the states of Washington and Massachusetts leave the issue up to the discretion of the individual judges. In the late 1970s California led the country when it allowed the blind and the deaf to be included on the jury lists, although lawyers can excuse them from a particular case. "California Law Allows Deaf Jurors," *Trial*, November 1980, p. 14.

An additional problem for the deaf is the fact that for more than four hundred years jury deliberations have been conducted in secret, with no one but the twelve jurors being permitted in the jury room. If there is a blind or deaf juror, a "thirteenth person" must be allowed into the jury room to interpret and make it possible for him to take into consideration what the other jurors say and allow the other jurors to know what the handicapped juror has in mind. "Should Deaf, Blind Serve as Jurors?" 66 *ABA Journal* 133 (1980).

Some, like Stanley Flashman, a Los Angeles attorney who has represented handicapped people who have sought the right to serve as jurors, have argued that the handicapped compensate for their disability with their keener, remaining senses. The blind may hear in the inflection of a voice or the deaf may notice in the body language of a gesture something that betrays a lie that the nonhandicapped misses altogether. "Should Deaf, Blind Serve as Jurors?" 66 *ABA Journal* 133 (1980).

pp. 25–26 The information about a juror's pay comes from No. 2 *Center for Jury Studies Newsletter*, 6 (March 1980). The small fees mean that few people making more than the minimum wage can afford the low income imposed by jury service. As a result, many jurisdictions excuse laborers, sales people, and sole proprietors of small businesses on the basis of economic hardship. Only those with an employer who will continue to pay their salary can participate in jury service without a major economic sacrifice. This reduces the representativeness of the jury pool and transfers a significant portion of the costs of public service to private industry. The overwhelming majority of major labor agreements include a provision for payment for jury leave. It has been estimated that as much as 68 percent of the jury system costs are being absorbed by private industry. No. 2 *Center for Jury Studies Newsletter*, 6 (March 1980), p. 2; *Lewis* v. *United States*, 146 U.S. 370, 378 (1892).

p. 26 Jurors are compensated $200 million annually, and their absence from work costs the nation an estimated $1 billion. "We, the Jury, Find . . . ," *Time*, September 28, 1981, p. 44.

p. 27 In the 1970s people between 21 and 25 constituted 13 percent of the population but made up only 3 percent of the jurors, according to a study by the New York Supreme Court.

The discrimination of the young begins at the beginning of the process and continues at every stage. Six states require jurors to be older than 18 years of age, and in some states the minimum age is 25. Even if allowed by statute, young people are underrepresented on the jury rolls based on voter lists; 59 percent of persons aged 18–24 are registered to vote as compared to 80 percent of those aged 55–64. U.S. Bureau of the Census, *Current Population Reports,* Series P-20, No. 253, "Voting and Registration and the Election of November 1972" (1973).

The maintenance of permanent juror lists adds to the underrepresentation of the young. Each federal district, for example, maintains the same juror lists for up to four years, which means that people 18 to 21 are totally excluded from service by the lists' fourth year of use. D. Zeigler, "Young Adults as a Cognizable Group in Jury Selection," 76 *Michigan Law Review* 1045, 1046–1047 (1978).

From the point of view of the lawyers picking jurors, a person's age affects his perceptions of and attitudes toward such things as law and order. Young people are less likely than older people to think law enforcement agencies should be tougher than they are now in dealing with crime and lawlessness; in one study, some 66 percent of those between 18 and 20 favored tougher enforcement, while 85 percent of those over 50 held that opinion. M. Hindelang, M. Gottfredson, C. Dunn, and N. Parisi, *Source Book of Criminal Justice Statistics* (1976).

p. 28 Twenty-one states prohibit people beyond a certain age, generally sixty-five or seventy. Van Dyke, *Jury Selection Procedures: Our Uncertain Commitment to Representative Panels,* Appendix A; and W. Macauley and E. Heubel, "Achieving Representative Juries: A System That Works," 65 *Judicature* 126, 133 (1981).

p. 28 Sixteen states in New England and the South use the once more popular "key-man" system. H. Dogin and D. Tevelin, "Jury Selection in the Eighties: Toward a Fairer Cross Section and Increased Efficiency," 11 *University of Toledo Law Review* 939 (1980).

p. 28 The "key-man method has often produced social peers of the commissioners." I. Kaufman, "A Fair Trial—The Essence of Justice," 51 *Judicature* 88 (1967).

p. 28 The 1968 federal legislation that replaced key men with voter lists is called the Jury Selection and Service Act, which was passed to guarantee a trial by a fair and impartial jury in the federal district courts. The Act prohibits discrimination in jury service on the basis of race, color, religion, sex, national origin, or economic status. The Act also specifies how a random jury is to be chosen. Each federal district court is to compose its own plan under the guidelines set forth in the Act. The basic source of names for jurors must be either a voter registration or actual voting list. If there is any reason to believe that these lists are not sufficiently representative, they must be supplemented from other sources. Names must be selected randomly from these lists and put in a master jury wheel from which names are randomly drawn for jury service. The wheel itself must be refilled at least every four years.

The Jury Selection and Service Act was necessary, in part, to replace the key-man system of obtaining federal juries. "If [the jury's] composition is a sham, its judgment is a sham. And when that happens justice itself is a fraud, casting off the blindfold and tipping the scales one way for whites and another way for Negroes." So said President Johnson in support of the Act. "Juries: Cornerstone or Millstone to Justice?" *Senior Scholastic,* January 7, 1966, p. 18.

Some critics opposed the new federal legislation, arguing that too many cases were too technical, too complex for the average or below-average intelligence of most jurors. The new law required only a minimum test of literacy and knowledge of English. "The idea apparently being that the jury system has long rested its ultimate faith in man's common sense, a quality that is not necessarily limited to the educated." "Everyman on Juries," *Time,* March 29, 1968, p. 68.

p. 29 Less than three quarters of eligible voters in 1984 were registered—in some states the level was below 60 percent. *1985 Statistical Abstract of the United States,* U.S. Government Printing Office. "And those who do register are not a random group: whites, the middle-aged, and the better educated are overrepresented, while nonwhites, the poor, the young, the old, and the less educated are underrepresented." H. Dogin and D. Tevelin, "Jury Selection in the Eighties: Toward a Fairer Cross Section and Increased Efficiency," 11 *University of Toldeo Law Review* 939 (1980).

The studies showing the percentages of people who do not vote in order to avoid jury duty are cited in "The Constitutionality of Calling Jurors Exclusively From Voter Registration Lists," 55 *New York University Law Review* 1266, 1268–9 (1980), and are referring to a survey published on January 9, 1977, in the *Los Angeles Times* of 253 unregistered voters and a 1980 Eagleton Institute of Rutgers University survey of 118 unregistered voters. If the threat of jury duty deters 5 percent of potential voters in states that call jurors exclusively from voting rolls, the number of eligible voters deterred exceeds 750,000. Note, "The Constitutionality of Calling Jurors Exclusively from Voter Registration Lists," 55 *N.Y.U. Law Review,* 1266 (1980).

p. 29 Voter lists are defended on the grounds that they screen out incompetent jurors by eliminating those unqualified to vote or without sufficient interest in the world around them to do so. The voter list is an inexpensive, readily available source of names compiled without anyone deliberately trying to discriminate against any class, and those who choose to stay away from the political process, it is argued, should forfeit their right to serve on juries. Alker, Hasticka, and Mitchell, "Jury Selection as a Biased Social Process: The Case of Eastern Massachusetts," 9 *Law and Society* 41, 237 (Fall 1976) and J. Ashby, "Juror Selection and the Sixth Amendment Right to an Impartial Jury," 11 *Creighton Law Review* 1137, 1148 (1970).

But if a defendant does not get a fair trial or if certain groups in our society do not get the same opportunity to be part of juries, whether the voter lists discriminate intentionally or unintentionally is irrelevant. By ignoring the biases of the voter lists, the courts have allowed the theory behind the key-man system to be reintroduced: only those people with an "interest" in society should make decisions affecting it.

No evidence demonstrates that nonvoting citizens would be less competent as jurors than those who do vote. Nonvoters should have the same rights and they certainly do have the same burdens as citizens, such as paying taxes and being drafted, that voters enjoy. Alker, Hasticka, and Mitchell, "Jury Selection as a Biased Social Process: The Case of Eastern Massachusetts," 9 *Law and Society* 41, 235–236 (Fall 1976) and J. Barnard, "Procedural and Social Biases in the Jury Selection Process," 3 *Justice System Journal* 220 (1978).

According to a 1982 report of the Committee on Jury Standards of the American Bar Association, practical limitations make it impossible to compile lists that include 100 percent of the eligible population, and experts believe 85 percent would be a reasonable goal. H. Dogin and D. Tevelin point out in "Jury Selection in the Eighties: Toward a Fairer Cross Section and Increased Efficiency," 11 *University of Toledo Law Review* 939 (1980), that with 84 percent of the driving-age population in the United States licensed to drive, the lists of drivers offer a simple way to draw more people into the pool.

Some of the proposed supplementary lists have serious drawbacks. Women, minorities, the young, and the poor are underrepresented, for example, from real estate and income tax lists. J. Ashby, "Juror Selection and the Sixth Amendment Right to an Impartial Jury," 11 *Creighton Law Review* 1137, 1150 (1970). Federal Judge Alfred C. Hagan of Boise, Idaho, has recommended that lists indigenous to the local populations be used such as tribal rolls in areas containing Indian reservations and employee lists in areas containing large migrant worker populations. Quoted in Van Dyke, *Jury Selection Procedures: Our Uncertain Commitment to Representative Panels,* p. 104.

p. 29 According to the September 28, 1981, issue of *Time* ("We, the Jury, Find . . ." p. 44), over three million people are summoned every year in America to jury duty. In New York, where jury delinquency can draw a $250 fine or five days in jail, a full 20 percent of those summoned never reply. "It's bad publicity to prosecute," New York Court Clerk Norman Goodman admitted, "and besides, the number of delinquents is too large and the court staff too small." "Twelve Missing Men," *Newsweek,* June 10, 1968, p. 58.

The United States census, which theoretically includes all citizens, has been suggested as a primary source for the jury rolls. Legislation would be required to allow the census to be used for other than demographic purposes, and critics of this alternative make the same argument as those opposed to using voter lists: if the burden of jury service were attached to giving information to census-takers, fewer citizens might cooperate. J. Ashby, "Juror Selection and the Sixth Amendment Right to an Impartial Jury," 11 *Creighton Law Review* 1137, 1150 (1970). In some Massachusetts towns the police conduct an annual door-to-door census to compile a list of residents for their jury pool, but this kind of survey is expensive. Van Dyke, *Jury Selection Procedures: Our Uncertain Commitment to Representative Panels,* p. 100.

pp. 29–30 The United States Supreme Court stopped the Georgia practice of placing the names of white potential jurors on white cards and the names of blacks on yellow cards in 1953. *Avery* v. *Georgia,* 345 U.S. 559 (1953).

p. 30 The Supreme Court referred to the absence of women on juries as the loss of "a flavor, a distinct quality," in *Ballard* v. *United States,* 319 U.S. 187, 193 (1943).

p. 30 A thorough discussion of how the various age groups differ in important attitudes can be found in D. Zeigler, "Young Adults as a Cognizable Group in Jury Selection," 76 *Michigan Law Review* 1045, 1075 (1978).

p. 30 According to a 1972 Gallup poll 44 percent of those between 18 and 24 opposed the death penalty, while only 27 percent of those over 50 opposed it. Van Dyke, *Jury Selection Procedures: Our Uncertain Commitment to Representative Panels,* p. 38.

p. 31 On April 10, 1201, King John signed a charter giving Jews on trial the right to have juries composed of equal numbers of Jews and Christians. L. LaRue, "A Jury of One's Peers," 33 *Washington and Lee Law Review* 841 (1976). During the late 1600s Indians were added to juries of English settlers at the Plymouth Colony in Massachusetts in cases involving the natives. Van Dyke, *Jury Selection Procedures: Our Uncertain Commitment to Representative Panels,* p. 10.

p. 31 The Supreme Court case that discussed mixed juries was *Virginia* v. *Rives,* 100 U.S. 313 (1880).

pp. 31–32 The various cases in which mixed juries were involved is discussed in L. LaRue, "A Jury of One's Peers," 33 *Washington and Lee Law Review* 841 (1976).

p. 32 The Supreme Court rejected the arguments of a woman convicted of murdering her husband that she had been denied a fair trial because her jury had been all male in the case of *Hoyt* v. *Florida,* 368 U.S. 57 (1961).

CHAPTER II

p. 37 In most instances where a person has a right to be tried by a jury, he also has two ways to waive that right. A defendant can choose to be tried by a judge without a jury in what is sometimes called a bench trial. He could also plead guilty to the charges or, if the prosecutor agrees, enter into plea bargain by which he would plead guilty to some lesser charge.

The Supreme Court has ruled that the Constitution's provisions for a jury were not intended to establish a tribunal that could be forced on a defendant; those provisions were intended as a valuable privilege bestowed on the person accused of the crime for the purpose of safeguarding him against the oppressive power of an overzealous or corrupt prosecutor or judge. In light of this it seemed reasonable to the Supreme Court to conclude that a prosecutor cannot waive the jury without the consent of the defendant, and unless there was some compelling reason otherwise, this protection of the accused could be waived by him.

To waive his trial by jury, a defendant must convince a judge that he has been advised by counsel of his rights, or if he is without counsel, he must demonstrate that his waiver is voluntary and based on an understanding of the nature and consequences of his act. The defendant's intelligence, occupation, education, and comprehension of the seriousness of his position are all factors that are considered to determine whether he knows what he is doing. The defendant must personally express his desire to waive the jury in open court; a statement by his lawyer is insufficient.

Once a defendant has waived a jury, a judge, in his discretion, may permit him to withdraw that waiver and reinstate the case for a jury trial. Usually a judge will allow a defendant to change his mind and withdraw his waiver of a jury if it doesn't substantially delay the trial.

The Supreme Court has ruled that a person cannot be coerced into waiving his right to a jury. In a 1968 case, a defendant charged under the Federal Kidnapping Act moved to have the charge against him dismissed on the grounds that the Act made the risk of death the price of exercising his constitutional right to a jury. The Act was worded in such a way that no death sentence could be imposed except by a jury. Waiver of a jury trial thus guaranteed that the maximum penalty would be life imprisonment. The Supreme Court agreed with the defendant and held the federal statute unconstitutional. *United States* v. *Jackson* 390 U.S. 570 (1968).

Whether or not to waive a jury is often a difficult decision for a defendant to make. Obviously, defendants choose jury trials in those instances where they think they would be better off than with a judge. There is an old piece of lawyer's advice: if not guilty, be tried by a judge; if guilty, be tried by a jury. In some cases, a cynical opinion of a jury's intelligence or their ability to be swayed by emotion may incline a lawyer with a clearly guilty client to rely on a jury.

p. 39 The jury trial in England in the fifteenth century had all the essential features of what now exists with one exception: today, prospective jurors would be excused from serving on a case if they knew any of the parties or witnesses involved in the case. Jurors then were not neutral judges of disputes; they were witnesses who knew the parties and decided cases on the basis of the reputation of the parties and facts they already knew.

It may have been as early as the year 1200 that if the authorities felt that a jury had reached an improper decision, they would convene a second jury to convict the first panel of "attaint," the crime of having been false witnesses who had rendered a false verdict. The penalty was often the forfeiture of their property and liberty. W. Blackstone, 4 *Commentaries on the Laws of England* (Cooley ed., 1899), p. 349; Justice William Douglas in his dissenting opinion in *McKeiver* v. *Pennsylvania,* 403 U.S. 528, 563 (1970).

By the late Middle Ages during the reign of Edward III, as society became more complex and jurors were less likely to have sufficient personal knowledge of the parties or the disputes, judges began to allow witnesses to testify in court. With the arrival of witnesses came the need for rules of evidence to determine what would be proper testimony, what would or would not be admissible to determine guilt. But it was not until the reign of George III at around the time of the American Revolution that the practice was abandoned where jurors should "not be wholly strangers to the fact." F. X. Busch, *Law and Tactics in Jury Trials,* Encyclopedia Edition Vol. 1 (1959), p. 10. The principle was established that only jurors without personal knowledge of the facts or the parties should sit on a case. W. R. Cornish, *The Jury* (1968), p. 12.

p. 40 According to the Declaration of Independence one of the reasons for separating from England was that George III made

"Judges dependent on his Will alone, for the tenure of their offices, and the amount and payment of salaries," and "depriving us in many cases, of the benefits of Trial by Jury."

Those who opposed the Constitution's adoption argued that the proposed words regarding jury trials would allow secret trials, or indefinite postponements to suit the purposes of the government, or the transfer of the trial to a state or district other than where the crime was committed. Jefferson insisted on a "bill of rights," and in a letter to James Madison he proposed an amendment providing for "trial by juries in all matters of fact triable by the law of the land."

The framers of the Constitution claimed that the general language of the original draft—which said that the trial of all crimes be by jury—was intended to cover all the guarantees demanded by the opponents, but they agreed to spell out the details in an amendment. Madison used the words of the Virginia Constitution that spoke of "all criminal prosecutions," and that was the language eventually adopted in the Sixth Amendment. The focus of the Sixth Amendment was not about the *right* to a jury trial, but about the details surrounding that right. There is no evidence that the scope of the rights protected by the Sixth Amendment increased what had already been included by implication in Article III. F. Frankfurter and T. Corcoran, "Petty Federal Offenses and Trial by Jury," 39 *Harvard Law Review* 917, 971 (1926).

p. 41 The Supreme Court case that concluded that states may have juries made up of less than twelve members was *Williams* v. *Florida,* 399 U.S. 78 (1970), and the cases that found that less than unanimous verdicts are permissible were *Johnson* v. *Louisiana,* 406 U.S. 356 (1972), and *Apodaca* v. *Oregon,* 406 U.S. 404 (1972).

p. 41 The 1968 case that ruled that a jury trial was constitutionally required in all criminal cases in which the penalty could exceed six months was *Duncan* v. *Louisiana,* 391 U.S. 145 (1968).

p. 42 The American Bar Association Committee on Jury Standards recommended that an individual who is so mentally retarded so as to be unable to receive and assess the evidence and arguments and participate in the deliberations with other jury members should be excused, and such a person should be excused only by a judge. The only other basis of excuse recommended by the committee was if the person had service within the previous twenty-four months as a juror. The last grounds for excuse would be that the jury service would cause a genuine personal hardship either to the individual requesting the excuse or to members of the public whom that individual serves. Few courts have uniform guidelines with specific criteria to govern the granting of excuses. As a result, many permit excuses on ad hoc bases leading to a great lack of uniformity.

p. 42 The prospective juror who reported to a San Francisco court toting two birdcages containing twenty canaries was described in "Twelve Missing Men," *Newsweek,* June 10, 1968, p. 58.

p. 47 Statistics show that the higher the chance of a jury's acquitting, the less likely it is that the defendant will plead guilty. Manslaughter and assault, for example, rank high as trials leading to acquittals, 46 percent and 37 percent, and rank low as crimes where defendants plead guilty, 52 percent and 56 percent. On the other hand, crimes like burglary and forgery have the lowest odds of an acquittal, 22 percent and 15 percent, and they rank highest in percentage of guilty pleas, 82 percent and 90 percent.

Plea bargaining has been the principal means of settling criminal cases since the mid-1800s, and today defendants in about three quarters of all cases plead guilty to something rather than face a jury. Less than 10 percent of all felony charges and an even smaller percentage of misdemeanor charges are tried before a jury. C. Silberman, *Criminal Violence, Criminal Justice,* Random House (1978), pp. 376–81.

"If the case against the defendant has overwhelming evidence and it is clear that the defendant will draw a long prison term, whether by conviction after a trial or by pleading guilty, then the defendant has little to risk in going to trial, since there is always a possibility, some possibility, of acquittal. In general, therefore, the more serious the offense, the larger proportion of cases that go to trial." Silberman, *Criminal Violence, Criminal Justice,* p. 382.

p. 49 Almost a quarter of the people called for jury duty every year never wind up serving on an actual jury, and 80 percent of the prospective jurors summoned to the courthouse have never served on jury duty. N. Lewis, W. Bundy, and J. Hague, *An Introduction to the Courts and the Judicial Process* (1978), pp. 202–3.

p. 52 According to some experts the optimum use of juror time that can be expected for the continuous operation of the courts is regarded at about 70 percent. M. Graham and R. Pope, "One Day/One Trial or a One-Week Term of Jury Service: The Misleading Marketing of Modern Jury Management Systems," 45 *Missouri Law Review* 255, 270 (1980).

p. 52 The usefulness of a jury waiting in the wings is discussed in F. Merill and L. Schrage, "A Pilot Study of Utilization of Jurors," quoted by M. Graham and R. Pope, "One Day/One Trial or a One-Week Term of Jury Service: The Misleading Marketing of Modern Jury Management Systems," 45 *Missouri Law Review* 255, 258 (1980).

pp. 53–54 In 1961 the United States Commission on Civil Rights reported that total or partial exclusion of blacks from jury service was commonplace in America. The same commission concluded in 1970 that "serious and widespread underrepresentation of Mexican-Americans on grand and petit juries existed in state courts in many areas of the Southwest. H. Alker, Hasticka, and Mitchell, "Jury Selection as a Biased Social Process: The Case of Eastern Massachusetts," 9 *Law and Society* 41 (Fall 1976).

The Supreme Court ruled in 1880 that excluding blacks from juries endangered the defendant's right to a fair trial. "It is well known that prejudices often exist against particular classes in the community, which sway the judgment of jurors, and which, therefore, operate in some cases to deny persons of those classes the full enjoyment of that protection which others enjoy." *Strauder* v. *West Virginia*, 100 U.S. 303, 309 (1880). The Court said it would not limit its ruling only to cases involving blacks. "Nor if a law should be passed excluding all naturalized Celtic Irishmen [from jury service], would there be any doubt of its inconsistency with the spirit of the Fourteenth Amendment [which gave all citizens the right to the equal protection of the law]. *Strauder* v. *West Virginia*, 100 U.S. 303, 310 (1880).

The Court also maintained that the particular black defendant was not the only one injured by West Virginia's blatant discrimination. To deny "the privilege of participating equally in the administration of justice" stigmatized the entire excluded group by implying they were unfit for service. It was "practically a brand upon them . . . an assertion of their inferiority." *Strauder* v. *West Virginia*, 100 U.S. 303, 308 (1880).

A state was still allowed, under the Court's ruling, to make discriminations so long as they didn't violate the equal protection clause of the Fourteenth Amendment. A state "may confine the selection to males, to freeholders, to citizens, to persons within certain ages and to persons having educational qualifications. We do not believe the Fourteenth Amendment was ever intended to prohibit this." *Strauder* v. *West Virginia*, 100 U.S. 303, 308 (1880).

In 1946 the Supreme Court sustained the challenge to the jury selection procedures in the Southern District of California on the grounds that women were being systematically excluded. Without requiring proof, the Court assumed that women were a cognizable group sharing distinct attitudes and perspectives, and the male defendant in that case did not have to prove actual prejudice because "the injury is not limited to the defendant—there is injury to the jury system, to the law as an institution, to the community at large, and to the democratic ideal reflected in the process of our courts." *Ballard* v. *United States*, 329 U.S. 187, 193–194 (1946).

In 1946 a man named Thiel made a claim in his civil case that lower-class working people had been systematically excluded from his jury rolls when jury officials had deliberately excluded everyone who worked for a daily wage, leaving businessmen and others more disposed toward an employer's point of view. The Supreme Court agreed that Thiel had a legitimate grievance, and concluded that he did not have to carry the difficult, if not impossible, burden of proving that he had suffered actual prejudice by the jury with which he had wound up; the mere danger of prejudice was enough to justify a new trial. *Thiel* v. *Southern Pacific Company*, 328 U.S. 217, (1946).

The Court in *Thiel* assumed there was a range of distinct and identifiable groups whose members share attitudes and experiences that may not be adequately represented on a jury without those members, and unless the jury represents a cross section, there is a danger that it will become "the instrument of the economically and socially privileged" and representative of "narrow class interests." *Thiel* v. *Southern Pacific Company*, 328 U.S. 217, 223–224, (1946).

A cognizable group has been defined as such a group that has a definite composition with members who share common attitudes, ideas, or experiences and have a community interest that cannot adequately be protected by the rest of the population. *United States* v. *Guzman*, 337 F. Supp. 140 (S.D.N.Y. 1972), aff'd, 468 F. 2d 1245 (2d Cir. 1972) cert. denied, 410 U.S. 937 (1973). In addition to blacks, women, and wage earners, the Supreme Court and lower courts have identified other "cognizable" groups entitled to protection from restrictions on jury service: Native Americans—*State* v.

Plenty Horse, 85 S.D. 401, 184 N.W. 2d 654 (1971) and *United States* v. *Freeman,* 514 F. 2d 171 (8th Cir. 1975); common laborers—*Simmons* v. *State* 182 So 2d 442 (Fla. App. 1966); "hourly wage earners"—*People* v. *White,* 278 P. 2d 9 (1954); nontheists—*State* v. *Madison,* 240 Md 265, 213 A. 2d 880 (1965); students and professors—*United States* v. *Butera,* 420 F. 2d 564 (1st Cir. 1970); persons who object in principle to the death penalty—*Witherspoon* v. *Illinois,* 391 U.S. 510 (1968); Puerto Ricans in St. Croix, Virgin Islands—*United States* ex rel. *Leguillo* v. *Davis,* 115 F. Supp. 392 (D.V.I. 1953); and non-Caucasians in Hawaii—*United States* v. *Fujimoto,* 105 F. Supp. 727 (D. Hawaii 1952). Some courts have stated without discussion that Jews *(Schowgurow* v. *State,* 240 Mv. 121, 213 A. 2d 475 [1965]), Catholics *(United States* v. *Suskin,* 450 F. 2d 596 [2d Cir. 1971]), and persons who do not believe in a Supreme Being *(Juarez* v. *State,* 277 S.W. 1091 [1925]) are also protected groups.

In 1975 the Court held that the Sixth Amendment prohibited the practice in Louisiana and in a number of other states of permitting women to serve on juries only if they volunteered, which had resulted in their complete exclusion from the jury rolls. The Court was not at all dissuaded by the prosecution's argument that compulsory jury service would interfere with the "distinctive role in society" served by women. *Taylor* v. *Louisiana,* 419 U.S. 522 (1975).

Taylor was particularly important in the development of the right to a jury drawn from a cross section because it relied on the Sixth Amendment. In 1968 the Court had decided the case of *Duncan* v. *Louisiana* in which the Sixth Amendment was interpreted for the first time as binding on the states by virtue of the Fourteenth Amendment. The *Taylor* case defined the state's obligations more specifically when it held that "the selection of a petit jury from a representative cross section of the community is an essential component of the Sixth Amendment right to a jury trial." *Taylor* v. *Louisiana,* 419 U.S. 522 (1975).

Not only was community participation in the administration of criminal law essential for the fairness of the verdicts, but it was also critical in establishing the appearance of fairness, without which the public's confidence in the justice system would be undermined. *Taylor* v. *Louisiana,* 419 U.S. 522 (1975).

This last point was a recognition that a key purpose of the fair cross section requirement is that it lends legitimacy to the trial process. "When large classes of people are denied a role in the legal process, even if that denial is wholly unintentional or inadvertent, there is bound to be a sense of alienation from the social order." I. Kaufman, "The Judges and Jurors," in *Justice on Trial* 91 (1973), quoted by J. Ashby, "Juror Selection and the Sixth Amendment Right to an Impartial Jury," 11 *Creighton Law Review* 1137, 1139 (1970). "Of course, the individual defendant experiences a greater sense of injustice, since it is he who is sent to prison by an unrepresentative jury." J. Ashby, "Juror Selection and the Sixth Amendment Right to an Impartial Jury," 11 *Creighton Law Review* 1137, 1139 (1970).

p. 54 In 1935 in the second "Scottsboro Case" the Supreme Court finally said that public officials could not use their authority to exclude blacks. *Norris* v. *Alabama,* 294 U.S. 587 (1935).

p. 54 The Supreme Court decided that juries must reflect a fair cross section of the community in *Smith* v. *Texas,* 311 U.S. 128 (1940).

p. 56 Crimes considered "petty" are disposed of by a judge without a jury, and there is quite a squabble among legal scholars over what constitutes "petty." The question of what is meant by a "petty" as opposed to a "serious" crime has varied at different times and from place to place. Before we became a republic, the "petty" exception to the right to a jury trial existed in England, which extensively used magistrates without juries and made very limited use of jury trials.

Although offenses tried without juries were called petty, the punishments were frequently very harsh, sometimes even involving corporal punishment. The "common player of interludes who should perform or cause to be acted any interlude, tragedy, opera, play, farce or other entertainment" could be considered a vagabond and whipped by the local justice before being committed to a jail. The smuggler's wharfhands and the keeper of the gaming house could be indefinitely jailed unless a heavy bond were posted assuring their indefinite good behavior. "The rum runner's scout caught waiting the arrival from sea of illicit goods suffered a month of hard labor, with severe whippings occasionally added; the gamekeeper who poached on the side risked three months in jail; the dissenting preacher who had not taken the oath of allegiance, six months. The false prophet who advanced any fond fanatical or false prophesy to the disturbance of the realm, the unmarried mother, the lottery agent, the servant assaulting his master, the destroyer of bent grass" were incarcerated for a year. F. Frankfurter and T. Corcoran, "Petty Federal Offenses and Trial by Jury," 39 *Harvard Law Review* 917, 923–933 (1926).

After arriving in America the settlers adapted the English law to the American soil: "the old material had to be transformed, not merely transplanted. . . . The colonies did not blindly reproduce English procedure. . . . The need for criminal legislation in the colonies was comparatively narrow; and their sparsely settled homogeneous societies were peculiarly adapted for dealing with wrongdoers through popular forms of justice. Inevitably, therefore, the colonies entrusted fewer matters to justices than did the contemporary English law. Inevitably, also, the English magistrates exercised wider powers of punishment than the colonies gave to their magistrates. . . . Nor did the colonies work out uniform rules among themselves. . . . Different environments evolved different applications of trial by jury and its limits. The isolation of the scattered communities, differences in the composition of their settlers, the paucity of trained lawyers, fostered in each colony distinctive features of a common system. . . . Despite these differences all the colonies . . . resorted to summary jurisdiction for minor offenses with full loyalty to their conception of the Englishman's right to trial by jury." Frankfurter and Corcoran, "Petty Federal Offenses and Trial by Jury," 39 *Harvard Law Review* 917, 935–936 (1926).

Although there were few federal offenses that were prohibited from the start of our republic, those that existed were very serious and usually called for jury trial. In 1888 while ruling that the charge of conspiracy was not petty, the Supreme Court acknowledged for the first time that petty offenses did not require a jury. *Callan* v. *Wilson,* 127 U.S. 540, 547 (1888).

In 1966 the Supreme Court ruled, over the strenuous objections of two justices, that no jury was required in a federal trial for contempt where the punishment was less than six months. *Cheff* v. *Schnackenberg,* 384 U.S. 373 (1966).

In 1969, at the end of a decade of political turbulence, the Court concluded that a sentence of three years of probation did not turn a criminal contempt charge into a "serious" crime requiring a jury trial. *Frank* v. *United States,* 395 U.S. 147 (1969). Chief Justice Earl Warren wrote a blistering dissent attacking the majority for putting "a new weapon for chilling expression in the unrestrained hands of trial judges." He felt that without the safeguard of the jury system, local judges could control groups with unpopular views by using injunctions, their contempt power, and long probationary sentences. Warren envisioned the possibility that a large number of civil rights advocates, labor unionists, or student demonstrators could be brought into court on minor trespass or disturbance charges, and, without a jury's conviction, the court could control the lives of these defendants by imposing a lengthy probation sentence with all sorts of oppressive conditions. A trial judge could simply issue a blanket injunction against an unpopular group without waiting until laws are violated; he could then cite its members for contempt for the slightest injunction violation and, by imposing strict conditions, effectively deprive them of any meaningful freedom for a period of years. The terms of a probationary sentence could require defendants to keep "reasonable hours" and prohibit them from leaving the court's jurisdiction without the probation officer's permission, thereby virtually nullifying a person's freedom of movement. A judge could also insist that a defendant "work regularly," and thereby regulate his working life as well. Finally, a court can order a defendant to associate only with "law-abiding" persons, thereby significantly limiting his freedom of association. *Frank* v. *United States,* 395 U.S. 147, 152–154 (1969).

In the same contempt case in which Warren dissented so vehemently, Justice Hugo Black, joined by Justice William Douglas, went even further: "To my way of thinking, when a man is charged by a governmental unit with conduct for which the Government can impose a penalty of imprisonment for any amount of time, I doubt if I could ever hold it petty. . . . Nor do I take any stock in the idea that by naming an offense for which a man can be imprisoned a 'contempt,' he is any the less charged with a crime. . . . Those who commit offenses against courts should be no less entitled to the Bill of Rights than those who commit offenses against the public in general." *Frank* v. *United States,* 395 U.S. 147, 160 (1969).

The following year Black wrote again on the subject of petty crimes. "Many years ago," Black said, "this Court, without the necessity of an amendment pursuant to Article V, decided that 'all crimes' did not mean all crimes, but meant only 'all serious crimes.' . . . Those who wrote and adopted our Constitution and Bill of Rights engaged in all the balancing necessary. They decided that the value of a jury trial far outweighed its costs for 'all crimes' and 'in all prosecutions.'" *Baldwin* v. *New York,* 399 U.S. 66, 75 (1970).

The Court in the *Baldwin* case threw out a New York statute that authorized a one-year imprisonment for "jostling." While the Court had previously held that no jury was required for the trial of a charge where the punishment was less than six months, it was finally made clear that no offense in any court, federal or state, can be deemed "petty" for purposes of the right to a jury trial where imprisonment for more than six months is authorized. *Baldwin* v. *New York*, 399 U.S. 66, 73 (1970).

p. 56 According to the Supreme Court in *McKeiver* v. *Pennsylvania*, 403 U.S. 528 (1971), juries have generally not been used in military trials, and states have been permitted to try juveniles without juries.

p. 56 The purpose of the jury, as the Supreme Court sees it, is "to guard against the exercise of arbitrary power—to make available the common-sense judgment of the community as a hedge against the overzealous or mistaken prosecutor and in preference to the professional or perhaps overconditioned or biased response of a judge." *Taylor* v. *Louisiana*, 419 U.S. 522, 530 (1975).

pp. 56–57 "In the 13th century if a defendant stood mute when asked to plead to a crime or submit to a trial jury, the defendant was subjected to punishment . . . three morsels of the worst bread and . . . three draughts of standing water . . . and in this situation the person should remain til he died or til he answered." R. von Moschzisker in *Trial by Jury* (1922), p. 45, and M. Bloomstein, "The American Jury System," *Current History*, June 1971.

Part Two: Those Chosen to Judge

CHAPTER III

p. 62 The effects of the physical characteristics of courtrooms on the responses of jurors is discussed in D. Suggs and B. Sales, "Juror Self-Disclosure in the Voir Dire: A Social Science Analysis," 56 *Indiana Law Journal* 245, 264–268 (1981).

p. 62 Nationally 73 percent of those who face juries are white and 93 percent are male, but women confront juries in 11 percent of the murder trials and blacks constitute 43 percent of the defendants. H. Kalven and H. Zeisel, *The American Jury* (1966), pp. 195–97.

p. 64 Voir dire means "true talk," the word *voir* being a corruption of the Latin *verus,* which means "true." H. Zeisel and S. Diamond, "The Effect of Peremptory Challenges on Jury and Verdict: An Experiment in a Federal District Court," 30 *Stanford Law Review* 491, 492 (1978).

p. 64 The varied functions of the voir dire are described by Professor A. Ginger in *Jury Selection in Criminal Trials* (1975).

p. 67 The effect of a defendant's unattractiveness on the jurors' view of his credibility is discussed in Kalven and Zeisel, *The American Jury,* pp. 381–85.

p. 73 "If you don't like a juror's face, chances are he doesn't like yours either—and you'd better get rid of him." H. Fahringer, "In the Valley of the Blind: A Primer on Jury Selection in a Criminal Case," 43 *Law and Contemporary Problems* 116 (1980), and R. Cartwright, "Jury Selection," *Trial,* December 1977, p. 29.

p. 73 The story of a lawyer wearing a tie to match that of a juror was reported in H. Robinson, "Would a Lawyer Pick You as a Juror?" *Argosy,* September 1945, reprinted in *Reader's Digest,* September 1945, p. 86.

pp. 73–74 A discussion of studies by psychologists of speech patterns and physical cues can be found in T. Salisbury, "Forensic Sociology and Psychology: New Tools for the Criminal Defense Attorney," 12 *Tulsa Law Journal* 274 (1976); J. Conley, W. O'Barr, and E. A. Lind, "The Power of Language: Presentational Style in the Courtroom," 1978 *Duke Law Journal* 1375; H. Fahringer, "In the Valley of the Blind: A Primer on Jury Selection in a Criminal Case," 43 *Law and Contemporary Problems* 116 (1980); and D. Suggs and B. Sales, "Using Communication Cues to Evaluate Prospective Jurors During the Voir Dire," 20 *Arizona Law Review* 629 (1978).

p. 75 A summary of the cases where friends of key witnesses or victims have served as jurors can be found in *State* v. *Singletary,* 156 N.J. Super. 303 (App. Div. 1978).

p. 77 A juror's identification with the lawyer, whether by religion, ethnicity, or personality, can influence the juror's attitude to that lawyer and his arguments. H. Fahringer, "In the Valley of the Blind: A Primer on Jury Selection in a Criminal Case," 43 *Law and Contemporary Problems* 116 (1980).

p. 84 Some judges feel that on balance voir dire cannot produce results justifying very large expenditures of court time. For example, in *United States* v. *Dennis,* 183 F. 2d 201, 227 (2d Cir. 1950), aff'd, 341 U.S. 494 (1951), Judge Learned Hand said: "Nothing but an examination, utterly impracticable in a courtroom, will disclose [our deepest antipathies], an examination extending at times for months, and even then unsuccessful. No such examination is required. . . . If trial by jury is not to break down by its own weight, it is not feasible to probe more than the upper levels of a juror's mind." Jerome Frank (in *Courts on Trial* [1949], p. 204) is among those judges who believe that the voir dire can disclose merely superficial information about a juror. Louis Nizer (in "The Art of the Jury Trial," *Cornell Law Quarterly* 59 [1946]) is among the others who feel that as long as we want jurors to try cases, the voir dire is the only practical approach and is worth spending some time on. See also H. Fahringer, "In the Valley of the Blind: A Primer on Jury Selection in a Criminal Case," 43 *Law and Contemporary Problems* 116 (1980).

p. 84 The 1881 Supreme Court case that decided that Mormons could be excluded from a jury in the trial of a Mormon accused of bigamy was *Miles* v. *United States,* 103 U.S. 304 (1881). The 1968 prosecution in which taxicab drivers and those related to taxicab drivers were considered unqualified as jurors was *Sims* v. *United States,* 405 F. 2d 1381 (D.C. 1968). Being a Catholic did not prevent a juror from serving in a case involving a bishop in *Searle* v. *Roman Catholic Bishop,* 203 Mass. 493, 89 N.E. 809 (1909). Being a union textile worker did not automatically disqualify a juror in a prosecution growing out of a unionization struggle in *State* v. *Royster,* 181 S.C. 269, 186 S.E. 921 (1936).

A controversial case in 1950 left the Supreme Court in sharp disagreement over who should be qualified as jurors. The general secretary of the United States Communist Party was being prosecuted for failing to appear before the House Un-American Activities Committee, and he argued that, given the atmosphere in Washington at the time and the pressure on government workers to demonstrate their loyalty, all government employees should be excused as jurors for implied bias. The majority of the Court held that government employees who said they could render a fair verdict were permitted to serve as jurors. In dissent, Justice Frankfurter attacked this reluctance to presume bias from class status: "The reason for disqualifying a whole class on the ground of bias is the law's recognition that if the circumstances of that class in the run of instances are likely to general bias, consciously or unconsciously, it would be a hopeless endeavor to search out the impact of these circumstances on the mind and judgment of a particular individual. This is the reason why the influences of consanguinity or of financial interest are not individually canvassed. Law as a response to life recognizes the operation of such influences even though not consciously or clearly entertained. The appearance of impartiality is an essential manifestation of its reality." *Dennis v. United States,* 339 U.S. 162, 181–182 (1950).

pp. 84–85 The amount of information disclosed by investigations and the restrictions placed on lawyers in their contact with jurors is discussed in D. Silver, "A Case Against the Use of Public Opinion Polls as an Aid in Jury Selection," 6 *Journal on Computer and Law* 175, 195 (1978). C. Callendar, in his book *The Selection of Jurors* (1924), described the practice of investigating jurors in the Philadelphia District Attorney's Office where patrolmen from the juror's district reported on his reputation, drinking habits, and "habits as to morality." Boston police in 1928 were required to provide personal endorsements of prospective jurors. *Commonwealth v. Cero,* 264 Mass. 264, 162 N.E. 349 (1928).

Some lawyers believe that juror investigators operate no differently from a news reporter, but ultimately the courts may be forced to balance the privacy of jurors performing a public service against the right of a defendant to the most thorough defense possible.

The government can gather information ranging from simple census data, to FBI reports, to industrial security files, to the very detailed information available in the personnel files of 25,575,000 veterans, 2,903,000 civilian employees of the federal government, and 8,618,000 employees of state and local governments, in addition to the detailed financial information on the nearly 70 million individuals who annually file federal income tax returns.

Access to some record systems is restricted and others may even be illegal, but the potential for abuse is great and so is the profit incentive to get that information. Up to now the courts have provided little protection of the juror's privacy rights. The future litigant without access to this information may find himself at a great disadvantage in obtaining an impartial jury against an adversary who does have access.

Simply assembling a quantity of materials about a prospective juror may represent a damaging invasion of his privacy. Usually the juror does not even know about the invasion of his privacy. He is deprived of control over inaccuracies that may create an erroneous or scandalous impression of him.

While a person may decline to discuss his neighbor's personal affairs with an inquiring private detective, the same person may be reluctant to withhold that information from an FBI agent. Most people do not realize that the agent has no more legal right to question them than the private detective, but displaying FBI credentials is usually enough to guarantee full disclosure. Private investigators know they will be punished by the court if they step over certain limits, even when they make an innocent error in judgment. It is hard to imagine that a government agent, acting under orders, has ever been punished for the manner in which he investigated a juror. In effect, a prosecutor is really left to set his own limits in an area where the boundaries are admittedly gray.

Although the government has a great and unfair advantage in using the information available to it, courts have found that the government, because of the adversary nature of our trials, has no obligation to share the information with defense counsel. R. Moskitis, "The Constitutional Need for Discovery of Pre-Voir Dire Juror Studies," 49 *Southern California Law Review* 597 (1976); J. Okun, "Investigation of Jurors by Counsel: Its Impact on the Decisional Process," 56 *Georgetown Law Journal* 839 (1968); J. Wanamaker, "Computers and Scientific Jury Selection: A Calculated Risk," 55 *Journal of Urban Law* 345, 356 (1978).

p. 85 A sensational case in 1956 raised many of the issues involved in investigating jurors. The mobster Frank Costello was being prosecuted for tax evasion, and the prosecutor requested an Internal Revenue agent to check the tax returns of all prospective jurors. The tax returns revealed information about business dealings, marital status, source of income, amount of income, individual deductions, number of dependents, tax paid, refund, and any apparent irregularity.

The prosecutor argued that the information was important "to find out whether any of the prospective jurors had income tax troubles of their own or had other reasons to be unfavorably disposed to the government." The government used the information to rank the jurors; people with little or no contact with the IRS, aside from the filing of their annual returns, were considered the most favorable, and the jury as finally constituted consisted of eight such jurors.

Appealing the conviction, Costello claimed that the use of the income tax returns violated the privacy of the jurors because of the confidential nature of the returns, that the practice would intimidate future jurors, and that through the use of the returns the prosecution had obtained a jury "specially conditioned" to find him guilty.

The government was unembarrassed to argue to the court that inspection of tax returns could have no adverse effect on the jury system because citizens would welcome the opportunity to prove to the IRS that their returns were an accurate reflection of their financial lives.

The defense responded that most taxpayers, even the most scrupulous and accurate, not only do not welcome this "opportunity" but in fact dread it. The court decided that jurors would not be discouraged from "cheerful" jury service if they had filed honest tax returns. The court did not believe that scrutiny of tax returns would deter "a good citizen from service in the judicial establishment any more than the fierce publicity which beats upon the private affairs of the citizen appointed to high office in the executive department deters acceptance of such appointment."

In affirming Costello's conviction, the court also concluded that the defendant had no standing to raise the issue of jurors' privacy. If there was a grievance at all, it was for the juror himself to raise it, not the defendant, and besides, the jurors in the Costello case did not have knowledge that their records had been acquired. As far as the threat of intimidating future jurors, the court called that "farfetched bogies."

When the Costello case was appealed to the Supreme Court, the Solicitor General conceded that knowledge of the government's practice might cause some persons to wish to avoid jury service, and the Supreme Court was informed that "to avoid any possible problems in this respect in future cases, United States Attorneys are being instructed not to engage in this practice." In other words, the Supreme Court was told that any danger to the jury system that may have existed had been removed.

Costello's conviction was not disturbed by the Supreme Court. Instructions were issued to U. S. Attorneys not to inspect federal income tax returns of prospective jurors in income tax prosecutions, and these instructions are still in force. And a juror is left with little he can do to protect his privacy. *United States* v. *Costello,* 255 F. 2d. 876 (2nd Cir.) cert. denied 357 U.S. 937 (1958).

p. 85 A report on the efforts to investigate potential jurors in the T. Cullen Davis case was made in "Juror Privacy," *Newsweek,* April 10, 1978, p. 89.

p. 85 The need for new legislation to prevent access to business and personal records to prevent a governmental surveillance system is argued in J. Wanamaker, "Computers and Scientific Jury Selection: A Calculated Risk," 55 *Journal of Urban Law* 345, 358 (1978).

p. 86 *Ham* v. *South Carolina,* 409 U.S. 524 (1973).

p. 88 The Supreme Court case in which the Court concluded that questions about race had not been required because racial issues had not been "inextricably bound up" with the conduct of a trial was *Ristaino* v. *Ross,* 424 U.S. 589 (1976).

p. 88 Questioning jurors about political affiliations was disallowed in *Connors* v. *United States,* 158 U.S. 408 (1895). In *United States* v. *Hamling,* 481 F. 2d 307, 314 (9th Cir. 1973), aff'd. 414 U.S. 1143 (1974) the refusal to question jurors about views toward sex and obscenity was proper in an obscenity prosecution; in *United States* v. *Goodwin,* 470 F. 2d 893, 897 (5th Cir. 1972), cert. denied, 411 U.S. 969 (1973) the refusal to question jurors about attitudes toward defendant's refusal to take stand was proper; in *United States* v. *Workman,* 454 F. 2d 1124, 1128 (9th Cir. 1972) cert. denied, 409 U.S. 857 (1973) the refusal to question jurors about attitudes toward drug use, political activists, and antiwar demonstrators was proper in prosecution of antiwar demonstrator for assault on policeman and destruction of government property; in *United States* v. *Mattin,* 419 F. 2d 1086 (8th Cir. 1970) the refusal to question jurors about their attitudes toward antiwar demonstrators was proper in prosecution for failing to register for draft; in *United States* v. *Hoffa,* 367 F. 2d 698, 710 (7th Cir. 1966), vacated on other grounds, 387 U.S. 231 (1967) the refusal to question jurors about political affiliations and encounters with union pickets was proper in prosecution of union officer; in *Maguire* v. *United States,* 358 F. 2d 442, 444–45 (10th Cir. 1966), cert. dismissed, 385 U.S. 801, cert. denied, 385 U.S. 870 (1967) the refusal to question jurors about bias against homosexuals was proper in a case in which the defense to a charge of auto theft was that the car owner gave defendants the auto after they had threatened to expose his sexual advances on them; in *Bellard* v. *United States,* 356 F. 2d 437, 439 (5th Cir. 1966), cert. denied, 385 U.S. 856 (1966) the refusal to question jurors about prior jury service was proper. But see *United States* v. *Dellinger,* 472 F. 2d 340, 367 (7th Cir. 1972), cert. denied, 410 U.S. 970 (1973) where the prosecution's argument that voir dire may be limited to matters falling within a challenge for cause was rejected.

A number of cases have held that unless religion is an issue in the case, the trial judge had the right to prohibit questioning jurors about it. In an obscenity prosecution prospective jurors were not allowed to be asked if they entertained any religious beliefs that would affect their impartiality. The Supreme Court has said that, as "to religion, our jury selection system was not designed to subject prospective jurors to a catechism of their tenets of faith, whether it be Catholic, Jewish, Protestant, or Mohammedan, or to force them to publicly declare themselves to be atheists. Indeed, many a juror might have a real doubt as to the particular religious category into which they could properly place themselves." *Swain* v. *Alabama,* 380 U.S. 220 (1965).

In *Kuzniak* v. *Taylor Supply Co.,* 471 F. 2d 702 (6th Cir. 1972) the trial court erred in refusing to question jurors about prejudice against Austrian nationals where one party was an Austrian national; in *United States* v. *Napoleone,* 349 F. 2d 350 (3d Cir. 1965) the trial court erred in refusing to ask prospective jurors whether they had such moral or ethical repugnance toward liars that they could not objectively evaluate testimony of defendant, a private investigator who regularly lied about the purpose of his investigations; in *United States* v. *Daily,* 139 F. 2d 7 (7th Cir. 1943) the trial court was correct in asking whether prospective jurors were prejudiced against Jehovah's Witnesses where the defendant, in a prosecution for failing to report for induction, was a Jehovah's Witness.

When the information sought from the prospective jurors seems specifically related to the facts of the case, questioning has been allowed. In a 1968 manslaughter prosecution arising out of an abortion, an Oregon court held that questions regarding religious beliefs were appropriate where the defendant was accused of murder since "[t]here is a widely accepted belief that certain religious faiths feel more strongly about abortion than do others."

p. 88 The Chicago Seven case is cited as *United States* v. *Dellinger,* 472 F. 2d 340, 367 (7th Cir. 1972), cert. denied, 410 U.S. 970 (1973).

p. 88 In most federal courts, judges conduct a voir dire examination but permit additional questions to be submitted by the lawyers, either directly or through the judge. Judges in thirteen states conduct the voir dire themselves with no direct participation by counsel. Eighteen states give primary control over the voir dire questioning to the lawyers. In the remaining states, the questioning is conducted by both judge and counsel. National Center for State Courts, *The State Organization: 1980,* Table 42 (1981), p. 114. The different answers obtainable from jurors by the way questions are phrased is discussed in D. Suggs and B. Sales, "Juror Self-Disclosure in the Voir Dire: A Social Science Analysis," 56 *Indiana Law Journal* 245, 258–261 (1981).

Several reasons exist for jurors' silence when honesty requires a reply, or for their outright deception. Sometimes the judge frames the question so as to intimidate jurors. One judge, when describing what constituted a fixed opinion requiring excuse for cause, stated: "Now, a fixed opinion . . . means a buttheaded opinion. . . . It means the kind of buttheadedness that you find in a man with a head the shape of a baseball." *Fuller* v. *State,* 269 Ala. 312, 391, 113 So. 2d 153, 158 (1959).

p. 89 Dale Broeder described the jurors in the various cases who had clear conflicts of interest in his study reported in "Voir Dire Examinations: An Empirical Study," 38 *Southern California Law Review* 503 (1965).

p. 90 The case against Aaron Burr was reported in *United States* v. *Burr,* 24 F. Cas. 49 (D. Va. 1807).

p. 91 The survey conducted by the National Jury Project Study of New York in the Joanne Chesimard murder prosecution was discussed in H. Fahringer, "In the Valley of the Blind: A Primer on Jury Selection in a Criminal Case," 43 *Law and Contemporary Problems* 116, 118 (1980).

p. 92 That Judge Sirica felt the people who had not heard of Watergate were probably the least qualified to sit on the jury was reported in J. Van Dyke, *Jury Selection Procedures: Our Uncertain Commitment to Representative Panels* (1977), p. 143.

CHAPTER IV

p. 95 The tactic of accepting the first jurors called to the jury box to impress the jurors is discussed in H. Robinson, "Would a Lawyer Pick You as a Juror?" *Argosy,* September 1945, reprinted in *Reader's Digest,* September 1945, p. 86, and R. Cartwright, "Jury Selection," *Trial,* December 1977, p. 29.

p. 98 Peremptory challenges allow judges to avoid being in the position of challenging the honesty of the prospective juror. J. Spears, "Voir Dire: Minimum Standards to Facilitate the Exercise of Peremptory Challenges," 27 *Stanford Law Review* 1493 (1975).

Peremptory challenges were allowed to defendants in the federal system from the beginning of the republic, being considered a part of the inherited common law. But there was disagreement as to whether the government had a similar right. The Supreme Court held in 1856 that federal prosecutors could challenge jurors peremptorily only if the state in which the court was sitting granted such a right to the local prosecutor. Congress did not grant the peremptory challenge to the federal prosecutor until 1865. Most of the states had not given peremptories to the prosecution until around 1870. Today in a number of states the defendant still has more peremptories than the prosecutor, which implies that more potential jurors have biases against someone accused of a crime than biases against the state. The number of peremptory challenges permitted a party varies widely. Some states permit as many as twenty-six per party in capital cases, fifteen in felony cases, thirteen in misdemeanor cases, and two in civil cases. J. Van Dyke, *Jury Selection Procedures: Our Uncertain Commitment to Representative Panels* (1977), pp. 155–56.

p. 99 Judge Whitaker was referring to *Swain* v. *Alabama,* 380 U.S. 220 (1965).

p. 102 Interpreting body language is discussed in D. Suggs and B. Sales, "Using Communication Cues to Evaluate Prospective Jurors During the Voir Dire," 20 *Arizona Law Review* 629 (1978).

p. 106 Percy Forman's and Louis Nizer's views on picking jurors were discussed in "Twelve Missing Men," *Newsweek,* June 10, 1968, p. 58, in *Time,* March 29, 1968, p. 64.

p. 106 Melvin Belli was quoted as saying that he prefers men to women jurors because "women jurors are too brutal" in N. Totenberg, "The Jury Picker," *Parade*, May 9, 1982, p. 12.

p. 106 Clarence Darrow's views on jury selection were disclosed in "Clarence Darrow: Ace Jury-Picker," *The Literary Digest*, May 16, 1936, p. 35.

p. 107 A prominent Louisiana attorney, a former president of the Louisiana Trial Lawyers Association, has stated: "It is part of a lawyer's job to utilize the prejudices of the community. These prejudices, whether against Negroes or other minority groups or economic interests, exist everywhere in the country." *Washington Post*, Nov. 22, 1965, p. 4. A study by Rita Simon, a sociologist at the University of Illinois, of the stereotypes relied on by prosecutors and defense lawyers was reported in "We, the Jury, Find . . . ," *Time*, September 28, 1981, p. 47.

p. 107 The assistant district attorney from Albuquerque, New Mexico, who wanted "to get the flaky weirdos off" the jury was quoted in Van Dyke, *Jury Selection Procedures: Our Uncertain Commitment to Representative Panels*, p. 154.

p. 107 Louis Nizer's attitude toward people who draw their mouths together too tightly was reported in "We, the Jury, Find . . . ," *Time*, September 28, 1981, p. 47.

pp. 108–9 Reports of what the psychologists were looking for in the Angela Davis case were reported in "Finding a Friendly Jury," *Newsweek*, August 26, 1974, p. 49.

p. 109 A detailed account of how the team of experts helped pick jurors for the Berrigan brothers is found in J. Schulman, "Recipe for a Jury," *Psychology Today*, May 1974, p. 44.

The techniques to measure prospective jurors' attitudes and biases have been in existence since the late 1920s. By 1970, sociologists and psychologists had developed personality scales that they could correlate with various demographic characteristics. With the arrival of computers, the potential for statistically selecting jurors went from "feasible to easy," and counsel was capable of learning what the prospective juror is likely to believe, despite the juror's insistence of being impartial. J. Wanamaker, "Computers and Scientific Jury Selection: A Calculated Risk," 55 *Journal of Urban Law* 345 (1978).

p. 110 The cost of jury surveys was discussed by E. Tivnan in "Jury by Trial," *The New York Times Magazine,* Nov. 16, 1975, p. 30.

p. 110 Some people feel that social scientists or experts in body language threaten the very idea of a random selection of jurors by stacking the deck. A. Etzioni, "Creating an Imbalance," *Trial,* November/December 1974, p. 28; E. Tivnan, "Jury by Trial," *The New York Times Magazine,* Nov. 16, 1975, p. 30; L. Andrews, "Mind Control in the Courtroom," *Psychology Today,* March 1982, p. 66.

p. 110 Supporters point out that the use of experts to observe the demeanor of prospective jurors is little more than what lawyers have always done but with more discipline. "The Defendant's Right to an Impartial Jury and the Right of Prospective Jurors," 48 *Cincinnati Law Review* 985 (1979).

p. 111 Joan Little's attorney was quoted as saying that he had "bought" the verdict in E. Tivnan, "Jury by Trial," *The New York Times Magazine,* Nov. 16, 1975, p. 30.

pp. 111–12 How the jury reached its verdict in the Mitchell-Stans trial was reported by Martin Arnold in "How Mitchell-Stans Jury Reached Acquittal Verdict," *The New York Times,* May 5, 1975, p. 1, and brilliantly analyzed by H. Zeisel and S. Diamond in "The Jury Selection in the Mitchell-Stans Conspiracy Trial," *American Bar Foundation Research Journal* (1976), p. 162.

p. 112 Edward Bennett Williams was quoted by E. Tivnan as calling the use of modern marketing techniques and applied social science "bunk" in "Jury by Trial," *The New York Times Magazine,* Nov. 16, 1975, p. 31.

p. 112 Scientific jury selection smacks of sinister manipulation. A. Etzioni, "Creating an Imbalance," *Trial,* November/December 1974, p. 28. Many judges are opposed to its use. M. Hunt, "Putting Juries on the Couch," *The New York Times Magazine,* Nov. 28, 1982, p. 70.

p. 112 Referring to the jury in the Jack Ruby case, Melvin Belli was quoted as saying, "I got a jury of bums." N. Totenberg, "The Jury Picker," *Parade,* May 9, 1982, p. 12. "Jury selection is a very, very unscientific business," F. Lee Bailey is quoted as saying. "It's a haphazard process. And those of us who run around lecturing on how to pick juries should really start out, if we're honest, by admitting that we really don't know much about them." E. Tivnan, "Jury by Trial," *The New York Times Magazine*, Nov. 16, 1975, p. 30.

p. 112 The voir dire was called an ineffective screening mechanism by Dale Broeder in "Voir Dire Examinations: An Empirical Study," 38 *Southern California Law Review* 503 (1965). Broeder found that the way many lawyers conduct a voir dire made it perfunctory, boring, and brief.

p. 112 The recent, ingenuous study that supports the view that some lawyers can select "favorable" jurors by relying on a sensitivity and intuition about people that is developed over time and experience was by Hans Zeisel and Shari Diamond, and reported in "The Effect of Peremptory Challenges on Jury and Verdict: An Experiment in a Federal District Court," 30 *Stanford Law Review* 491 (1978).

p. 114 There is a "core of truth" in some stereotypes. D. Broeder, "The Negro in Court," *Duke Law Journal* 19, (1965).

p. 116 The example of the Nazi defendant can be found in "The Prohibition of Group-Based Stereotypes in Jury Selection Procedures," 25 *Villanova Law Review* 339, 361 (1979–1980). The Supreme Court has said that a member of the Nazi Party should not be allowed to sit in judgment on a Jewish defendant. *Rosales-Lopez* v. *United States,* 451 U.S. 182, 197 (1981).

p. 117 A federal district court took judicial notice that lawyers in many southern states almost never raised the issue of systematic exclusion of blacks from juries. *United States* ex rel. *Goldsby* v. *Harpole,* 263 F. 2d. 71 (5th Cir.), cert. denied, 361 U.S. 838 (1959). For a discussion of the role of the white lawyer in the South see *"Swain* v. *Alabama:* A Constitutional Blueprint for the Perpetuation of the All-White Jury," 52 *Virginia Law Review* 1157, 1163 (1966).

p. 118 The California Supreme Court in *People* v. *Wheeler,* 583 P. 2d 748 (1978) and the Massachusetts Supreme Court in *Commonwealth* v. *Soares,* 387 N.E. 2d. 449 (1979) have disagreed with the *Swain* decision and ruled that if blacks are excused from a jury, it becomes the prosecutor's burden to prove that racial discrimination was not the reason. The state courts of Louisiana and Illinois have also disagreed with the *Swain* decision.

Part Three: The Trial

CHAPTER V

p. 126 In 1979 eleven defendants, including kingpin Leroy "Nicky" Barnes, were brought to trial for conspiracy to violate the federal narcotics laws. *United States* v. *Barnes,* 604 F. 2d. 121 (2d. Cir. 1979). Newspapers called Barnes "one of Harlem's most notorious drug dealers." The trial judge refused to permit questioning during voir dire of the names and street addresses of potential jurors. The judge's decision to impose anonymity was partly prompted by the wish to protect the jurors' privacy from interference by the media, but mostly the judge was concerned about the safety of the jurors.

The defendants claimed they were deprived of their right to an impartial jury because, they argued, to exercise peremptory challenges, a defendant needs to know the neighborhood and the ethnic and religious background of the prospective jurors. Prior to the *Barnes* case, some trial judges had refused to disclose names and addresses of potential jurors, and other judges had denied the right to inquire about the religious and ethnic backgrounds, but the *Barnes* decision was unprecedented in foreclosing counsel from inquiring into both of these areas in the same case.

The defendants were convicted after a ten-week trial. On appeal, Judge Moore, writing for the majority of the court of appeals, found that the "sordid history" of narcotics cases in New York, including threats to jurors and witnesses, necessitated all possible safety measures for the protection of prospective jurors, including complete juror anonymity. The court asked rhetorically how a juror's judgment can be free and impartial when he fears for his own life and the safety of his family. Prospective jurors, Judge Moore said, were not on trial. Furthermore, he warned that as attorneys seek more information in order to empanel jurors favorable to their clients, more and more people will refuse to serve on juries if they will be subjected to extensive inquiry about private matters.

"Appellate judges," Judge Moore wrote, "from the comparative security of their ivory towers, are not burdened, as was this trial judge (and, indeed, as are all trial judges), with the responsibility of providing for the protection of the jurors, witnesses, and counsel. It can be no answer that no untoward event had occurred up to the opening of the trial. The trial judge had to take such steps as might be necessary in advance to avoid such an event. Cases need not be cited to prove the adage of the futility of locking the barn door after the horse has escaped."

In a dissenting opinion Judge Meskill felt that the majority disregarded the fact that the trial judge had made his ruling without having been requested to do so by the prosecutor and with no showing that any juror would have felt threatened in the absence of the ruling. In fact no juror during voir dire even expressed such concern.

"Ironically, it may well be that the judge's instruction instituted a fear that the jurors prior to the instructions had never entertained," Judge Meskill wrote. "Instances abound where jurors, after having their names and addresses revealed in open court, promptly proceeded to convict some of the most notorious criminals in our history."

Judge Moore had found that the possibility of unfairness was neutralized since both the defense and the prosecution were equally disadvantaged by their lack of information about prospective jurors.

To some extent the inconvenience to a prospective juror caused by public disclosure of personal information can be overcome by a voir dire examination held in private. A balancing of interests is involved between the responsibility to defendants whose liberty may be at stake and the rights of privacy and safety of prospective jurors.

Lawyers usually infer the ethnic or religious background of a juror from that person's name. Although not scientifically accurate, this method is simple and often reliable. In the *Barnes* case, the trial court even precluded the use of this basic source of information.

The court took the position that the ethnic background of a juror was irrelevant since no ethnic group looks favorably upon the sale of drugs or the use of firearms. The court did not address, or perhaps decided to ignore, both social science studies and respected legal folklore that have demonstrated that certain ethnic groups are traditionally favored by the defense.

While jurors have occasionally been verbally threatened, physical injury to a juror has been traced to a defendant in only one case,

United States v. *Bentvena,* 319 F. 2d. 916 (2d Cir.) cert. denied, 375 U.S. 940 (1963). A mistrial was declared in the first *Bentvena* trial after the jury foreman broke his back under suspicious circumstances.

p. 130 According to a study done by the National Jury Project of New York, 25 percent of all jurors assume that if a grand jury returned an indictment, the defendant must have done something. H. Fahringer, "In the Valley of the Blind: A Primer on Jury Selection in a Criminal Case," 43 *Law and Contemporary Problems* 116, 123 (1980).

p. 133 The Chicago Jury Project confirmed that defendants, at times, have been treated more leniently when juries have felt that the victim had been at fault, or had in some way caused or tempted the defendant into committing the crime.

p. 137 Several states have begun to allow jurors to take notes in long or complicated cases, but it is still not allowed in most courts. Georgia has allowed jurors to take notes with the proviso that the court should not allow the jury to spend too much time doing so rather than focusing on their real duty. Woodcock, "Note-Taking by Jurors," 55 *Dickinson Law Review* 335, 336–7 (1951); V. Flango, "Would Jurors Do a Better Job if They Could Take Notes?" 63 *Judicature* 436 (1980).

p. 141 The Chicago Jury Project found that in income tax and perjury cases defense counsel were superior in 27 percent of the cases, in auto theft and carrying a concealed weapon cases the prosecution was superior in approximately 20 percent of the cases, and in murder, rape, narcotics, and burglary cases the two sides were roughly even.

pp. 142–43 Chief Justice Warren Burger's opinion of the incompetence of counsel was reported in 42 *Fordham Law Review* 227 (1973). The other studies that found trial judges holding a much higher regard for lawyers were reported in "The Trial Bar: Prognosis Improved," *The New Jersey Law Journal,* January 10, 1980, p. 4.

pp. 143–44 H. L. Mencken's view of lawyers was published in the January 1928 issue of the *American Mercury,* p. 35.

pp. 144–45 Our Supreme Court has been very aware of how the power of trial judges developed in this country. "Those who wrote our Constitution knew from history and experience," the Court has written, "that it was necessary to protect against unfounded criminal charges brought to eliminate enemies and against judges too responsive to the voice of higher authority. The framers of the Constitution strove to create an independent judiciary but insisted upon further protection against arbitrary action. Providing an accused with a right to be tried by a jury of his peers gave him an inestimable safeguard against a corrupt or overzealous prosecutor and against the compliant, biased, or eccentric judge . . . beyond this, the jury trial provisions in the federal and state Constitutions reflect the fundamental decision about the exercise of official power—a reluctance to entrust plenary powers over the life and liberty of a citizen to one judge or to a group of judges. Freedom from unchecked power, so typical of our state and federal governments in other respects, found expression in the criminal law and its insistence upon community participation in the determination of guilt or innocence." Justice White in *Duncan* v. *Louisiana,* 391 U.S. 145, 156 (1968).

p. 148 For some years before and after the Magna Carta, disputes were primarily settled three ways: (1) trial by ordeal where it was thought that there would be Divine intervention on the side of the party with the just cause; (2) trial by battle, introduced to England by William the Conqueror, where representatives of the disputants fought with sword, shield, and spear, often on horseback, until one side—with Divine help it was thought—succeeded in killing the other; and (3) trial by compurgation where each side would summon people to swear that they believed that the litigant who called them was telling the truth.

Trial by ordeal in its various forms was described by R. von Moschzisker in *Trial by Jury* (1922) and J. Proffatt in *Trial by Jury* (1877), p. 16. The ordeals were part of the early judicial procedure of practically all the early nations and tribes of Europe and Asia. F. X. Busch, *Law and Tactics in Jury Trials,* Encyclopedia Edition Vol. 1 (1959), pp. 2–3. That the original idea of the ordeals was encouraged by the clergy to strengthen their influence is discussed by P. Devlin in *Trial by Jury* (1956), p. 9.

Long before the Norman Conquest, a mode of proof prevailed in England as well as on the Continent by which one accused of a crime could clear himself by denying his guilt under oath, and by producing a given number of people, called compurgators, or "oath-helpers," who would support him by swearing he was telling the truth. This process was called trial by compurgation, sometimes referred to as the "wager of law."

In a trial by compurgation, the accusation of a prosecutor was sufficient to put one accused of crime to his defense. "By the Lord, I am guiltless both in deed and counsel of the charge of which X accuses me," the defendant would swear. Proffatt, *Trial by Jury,* p. 17.

The "oath-helpers" would be given credit according to their rank. "By the Lord, the oath is clear and unperjured which D has sworn," the oath-helpers would swear. Proffatt, *Trial by Jury,* p. 17. These witnesses, in other words, did not testify to matters within their own knowledge, but only vouched for the trust-worthiness of the oath of the accused. They were similar to character witnesses in today's trials. The usual number of compurgators was twelve, but it could be as high as forty-eight. If a sufficient number of "oath-helpers" made the required formal oath, the accused was acquitted. If they failed to do so, the accused was compelled to undergo one of the ordeals.

CHAPTER VI

p. 166 In very few instances in life do people make important decisions without asking questions. The 1981 Georgia Supreme Court decision that ruled out juror-questioning of witnesses was *State* v. *Williamson,* 279 S.E. 2d. 833. See also L. Harms, "The Questioning of Witnesses by Jurors," 27 *American University Law Review* 127 (1977).

p. 168 The frequency of testimony by expert witnesses was reported in H. Kalven and H. Zeisel, *The American Jury* (1966), p. 137.

p. 178 The Supreme Court in *Neil* v. *Biggers,* 409 U.S. 188, 199–200 (1972) acknowledged the unreliability of eyewitness accounts that are often based on brief encounters under stressful conditions. The Court set out a list of factors for evaluating such testimony. It has been found that eyewitnesses testify in 25 percent of cases. Kalven and Zeisel, *The American Jury,* p. 137.

p. 179 The study by Elizabeth F. Loftus of the differences between male and female eyewitnesses was discussed in "Who Was That Masked Woman? Ask a Woman," *Psychology Today,* February 1980, p. 24.

p. 180 A discussion of the use of "shadow juries," a group of twelve people demographically similar to the actual jury, and the "mock jury," a group of people with similar characteristics of the actual jury, can be found in E. Tivnan, "Jury by Trial," *The New York Times Magazine,* Nov. 16, 1975, p. 30.

p. 181 The debate between critics and supporters of the use of these modern techniques can be found in J. Waltz, "Juries and the Mass Media," *The Nation,* Nov. 16, 1974, p. 495, and E. Tivnan, "Jury by Trial," *The New York Times,* Nov. 16, 1975, p. 30. See also E. Thorne, "The Impartial Jury and the Social Sciences," 5 *Journal of American Contemporary Law* 43 (1978).

CHAPTER VII

p. 184 Defendants testify in 82 percent of all cases. H. Kalven and H. Zeisel, *The American Jury* (1966), pp. 144–45.

p. 191 In about half of all cases defendants have a prior criminal record. Defendants with a record reach the witness box 74 percent of the time. Kalven and Zeisel, *The American Jury,* p. 146.

p. 201 Surveys by the National Jury Project Study of New York suggest that young people, single and not deeply rooted in the community, are best for the defense. Older people, entrenched in the establishment, are more likely to feel threatened by a defendant, and will more quickly identify with a victim and find for the prosecution. H. Fahringer, "In the Valley of the Blind: A Primer on Jury Selection in a Criminal Case," 43 *Law and Contemporary Problems* 116, 135 (1980).

p. 201 The conviction rate in an Oregon county dropped from 62 percent to 41 percent after 1922 when women were added to previously all-male juries. J. Van Dyke, *Jury Selection Procedures: Our Uncertain Commitment to Representative Panels* (1977), p. 42.

p. 201 Anne Rankin Mahoney, "Sexism in Voir Dire" in W. Hepperle and L. Crites, *Women in the Courts,* National Center for State Courts (1978), quoted in Ruth Simon, *The Jury: Its Role in American Society,* Lexington Books, 1980, p. 39.

p. 201 Women jurors were more sympathetic than men toward the defense of insanity when male defendants were charged with housebreaking but were more likely than men to convict when a plea of insanity was introduced to a charge of incest. Ruth Simon, *The Defense of Insanity,* p. 109. Housewives were more likely to convict than working women. Simon, *The Jury: Its Role in American Society,* p. 39.

pp. 201–2 When the percentage of blacks on juries was increased in Baltimore from 34 percent to 46 percent, the rate of conviction dropped from 83 percent to below 70 percent. Van Dyke, *Jury Selection Procedures: Our Uncertain Commitment to Representative Panels,* p. 33.

p. 202 The generalizations believed by several social scientists and many experienced criminal lawyers about the ethnic background of people that do seem to hold up are discussed in D. Broeder, "University of Chicago Jury Project," 38 *Nebraska Law Review* 744, 747–48 (1959).

pp. 202–3 Studies have shown that the greater the disparity in socioeconomic status between jurors and the accused, the greater the likelihood of conviction. F. Adler, "Empathy as a Factor in Determining Jury Verdicts," 12 *Criminology* 127 (1974). The Chicago Jury Project found that people of higher-status jobs, more income, and more education were less likely to give a defendant the lenient verdict of acquittal by reason of insanity than were people of lower socioeconomic status.

p. 203 One study found that in seventeen cases in which a wife was accused of killing her husband, juries acquitted 41 percent of the time; on the other hand, in twenty-seven cases, husbands were acquitted only 7 percent of the time. Kalven and Zeisel, *The American Jury,* p. 202.

p. 203 A number of cases in which judges attributed acquittals to the sympathy generated by the defendants was reported in Kalven and Zeisel, *The American Jury,* p. 202.

p. 203 The case in which the woman defendant wore a white mask throughout the trial was reported in Kalven and Zeisel, *The American Jury,* p. 201.

p. 203 The other attributes of the defendant that have aroused sympathy in jurors are discussed in Kalven and Zeisel, *The American Jury,* pp. 193–218.

p. 204 A discussion of cases in which juries have acquitted defendants as a means of protesting the behavior of the police or prosecution that it considers improper can be found in Kalven and Zeisel, *The American Jury,* pp. 318–23.

p. 205 The bankers of England petitioned Parliament in 1819 to remove the death penalty for forgery because it had become nearly impossible to get juries to return convictions for that crime. Kalven and Zeisel, *The American Jury,* pp. 310–11.

p. 205 Other factors that arouse sentiments in juries that cause them to lean toward acquittals are discussed in Kalven and Zeisel, *The American Jury,* pp. 301–71.

p. 205 Juries have been more lenient toward defendants charged with the so-called victimless crimes, where it is hard for juries to see any harm done by the criminal conduct, and where the government seems to be imposing its morality. Kalven and Zeisel, *The American Jury,* pp. 286–97.

p. 205 The effect of restitution, the reluctance of the complaining witness to prosecute, the resumption by a victim of a relationship with a spouse or business partner are discussed in Kalven and Zeisel, *The American Jury,* pp. 269–85.

p. 206 That juries represent a subtle distribution of political power is discussed in Kalven and Zeisel, *The American Jury,* p. 498.

Part Four: Judgments

CHAPTER VIII

p. 223 "Reasonable doubt" has also been called an "almost heroic commitment to decency," a value judgment made by society that it would rather let ten guilty go free than convict an innocent man. H. Kalven and H. Zeisel, *The American Jury* (1966), p. 189.

p. 223 The story of the defense attorney who told the jury during a summation that the alleged murder victim would be walking into the courtroom in the next few seconds is attributed to TV actor Don Adams.

p. 223 Judge Tim Murphy of the District of Columbia Superior Court was quoted by D. Ranii, "Judges Push Increased Jury Role," in *The National Law Journal,* August 16, 1982, p. 1, as saying if jurors heard instructions three or four times, maybe then they would "tend to get it straight." See also D. Broeder, "The Functions of the Jury: Facts or Fictions?" 21 *University of Chicago Law Review* 386, 391–92 (1954).

pp. 224–25 D. Ranii reported a study by D. Sales concluding that juries that receive no instructions make about the same number of misinterpretations of the law as do juries that do receive instructions from the judge. "Written, Pretrial Instructions Needed by Jury, Study Says," *The National Law Journal,* June 15, 1981, p. 8.

p. 225 The case in which a defendant's conviction was reversed because a juror had consulted a dictionary as an aid to understanding the judge's instructions took place in Colorado, *Alvarez* v. *People,* and was reported in "Juror's Use of Dictionary Helps Defendant Win Reversal," in *The National Law Journal,* January 3, 1983, p. 43.

p. 225 The study of the impact on the jury of different definitions of the defense of insanity was conducted by the Chicago Jury Project. D. Broeder, "University of Chicago Jury Project," 38 *Nebraska Law Review* 744, 755 (1959).

p. 226 J. Frank has been critical of what a jury can understand in "The Jury System on Trial," *Senior Scholastic,* March 20, 1964, p. 8.

CHAPTER IX

p. 236 Lord Devlin recalls a trial in which after the verdict was rendered, two jurors were discovered to be unable to speak English. P. Devlin, *Trial by Jury* (1956), p. 35. But flaws will be found in any system. It took an appellate court to reverse a conviction in which a juror had complained to the district attorney of hearing "vibrations" throughout the trial and the vibrations were particularly intense in the jury room; the voices had been telling him that the defendant was not a murderer, but the juror was convinced the voices were trying to deceive him. *Sullivan* v. *Fogg,* 613 F. 2d. 465 (2nd. Cir. 1980).

p. 236 The differences in the way men and women behave in the jury was studied by F. Strodtbeck and R. Mann, "Sex Role Differentiation in Jury Deliberations," 19 *Sociometry 3,* March 1956, quoted in R. Simon, *The Jury: Its Role in American Society* (1980), p. 41.

p. 237 An excellent summary of the research on the decision-making process of juries can be found in Simon, *The Jury: Its Role in American Society,* pp. 49–107.

p. 237 The Chicago Jury Project gathered together the data on the percentage of hung juries in civil cases in various states. What emerged is a picture that showed hung juries being very rare, occurring in only 4.5 percent of those cases. The percentage of hung juries is only slightly lower in those jurisdictions where the verdict does not have to be unanimous. Three percent of the juries hung in nonunanimity jurisdictions and only 6 percent in jurisdictions requiring unanimity. "It would appear that the abolition of the unanimity requirement would not greatly reduce the number of hung juries which, from a statistical standpoint, are not much of a problem anyway." D. Broeder, "University of Chicago Jury Project," 38 *Nebraska Law Review* 744, 746 (1959).

p. 238 Many romantic explanations have been offered for why a petit jury has twelve jurors. The Supreme Court in *Williams* v. *Florida,* 399 U.S. 78, 87 (1970) found no clear source of twelve-man rule as it traced its history. Some writers trace the number of jurors to astrology or numerology, to history or religion. Jacob had twelve sons, who became the twelve patriarchs of the twelve tribes of Israel; twelve officers of Solomon, reported in the Book of Kings, reflected Solomon's wisdom; and twelve Apostles revealed and preached the truth. Perhaps twelve was considered a sufficient number of men to create a favorable public opinion and still was not so large as to end in a brawl. T. Clark, *Valparaiso Law Review* (Fall 1966).

The federal rules allow a jury of fewer than twelve persons to hear a criminal case if both sides agree prior to the return of the verdict. This rule was intended to be used where a juror must withdraw because of illness or other serious reason and no alternate is available to replace the departing juror.

The Supreme Court decided that a unanimous verdict was not required in all jury trials for all crimes in *Johnson* v. *Louisiana,* 406 U.S. 356 (1972) and *Apodaca* v. *Oregon,* 406 U.S. 404 (1972).

The origin of the rule of unanimous juries is also "shrouded in obscurity," although it was only in the latter half of the fourteenth century that it became settled that a verdict had to be unanimous. See footnote 2 in *Apodaca* v. *Oregon,* 406 U.S. 404, 409 (1972) for a discussion of the various explanations of the development of unanimity.

A majority verdict is allowed in Louisiana, Oregon, Idaho, Montana, Oklahoma, and Texas. J. Rooks, Jr., "'The Great and Inestimable Privilege': The American Criminal Jury," *Current History,* June 1976, p. 261. Seven states now permit juries of fewer than twelve to decide noncapital felony cases, and some twelve states permit the use of smaller juries in misdemeanor cases. J. Van Dyke, *Jury Selection Procedures: Our Uncertain Commitment to Representative Panels* (1977), Appendix C.

After the Supreme Court decision, a number of studies were conducted to determine the effect of the size of juries on the decision-making process. R. Lempard, "Uncovering 'Nondiscernible' Differences: Empirical Research and the Jury Size Cases," 73 *Michigan Law Review* 643 (1975). According to an American Bar Association committee, the decisions of small juries tend to be less consistent and reliable. Also, the smaller the jury, the less likely that a member of a minority group will be a member of the jury. The committee recommended twelve-person juries where more than six months' imprisonment could be imposed.

p. 238 The differences in the way that quorum juries and unanimous juries deliberate was studied by R. Foss, and reported in "Trial by Quorum: Unequal Justice?" *Psychology Today,* July 1981, p. 20.

p. 239 The Supreme Court set six as the minimum number of jurors for nonunanimous verdicts. *Burch* v. *Louisiana,* 441 U.S. 130 (1980).

CHAPTER X

p. 241 The article Ryan read where a jury had returned after thirty minutes of deliberation not only with an acquittal for the defendant, but also with a $68 collection taken up for him was published in H. Kalven and H. Zeisel, *The American Jury* (1966), p. 304.

CHAPTER XI

p. 250 In a national survey of trial court judges, 1,030 respondents gave their opinion of the jury system: only 3 percent of the judges described juries as unsatisfactory. Judges were asked in another survey for their verdict on the juries' performance in 1,152 cases: 69 percent felt that the jury verdict was "quite correct," 8 percent thought it was a result a judge might also come to, 14 percent believed the verdict was tenable for a jury, and only 9 percent concluded that the jury's verdict was without merit. H. Kalven, "The Jury, the Law and the Personal Injury Damage," quoted in R. Simon, *Readings in Sociology of Law* (1968), p. 8.

How judges function as fact finders has not been studied much, but it would be fair to assume that judges have many of the same human characteristics and flaws as jurors. Our commitment to juries was not made for efficiency, but out of a belief, based in part on faith, that we are all better protected from government by the good sense of our fellow citizens rather than by any institutional or intellectual elite—an astonishing transfer of power from the rich and few to the common man. Kalven and Zeisel, *The American Jury*, p. 499.

Out of the 3,576 jury trials studied by the Chicago Jury Project, 30.3 percent acquitted, 64.2 percent convicted, and 5.5 percent hung. Kalven and Zeisel, *The American Jury*, p. 499.

Eighty percent of the jurors who actually sat on a case and suffered no economic hardship would like to serve again. Only 48 percent of the jurors who did not actually sit on a case and who did suffer economic hardship would like to serve again. D. Broeder, "The University of Chicago Jury Project," 38 *Nebraska Law Review* 744, 751 (1959).

A survey was conducted to determine if people preferred a judge or jury trial. Among the general public some 70 percent favored the jury, 21 percent were undecided, and only 9 percent favored trial by judge alone. Among those who had jury service within the previous year, 77 percent favored jury trial while those favoring bench trials rose to 15 percent. D. Broeder, "The University of Chicago Jury Project," 38 *Nebraska Law Review* 744, 752 (1959).

A 1983 nationwide survey titled "The American Public, the Media, and the Judicial System," sponsored by The Hearst Foundation, found that 89 percent of Americans favor the jury system, yet only 16 percent have ever served on a jury. 112 *New Jersey Law Journal* 676 (December 22, 1983).

APPENDIX: THE STATE OF JURY RESEARCH

p. 255 Over the years the jury has usually been portrayed in popular American literature as a collection of ignorant members of society who allow their personal prejudices and lack of concerns to affect their verdicts. "Why Do Solid Citizens Shrink From Jury Duty?" *Saturday Evening Post,* March 29, 1952, p. 10.

A bibliography of personal juror accounts can be found in 37 *Judicature* 83 (1979).

That few serious books have been written in England or the United States about the jury system describing its history or its present operation was a statement made by Lord Devlin. P. Devlin, *Trial by Jury* (1956), p. 167.

p. 256 Professor Kalven was quoted as calling the Chicago Jury Project "the most comprehensive study of the workings of the American jury ever undertaken." G. Ferguson, "Legal Research on Trial," 39 *Judicature* 78, 79 (1955).

pp. 256–57 Working with Professor Kalven in masterminding the project were two distinguished social scientists, Professor Hans Zeisel, former president of the American Statistical Society, and Professor Fred Strodtbeck, an expert on the behavior of small groups. D. Broeder, "The University of Chicago Jury Project," 38 *Nebraska Law Review* 744 (1962).

p. 257 Edward Levi was quoted by G. Ferguson, "Legal Research on Trial," 39 *Judicature* 78, 80 (1955).

pp. 259–60 The statement of Dean Albert J. Harno was quoted by G. Ferguson, "Legal Research on Trial," 39 *Judicature* 78, 82 (1955).

p. 260 Irving Ferman, Washington director of the American Civil Liberties Union, was quoted by G. Ferguson, "Legal Research on Trial," 39 *Judicature* 78, 82 (1955).

pp. 260–61 Senator Eastland was quoted in "Why Eavesdropping on Juries?" *U.S. News & World Report,* October 21, 1955, p. 28.

p. 261 In 1955 the Ford Foundation gave an additional $1 million so that the Jury Project could continue for another four years. D. Broeder, "The University of Chicago Jury Project," 38 *Nebraska Law Review,* 744 (1962).

INDEX